THE COMPLETE
OUTDOOR
GARDENING
MANUAL
DENYS DE SAULLES

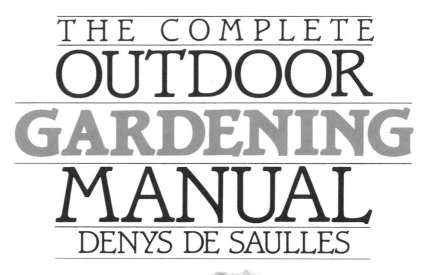

THE COMPLETE
OUTDOOR
GARDENING
MANUAL

DENYS DE SAULLES

Crescent Books
New York

1986 edition published by Crescent Books, distributed by Crown Publishers, Inc.

Library of Congress Cataloging-in-Publication Data
De Saulles, Denys
The complete outdoor gardening manual.
Includes index.
1. Landscape gardening. 2. Flower gardening.
3. Plants, Ornamental. 4. Gardening, I. Title.
II. Title: Outdoor gardening manual
SB473.D4 1986 635.9 85-21313

ISBN 0-517-60343-8

h g f e d c b a

Typeset by Wordsmiths, Street, Somerset
Origination by Rainbow Reproduction Ltd, London
Printed and bound in Great Britain by Purnell Book Production Ltd, Paulton, Bristol

This book was designed and produced by The Paul Press Ltd., 22 Bruton Street, London W1X 7DA

Designer: Marion Neville
Editors: Philippa Dyke, Barbara Horn
Art Assistants: John Graves, Aaron Thatcher
Picture Research: Maggie Colbeck
Illustrations: Caroline Pickles, Hayward and Martin Ltd, Janet Baker, The Maltings Partnership

Art Director: Stephen McCurdy
Editorial Director: Jeremy Harwood
Publishing Director: Nigel Perryman

Contents

Introduction 6

Know your garden 8

Garden problems 24

Lawns 52

Flowers 74

Roses 120

Shrubs 136

Trees 156

Water gardens 168

Index 186

Acknowledgments 192

Introduction

The myth of the "green fingers" still persists, as though the ability to grow plants and to create a beautiful garden belongs only to the privileged few. This is nonsense, of course, as countless beginners find to their delight every year when their own gardens burst into bloom for the first time. The most important qualities necessary for a successful gardener are not a magic touch, but common senses and a willingness to take care of all basic gardening requirements (particularly looking after the soil) before embarking on ambitious planting schemes.

However, no matter how much common sense you have, you will also need information or advice at times – for example, what are the needs of particular plants? How, when and why should certain tasks or regular garden routines be carried out? How do you deal with pests and diseases? These are the times when everyone wishes thay had an expert to hand.

The Complete Outdoor Gardening Manual provides exactly the type of guidance needed – clear and straightforward, and full of facts and detailed advice. Its purpose is to help another generation of gardeners to enjoy what must surely be the most rewarding of hobbies, whether they have a small town yard or a spacious country garden.

Know your garden

10 Assessing your garden
12 Understanding soil
14 Heavy soil
16 Sandy soil
18 Alkaline soil
20 Acid soil
22 Maintaining healthy soil

Assessing your garden

There are few places on earth where plants will not grow. Evolution has enabled them to come to terms with extremes of temperature and soil, rainfall and exposure. As a result, there are very few places where at least some plant species are not at home, while for most soils and situations there can be an embarrassment of riches.

For gardeners, the lesson must be to "swim with the tide", choosing plants that are attuned to the conditions they can provide. Of course, there is plenty that can be done about poor soil, excessive exposure and so on. Nevertheless, why try to grow moisture-loving plants in dry, sandy soil when there are so many others adapted to just such a habitat?

The first step is to assess exactly what your garden has to offer. This will provide a sensible basis for choosing plants and for putting worthwhile improvements in hand.

Sun and shade
Although a sunny garden would be most people's choice, there are plenty of attractive shade-loving plants. The choice is widest for beds overshadowed by walls or buildings, yet open to the sky, but narrows when the area is in the perpetual shadow cast by a large tree *(see pp30-1)*.

Position and aspect
Gardens in hollows or valleys often get an undue share of frost. This will mean that you will have to begin planting somewhat later in spring, and some tender plants will need protection *(see pp26-7)*. Before planning your garden, also try to assess which parts of the garden receive the most sun and which are exposed to any chill winds.

Exposure
This is a common problem on hillsides and by the sea. However,

Imagination was used to create this delightful garden for a small town house.

practical steps can be taken to reduce the effects of wind *(see pp26-7 and 32-3)*.

Soil
Practically any soil can be improved by adding humus (manure or compost, for example) and fertilizer. Acid soils can be sweetened with lime; clay can be broken down over a few seasons. However, poor drainage is a difficult problem to overcome, especially if the plot is surrounded by other gardens *(see pp14-15)*.

Weeds
These simply indicate neglect, not a particular category of garden – in fact, lush weed growth usually indicates fertile soil. Nowadays, there are simple and effective ways of destroying weeds *(see pp42-3)*.

Design details

In one sense, a garden is well designed if it pleases the person who has created it. There are no absolutes in aesthetics, only what satisfies the individual eye, and the making of a garden is an intensely personal matter. However, individual taste aside, today's preference is for less formal planting, for gentle curves that lure the eye to a striking focal point, and for an absence of excessive detail and geometric precision. Even so, when it comes to practicalities, there are a few ground rules about design to consider.

Patios
Ideally, a patio should be alongside the house, but this is pointless if it will be in the shade for much of the day. Choose a spot that receives plenty of sun, even if it is set away from the house. Then lay a path that provides easy access.

Utility corner
The compost heap and garden shed are usually consigned to the farthest corner of the garden,

Today's taste is for informality – and a hint of nostalgia.

necessitating long journeys to dispose of mowings or to collect tools. A more central site will save you a lot of time and effort. A screen of climber-covered trellis can easily be used to disguise the utility corner if you prefer.

Greenhouse
Abundant light is essential, and shelter from cold winds is a bonus. If this means placing the greenhouse in a prominent position, consider the attractive hexagonal designs and also the multi-faceted domed structures.

Paths
Good drainage and ample width are essential. Lay the path with its surface a little above ground level and preferably with a minimum width of 3ft. A narrow path looks mean and is awkward when you are trying to maneuver an overladen wheelbarrow on it.

Steps
A gentle slope is more convenient than steps if you are pushing a mower. However, steps are unavoidable on a sharp gradient.

Steps should be designed so that the height of each is no more than about 6in. For steps of this height, a tread depth of 12-15in is suitable, but this can be increased if the height of the riser is reduced.

Fences and screens
It is a pity to enclose your garden with a tall barrier, unless this is essential for privacy. A low wooden or wire fence is often adequate, perhaps with a topping of trellis, or a flowering hedge, which makes a particularly attractive but effective screen.

If a taller fence is required, there are alternatives to woven or lapped panels in the form of screens and hurdles formed from hazels, osiers and reeds.

Understanding soil

Soil is the gardener's chief asset, a marvelous amalgam of ground-down rocks, decayed organic matter, microorganisms, fungi, insects, earthworms – all the elements needed to sustain constant and balanced plant growth. However, unless you add more organic matter and fertilizers occasionally, the soil will become exhausted.

Decayed organic matter is needed to provide humus, the dark, spongy substance that improves the structure of every type of soil and serves as a slow-release reservoir for both moisture and nutrients. However, the nutrients themselves may not be particularly plentiful in such material as garden compost or even manure, so chemical fertilizers may be necessary.

These conditions apply principally to the topsoil, the surface layer through which plants extend their fibrous roots. Topsoil may be 10in deep, often less. Beneath this is the subsoil, which is a different color from the topsoil due to the absence of organic matter. It is important not to mix the two, although loosening the subsoil may assist plant growth.

Depending on the rocks and other material from which it was originally formed, the topsoil may be classed as clay (heavy), sandy (light), chalky (alkaline) or loam. There are variations on each, and both light and heavy soils may also be acid.

Although there are plants to suit every type of land, it is often possible to grow a wider range, and to grow better plants as well, by improving the particular type of soil you have. Practically anything will grow in good loam, which is midway between clay and sand and contains plenty of organic matter, but extreme soil conditions should be modified.

In the best of health – a mixed border flourishing in fertile soil.

Recognizing fertile soil

Plant development is the best guide to the state of the soil. Sparse, spindly plant growth and poor-colored foliage suggest that all is not well; lush growth and an abundance of strong shoots point to the opposite. On a neglected plot, plentiful, strong-growing weeds with a rich blend of greens, indicate good soil.

Water lying on the surface is an ominous sign of poor drainage. Turning over a few random forkfuls of soil will show you whether the soil crumbles readily or is hard and intractable. The latter suggests lack of humus, with clay, in particular, being prone to hardening as it dries.

Learn from the weeds

When viewing a plot for the first
time, the dominant types of weeds
can provide a good clue to the type
of soil. Like cultivated plants, many
of them are adapted to specialized
habitats. Note, though, that some,
such as chickweed and ground elder,
seem to thrive almost anywhere.

Weeds of heavy soil

Coltsfoot, speedwell,
creeping buttercup (**1**) and
groundsel (**2**) are particularly
at home on heavy, damp soil.
Horsetails are a sign that
drainage is poor.

Weeds of light soil

Free-draining, sandy soils,
often lacking in plant
nutrients, are a favorite
habitat of shepherd's purse
(**3**), knotgrass, pearlwort and
spurrey (**4**).

Weeds of acid soil

Sorrel (**5**) is nearly always to
be found on acid soil, often in
company with mayweed (**6**).
Plantains, too, grow on heavy
land, which is often acid.

Weeds of alkaline soil

The plants of chalk downland
include scarlet pimpernel,
lamb's tongue (**7**), dwarf
thistle (**8**) and bladder
campion. Look for lumps of
undissolved chalk in the soil.

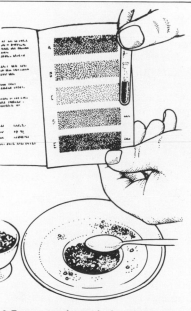

1 Pour soil and test solution into a test
tube.

2 Shake vigorously until thoroughly
mixed.

Soil testing

For a more positive and accurate
assessment of the condition of your
soil, there are simple test kits
available that require no skill to
use. The most basic test kit will
measure the soil's acid/alkaline
balance (called the pH value) but
there are also kits for checking the
levels of the main plant nutrients –
nitrogen, phosphate and potash.

As a rule, soil that has received
reasonable amounts of organic
material and balanced fertilizer is
unlikely to be very short of a
particular nutrient, but on most soil
it is worth doing a pH test
occasionally. If necessary, apply
lime to maintain a pH level of about
6.5 to 7, as measured on the scale of
values supplied with the kit.

3 Compare color with chart to check pH
level.

Clay, the extreme form of so-called 'heavy' soil, is made up of very fine particles, which fuse into a sticky, unworkable mass when wet – resulting in poor drainage – and set into a fair imitation of concrete when dry. Other types of heavy land share these characteristics to some degree, depending on the size of the soil particles. All are slow to warm up in spring, while the saturated conditions and lack of air in the soil may also cause plant roots to rot.

However, the situation is not as desperate as it may seem. There are a great many plants that actually require a moisture-retentive soil, provided that it is adequately drained. At the very least this means regular additions of compost or manure to open up the topsoil, but it also helps if grit and coarse sand are added – not just once, but regularly – while the rather laborious process of double digging will further assist drainage by breaking up the subsoil. Laying tile drains is often impractical under garden conditions, and should be seen as a last resort.

Many heavy soils are acid, so add lime if a soil test shows this to be necessary. Liming also helps to improve the soil structure.

It pays to keep off clay and other heavy soils while they are wet and sticky. Also, digging in late fall, and leaving the soil in unbroken lumps, exposes a large area to frost action and so ensures a crumbly tilth for seed-sowing in spring. It then needs no more than leveling out with a pronged cultivator and a rake.

Above all, you should apply frequent, generous dressings of bulky organic material to improve the structure of a heavy soil, making it more amenable to both the plants and the gardener. Spent mushroom compost, which contains lime, is excellent for this

Astilbes need constant moisture, and will grow in heavy, peaty soil that does not dry out in summer.

purpose. With this type of treatment, and the appropriate attention to drainage if necessary, heavy land will grow plants that are second to none.

Improving heavy soil

Double digging
The purpose is to loosen the subsoil and mix organic material with it. If manure is in short supply, however, save it for the topsoil.

Dig out a spade-deep trench across the plot. Dump the soil beyond the far end. Fork over the subsoil, adding compost or manure, and then dig out a second trench and place the soil on the forked-over subsoil. Loosen the subsoil in the second trench and continue as before. Fill the final trench with the dumped soil.

Liming
Ground limestone, a fairly bulky form of lime, should be applied at about 6oz per square yard. If you use hydrated lime, apply it at 4oz per square yard. (Hydrated lime acts almost immediately whereas ground limestone can take months to take effect.)

Always apply lime by itself, not mixed with fertilizer, and spread it on ground that has recently been cultivated. It will be washed into the soil by rain, so it is not necessary to dig it into the soil.

Drainage pipes
Agricultural drainage tiles, laid in trenches 18in deep and covered with a deep layer of coarse gravel, will have a dramatic effect. They must be laid with a gentle fall towards an open outlet, such as a ditch. For a broad area, angled side drains can lead to a main central drain in herringbone style.

Unfortunately, in many gardens it is not possible to provide the all-important drainage outlet, as a soakaway would soon become full.

Ribes will thrive in most soils, including well-drained heavy land.

Plants for moist soil

Although the plants mentioned here will grow in heavy, moisture-retentive soil, remember that few of them appreciate the wet, stagnant conditions caused by inadequate drainage.

Shrubs: Cornus (dogwood); Fothergilla; Hydrangea; Kalmia; Pieris; Rhododendron; Ribes (flowering currant).

Perennials: Astilbe; *Athyrium filix-femina; Caltha palustris* (marsh marigold); Convallaria (lily-of-the-valley); Gentiana (gentian); *Gunnera manicata;* Hosta; Lobelia; Lysimachia; Macleaya (plume poppy); Osmunda (royal fern); Primula.

Annuals: Ageratum; Althaea; Mimulus.

Bulbs: *Fritillaria meleagris; Iris sibirica;* Leucojum (snowflake).

Primula florindae, the giant cowslip, grows well in poorly-drained soil.

Sandy soil

This is the easiest type of soil to work. It is light, and can be dug without difficulty. Sandy soils are composed of coarse, gritty particles, which allow rainwater to drain freely between them. As a result, within only an hour or two of heavy rain, it is possible to make a seedbed or mow the lawn, as all the water will have drained away from the top soil. These jobs would not really be possible on heavy clay soil under the same conditions. Sandy soil can also be dug at any time of year.

Sandy soil warms up rapidly in the spring. This means it is possible to begin sowing and transplanting earlier in the year than usual.

However, there is another side to the coin, as sandy soil has some

Light sandy soil is ideal for a rock garden, where good drainage is essential. Create planting positions with a loamy compost.

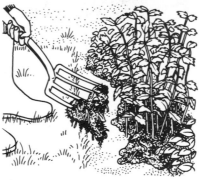

Manuring
If you cannot obtain farmyard or stable manure, use well-made garden compost, or spent mushroom compost. Leaf mold is also valuable, but it may take a couple of years to decompose properly.

Peat, hop manure, shoddy (waste from woollen mills) and even seaweed are other possibilities for manure. All should be dug into the topsoil.

Mulching
Materials used for manuring are also suitable for mulching. However, make sure that any manure has thoroughly rotted before doing this. Shredded bark also makes a good surface mulch.

Before applying a mulch, hoe or weed the ground thoroughly – preferably in late spring, after rain, when the soil is damp and warmer. Then spread the mulch. Renew it annually around shrubs and perennials.

Plastic mulch
Black plastic sheeting suppresses weeds, conserves moisture and keeps the soil warm. It may not look attractive but it will eventually be concealed by the plants. Specially-perforated sheeting is available that admits water but not light.

Lay the sheet on the ground and cover the edges with soil. Small plants or seeds can be inserted through slits cut in the plastic.

disadvantages. Light, sandy soil is frequently "hungry", as the coarse, open particles allow plant nutrients to be washed through into the subsoil by rain and watering. Sandy soil is also unsuitable for plant species whose roots require fairly moist conditions throughout the summer, again because water drains through it so quickly.

To improve sandy soil, you should apply plenty of humus-forming compost or manure – exactly the same treatment that is necessary for heavy soil. The humus helps to bind the sandy particles together and acts like a sponge, retaining moisture and dissolved nutrients.

Try to give the soil a good dressing every year, and be generous with fertilizers. Regular liming may also be necessary, although it is advisable to test the soil first *(see pp10-11)*, rather than apply lime indiscriminately.

Another way to improve sandy soil is to mulch as large an area as possible, especially around plants known to dislike dry conditions. Again, mulching involves spreading more organic material, but in this case it should be left on the surface around growing plants, rather than worked into the soil as you would do when manuring. By reducing evaporation, mulching helps to keep the surface layer of soil moist and encourages worm activity; it also acts effectively as a weed suppressant by depriving the weeds of the light and air they need to flourish.

A similar effect to that of mulching can be obtained by laying black plastic sheeting on the soil surface. You can then pierce holes through the sheeting with a trowel or knife for the plant stems. This type of treatment is particularly suitable for plants grown in rows, such as cuttings in a nursery bed or vegetables.

Suitable plants for sandy soil

Trees: *Acacia longifolia*; Arbutus (strawberry tree); *Banksia integrifolia*; Betula (birch).

Shrubs: Cistus (rock rose); Convolvulus; Cytisus (broom); Juniperus (juniper); Santolina (cotton lavender); Tamarix (tamarisk).

Perennials: Acanthus (bear's breeches); Achillea (yarrow); Dianthus (carnation); Kniphofia.

Annuals and biennials: Cheiranthus (wallflower); Felicia; Gazania; Gypsophila; Iberis (candytuft); Linum (flax); Mesembryanthemum (Livingstone daisy).

Bulbs: Crocus; Gladiolus; Hyacinthus (hyacinth); Nerine; Tulipa (tulip).

Nearly all alpines thrive in well-drained, sandy soil, so they are not listed separately here.

Santolina chamaecyparissus produces orange-yellow flowers in mid-summer.

Alkaline soil

Chalk land has its own distinctive flora of wild plants.

Most chalky or alkaline soils have much in common with sandy types of soil. In particular, they are free-draining and quick to warm up in spring. This means that nutrients are soon washed through into the subsoil by rain and watering, and also that the soil dries out rapidly during the spring and summer. In addition, chalky or alkaline soils tend to be shallow, often with only a few inches of meager topsoil over a base of solid chalk, although there are exceptions.

As with other types of soil, plentiful dressings of organic material will improve the soil's capacity for moisture retention and provide better conditions for root development. Fertilizer applications need to be frequent, while a mulch should be applied around growing plants before the soil dries out in spring.

A major limitation of alkaline soils is that certain 'lime-hating' (calcifuge) plants simply will not grow in them. Marked examples are rhododendrons, camellias and some species of lilies. If you particularly like any of these plants, you should grow them in pots or tubs containing an ericaceous compost or make a raised bed and fill it with soil that does not contain lime. An alternative way of coping with this problem is to treat the soil to increase its acidity. This can be done by applying flowers of sulfur, together with liberal dressings of peat.

Yellowing of the leaves, caused by iron deficiency and known as chlorosis, is a common condition of acid-soil plants that are grown in ground that contains lime, for although iron may be present in the soil, it is not available to the plants. The remedy for this is to apply a soluble compound called sequestered iron or iron chelates, which puts iron into the soil.

However, where possible, avoid growing the few lime-hating plants if you live in a chalk-soil area; there are so many alternatives that cause no problems.

Improving alkaline soil

Compost and manure

Much the same advice applies as
for sandy soil *(see pp16-17)*, but
avoid spent mushroom compost as
this contains a fair amount of lime.

The bulkier the dressing, the
better, as this increases the depth of
the soil, as well as adding to its
humus content. Apply the dressing
in spring, so that it is not washed
away during the winter.

Applying flowers of sulfur

This chemical reduces the pH level
of the soil to one where lime-hating
plants will grow quite satisfactorily.
Apply 6oz per square yard. It will
take some time for the flowers of
sulfur to take effect.

This treatment will keep the soil
acid for quite a long period but,
after a couple of years, test the soil
again to see if the pH level has risen
significantly. If so, apply more
flowers of sulfur.

Applying sequestered iron

This is applied as a diluted liquid
(ideally in late spring when the soil
is damp), or as a foliar spray.
Usually, an annual application
should be given (more frequently if
you use a spray) but follow the
instructions on the package. When
planting rhododendrons and other
lime-haters, work in plenty of peat
around the roots to promote initial
growth and help retain the
sequestered iron.

Suitable plants for alkaline soil

Verbenas will grow in chalky soil
provided it does not dry out in summer.

Most plants that grow in chalky soil
thrive just as well in any other well-
drained ground that is not deficient in
lime. Most rock plants and those listed
on *p17* are suitable, together with those
listed below.

Trees: Carpinus (hornbeam); Malus
(crab apple); Prunus; Sorbus.

Shrubs: Buddleia; Choisya (Mexican
orange); Cotinus (smoke tree);
Cotoneaster; Escallonia; Forsythia;
Lavandula (lavender); Lonicera
(honeysuckle); Philadelphus (mock
orange); Potentilla (cinquefoil);
Wisteria.

Perennials: Aster; Bergenia; Campanula
(bellflower); Dahlia; Delphinium;
Lupinus (lupin); Papaver (poppy);
Pulsatilla.

Annuals: Clarkia; Cosmos; Godetia;
Lathyrus (sweet pea); Nemesia; Salvia;
Verbena.

Bulbs: Anemone; Cyclamen; Iris;
Narcissus.

Wisterias will grow in fairly deep, and humus-rich alkaline soil.

Acid soil

Acid soils are not immediately recognizable, for both heavy and light soils may be acid. An acid soil simply lacks lime, owing to the type of rock from which it was formed. However, clay soils in particular are likely to be acid.

Just as rhododendrons and most heathers will not grow in a chalky soil, there are some plants – wallflowers, for example – that will not prosper in an acid soil. Fortunately, liming the soil is an effective solution to the problem so there is little that cannot be grown in acid soil. However, because lime is soon leached from some soils, especially during a wet winter, it pays to make regular checks on the soil's pH level with a proprietary test kit.

Soil is said to be acid when it registers below 7.0 on the pH scale. A reading of 6.5 indicates that a soil is slightly acid, which suits the majority of plants. If the reading is below 6.0, the soil will be too acid for most plants.

It is worth noting that, as well as lime, some materials reduce acidity while others increase it. Sulfate of ammonia, for instance, which is a nitrogenous fertilizer, increases acidity, whereas Nitro-chalk reduces it. Peat also makes soil more acid.

When testing the soil for acidity, take samples from several well-spaced points within the area concerned. Mix these together to provide the actual test sample: soil taken from just one point may give a misleading reading.

Occasionally a lawn may be affected by excessive acidity, resulting in weak growth and, usually, a great deal of moss. However, the pH level has to be very low for acidity to cause this.

Rhododendrons and azaleas need good drainage and prefer light shade.

Camellia 'Donation' has an erect habit and grows 6-8ft high.

Improving acid soil

Sandy, acid soil benefits from relatively frequent, light dressings of lime. Clay needs heavier but less frequent applications. On all soils ground limestone will have a longer-lasting effect than hydrated lime.

As a rough guide, an average dressing to help break down clay soil or to counteract slightly acid soil is 6oz of limestone per square yard or 4oz of hydrated lime. This should raise the pH level from 6.0 to 6.5.

The above amounts can be decreased by about 1oz for sandy soil. However, if the test pH reading is as low as 5.5, these quantities of lime should be doubled; for a reading of 5.0, they should be trebled.

Suitable plants for acid soil

Few plants require acid soil, although there are a great many plants that grow in neutral soil that will also tolerate a fair degree of acidity. Plants in the heather family – callunas, daboecias and ericas – come somewhere in between, for although they grow best in acid soil, they also grow quite well in other soils.

As you can see from the following plants, the majority of lime-haters are shrubs.

Trees: Eycryphia; Halesia; Nyssa; Picea.

Shrubs: Camellia; Clethra; Fothergilla; Gaultheria; Halesia; Kalmia; Lapageria; Leucothoe; Magnolia; Pernettya; Pieris; Rhododendron (including azalea); Vaccinium (bilberry, blueberry, cranberry).

Bulbs: Several lilies, including *Lilium auratum, Lilium canadense, Lilium rubellum* and *Lilium tigrinum*; *Nomocharis*.

Growing lime-haters in tubs

The easy way to enjoy plants, such as azaleas, heathers, camellias or pernettyas (even if your garden soil is chalky) is to grow them in a lime-free or ericaceous compost and to use rainwater for watering if your local supply is "hard" – that is, contains a good deal of lime.

A half-barrel or a large tub is suitable for shrubs with a height and spread no greater than 4ft. The container must have drainage holes in the base, covered with pieces of broken pot or tile, and the plants should be fed regularly.

Maintaining healthy soil

Successful gardening depends on developing an understanding of the soil and then on giving it the right care. Having identified the soil type in your garden, and improved its condition if necessary, your main task is to keep it in a healthy and fertile state.

Dig bare ground – beds where annuals are grown, for instance – at least once a year, working in compost or manure. Digging promotes fertility by aerating the soil, improving drainage and assisting the decomposition of organic material.

Forking between plants should be done annually in borders occupied by shrubs or perennials. Mix in compost and the remains of mulching material as you do so.

Fertilizers may be raked into the surface at planting time, or spread as a top-dressing around growing plants. Liquid fertilizers have a rapid but short-term effect, so frequent applications are necessary. Some, termed foliar feeds, are watered or sprayed over plants and absorbed by the leaves.

Balanced fertilizers contain all the main nutrients and are a good all-around choice. However, specific fertilizers may be needed for particular plants. Fertilizers are beneficial to plants only when in solution in the soil, so watering is essential during dry spells if the plants are not to go hungry.

Whenever necessary, remove dead leaves and other refuse from garden beds. Besides being a disease risk to your plants, they harbor slugs and other pests. Any material known to be diseased should be burned.

Keep off heavy soil while it is wet, otherwise the structure of the soil will be harmed – mud sticking to your boots is a danger sign. Occasional double digging of the soil (see pp14-15) is valuable if drainage is inadequate.

How to dig

1 Dig a trench the depth and width of a spade at one end of the plot.

2 Carry the soil from the trench to just beyond the end of the plot.

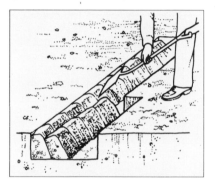

3 Dig the plot, turning over each spadeful and throwing it forwards and away from you to keep an open trench.

4 When you have finished digging, fill the final trench with the soil you removed initially.

Using a cultivator

Cultivators "dig" by means of rotating blades. They mix in manure or fertilizer evenly and break the soil finely, but do not bury weeds efficiently. They are particularly useful on light and medium soil but may spoil the texture of heavy land if used while it is wet. An adjustable depth skid controls the motion and depth of cultivation. Attachments, such as ridging plows and hoe blades, are available for some models.

Which fertilizer?

Balanced, general-purpose
fertilizers are often sold in granular
form and applied at about ½oz per
square foot. Liquid types are
available too. Formulations are also
sold under brand names.

Nitrogen

This is needed to promote healthy,
full-colored leaves and stems, but it
tends to leach out fairly quickly on
sandy soils. Sulfate of ammonia is a
quick-acting nitrogen fertilizer used
mainly as a top-dressing. However,
Nitro-chalk is a better choice on
acid soil than sulfate of ammonia
and, with nitrate of soda, acts more
quickly.
Organic nitrogenous fertilizers,
such as dried blood or hoof and
horn, have a slower, longer-lasting
effect, but are more expensive.

Phosphate

This helps root action, and the
formation and ripening of seeds.
Bonemeal is a slow-acting, long-
lasting source of phosphate and
helps to counteract acidity in the
soil. Superphosphate is another
widely-used, readily-available
source of phosphate.

Potash

This promotes the quality, size and
color of flowers and aids fruit
development. Sulfate of potash is
its most widely-used form. Wood
ash, from a wood stove or bonfire,
is another valuable source, but it
should be kept dry until spread on
the soil.

Making garden compost

Simply piling garden waste in a
sprawling heap will not produce
good compost. To achieve the even
and rapid rotting necessary, a
container of some sort is needed to
help the compost to retain its
warmth and moisture. A container
also saves space and looks tidier.

There are several types of
compost containers available.
Alternatively, make a container out
of wire mesh and line the sides
with plastic, or make a square box
out of wooden boards. Keep the
top covered to conserve the
compost's warmth and moisture.

Most garden waste that is not
diseased is suitable for compost.
However, woody prunings are
better burned and the dry ash
saved as a top-dressing for plants
needing potash. Brassica stalks and
the fibrous stems of herbaceous
plants can be included if they are
chopped into small pieces. There
are shredders specifically designed
for this purpose.

Mix the materials as much as
possible rather than piling up deep
layers of single substances, and
avoid putting on too many lawn
mowings at any one time. Water
any material that is excessively dry
before adding it to the compost
heap. Sprinkle on a proprietary
compost activator after every 9in or
so, or add some manure if it is
available. Keep the heap topped up
with fresh material as the compost
decomposes and sinks.

If possible, maintain two or three
compost heaps at the same time –
this not only provides a more
regular supply of finished compost,
but makes it easier to avoid thick
layers of one material by
distributing each between the
heaps. Wait until the heap is fully
decomposed before using any
compost. Transfer any unrotted
material from around its edges to
one of the other heaps.

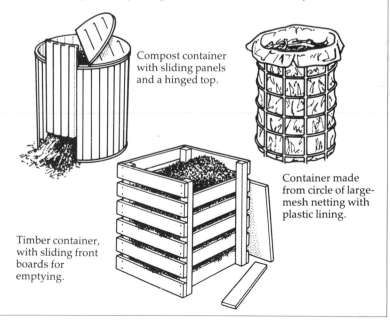

Compost container
with sliding panels
and a hinged top.

Container made
from circle of large-
mesh netting with
plastic lining.

Timber container,
with sliding front
boards for
emptying.

Garden problems

26 Cold and exposed gardens
28 Hot and dry gardens
30 Shady gardens
32 Coastal gardens
34 Town gardens
36 Neglected gardens
37 Labor-saving gardens
38 Annual weeds
40 Perennial weeds
42 Dealing with weeds
44 Ground-cover plants
46 Weedkillers
48 Bird and animal pests
50 The gardener's friends

Cold and exposed gardens

Cold and exposed gardens

Cold, and excessive exposure do not necessarily go together. The most severe frosts – and those occurring late in spring – are usually found in sheltered, low-lying spots where wind is seldom a problem. Conversely, quite tender plants may thrive in coastal areas that experience frequent gales and a great deal of rain but which also enjoy a relatively mild climate *(see pp32-3)*.

Latitude is also important. Even within a small area, plants in the north can be at least a week behind those in the south. And winter, of course, also comes earlier in some regions. If excessive cold is a problem, whether or not it is accompanied by strong winds, the answer is to choose shrubs and herbaceous plants that are reliably hardy. You should also protect precocious young growths and allow for frosts well into late spring when deciding dates for sowing and planting.

Where exposure to wind is the chief problem, temporary wind-breaks can be constructed in order to give a natural shelter belt of trees or shrubs a chance to become established. It is essential to plant trees and shrubs while they are small, so that they can develop below ground as well as above, and root securely in a suitably sturdy fashion. It is also advisable to stake young plants to give them extra support *(see pp32-3)*.

Windbreaks and shelter belts

Surprisingly, a tall wall or fence is not necessarily the most effective barrier against strong winds. The shelter they provide does not actually extend beyond more than about three times their heights. At this point strong eddies and back-

A windbreak of dogwood, spruce and pine is used here for a mountain garden.

drafts, which are just as troublesome as the unhindered wind, will occur.

In contrast, a hedge or a row of close-planted conifers or shrubs filters the wind. Although the wind will be still noticeable on the leeward side, its strength will be much reduced, with a minimum of turbulence. The perforated plastic material now available for making windbreaks also produces the same effect. It may be left in place permanently, if desired, or used to provide temporary shelter while a

hedge becomes established. The windbreak should be supported with sturdy posts so that it does not lean or sag.

A single windbreak along the windward side of the garden should be sufficient for a small garden. For a larger area, especially on an exposed hillside, smaller windbreaks within the garden are useful for protecting particular beds or plants, or to shelter a sitting area or patio. Also, protecting a greenhouse from the wind substantially reduces heat loss.

COLD AND EXPOSED GARDENS
Windbreaks and shelter belts ● Frost
pockets ● Plants for cold or exposed
gardens

Frost pockets

Cold air sinks, so frequent frosts are likely in hollows or valleys. These act as a kind of drainage sump for cool air that "flows" downhill from nearby higher ground. A tall hedge may also interrupt the flow of cold air and result in a frosty patch where the air collects. If your garden is in a frost pocket, you must take care to choose your plants accordingly. Beware of the late frosts and resist overeagerness when sowing or planting in spring.

Grevillea lavandulacea is a variable, but frost-hardy, shrub.

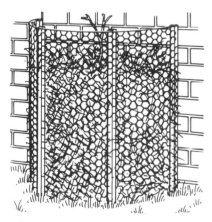

Protecting a wall shrub with straw and netting.

Extra-hardy trees and shrubs

Trees: Acer (maple); Betula (birch); Chamaecyparis; Crataegus (hawthorn); Laburnum; Picea (spruce); Pinus (pine); *Pyrus salicifolia; Sorbus aria* (rowan); *Sorbus aucaparia* (whitebeam).

Shrubs: Berberis; Elaeagnus; Forsythia; Gaultheria; Hedera (ivy); Kerria (Jew's mallow); Philadelphus (mock orange); Rosmarinus (rosemary); Spiraea; Syringa (lilac).

Melaleuca fulgens is a spreading shrub with red summer flowers.

Hot and dry gardens

The driest gardens and beds are those where there is little or no shade and the soil is light and free-draining. They warm up rapidly in spring but plant growth soon suffers in the absence of rain. Liberal watering is essential, but you should also aim to increase the soil's moisture-holding capacity by adding as much bulky organic material as possible. Mulching also helps to improve the condition of dry soil (*see pp16-17*).

Heat and dryness can also be a problem on heavy soil if there are corners of the garden that are rarely in the shade. Unless the ground is well supplied with manure or compost it will shrink, crack and become rock-hard.

For dry conditions suitable watering equipment is necessary. You need a hose-reel, a reinforced hose and a sprinkler.

Rotating sprinklers cover a fairly small, circular area and are a reasonable choice for small gardens. Oscillating sprinklers cover a square or rectangular area (often adjustable), and so avoid gaps or overlapping. Pulsating sprinklers have the longest throw and cover a full or part circle. There are two types of perforated hoses. Some are flat and lie straight, distributing a fine mist. Others consist of perforated plastic tubing and may be laid out in any pattern. They spout small jets of water on either side.

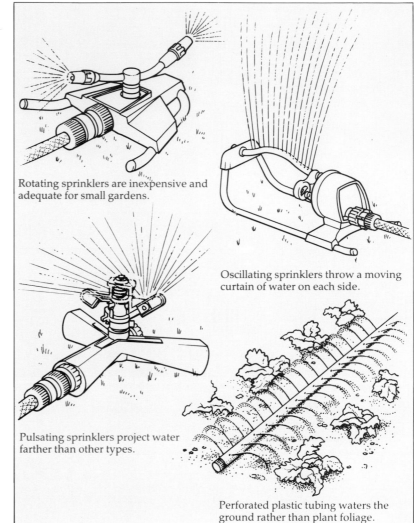

Rotating sprinklers are inexpensive and adequate for small gardens.

Oscillating sprinklers throw a moving curtain of water on each side.

Pulsating sprinklers project water farther than other types.

Perforated plastic tubing waters the ground rather than plant foliage.

Creating shade

Planting time is critical in gardens where the soil is unusually dry. In addition to watering in the plants, you should keep new plants well shaded from direct sunlight. Even a temporary covering of newspaper will improve their chances of survival while the new roots develop. However, something a little more substantial will provide better protection and save trouble in the long run.

Cloches sprayed with greenhouse shading material are ideal for shading plants. Leave the ends uncovered and place the cloches so that there are small gaps between them. For shrubs and small trees – especially evergreens – a temporary shelter can be created with a couple of hurdles, propped together in a tent shape.

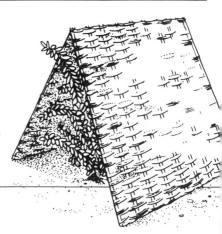

HOT AND DRY GARDENS
Combating drought ● Creating shade ●
Plants for dry soil

Hot, dry conditions suit the hypericums. This is *Hypericum patulum forrestii*.

Plants for dry soil

Shrubs: Berberis (barberry); Calluna (ling, heather); Ceanothus; Convolvulus; Elaeagnus; Erica (heath, heather); Escallonia; Hypericum (St John's wort); Ilex; Lonicera (honeysuckle); Rosmarinus (rosemary); Spartium (Spanish broom); Weigela.

Perennials: Achillea (yarrow); Agapanthus (African lily); *Alyssum saxatile*; Armeria (thrift); Bergenia; Centaurea; Cortaderia (pampas grass); Doronicum (leopard's bane); Echinops (globe thistle); Eryngium; Gaillardia (blanket flower); Geranium; Gypsophila; Helianthemum (rock rose); Hemerocallis (day lily); Hypericum (St John's wort); Iris; Linaria (toadflax); Nepeta; Papaver (poppy); Penstemon; Salvia; Sedum; Stachys; Thymus (thyme); Verbascum (mullein).

Achillea filipendulina produces deep yellow flowers, however hot the summer.

Shady gardens

Foliage provides much of the texture and color in this shaded garden.

Open shade

Quite a wide range of plants may be grown in gardens or beds that receive little direct sunlight but are open to the sky. By choosing a mixture of suitable evergreens and deciduous shrubs with colorful foliage, and covering the walls with climbers, a walled town garden can be turned into a peaceful haven from the bustle of the city.

Dappled shade

Woodland plants grow naturally in dappled shade beneath trees whose leaves and branches form an open, lacy pattern. There are many plants that appreciate partial shade of this sort, where conditions are neither too hot nor too gloomy and the drip from trees is rarely very prolonged. These include both species of periwinkle. The conditions created by dappled shade are also ideal for rhododendrons and azaleas.

Dense shade

Closely-planted trees and those with overlapping branches and leaves, such as the common beech, create dense shade. Few flowering plants can survive in such a gloomy environment, but many woodland species of shrubs, and some ground-cover plants will flourish in relatively dense shade. Several types of fern, notably the many species of dryopteris, are also suited to these conditions.

Plants for open shade

Bulbs: Colchicum (autumn crocus); Fritillaria (fritillary); Leucojum (snowflake); Narcissus.

Flowers: Anemone; Astilbe; Centaurea; Geranium; Geum; Hemerocallis (day lily); Meconopsis; Phlox; Rudbeckia (coneflower); Solidago (golden rod); Stachys; Trollius; Veronica (speedwell).

The periwinkle is a ground-cover plant that grows well in dappled shade.

The many species of dryopteris are adapted to dense shade.

The delightful *Anemone blanda* flourishes in open shade.

Ground cover: Euonymus (spindle tree); Gaultheria; Hypericum (St John's wort); Lamium (dead nettle).

Shrubs: Berberis (barberry); Camellia; Chaenomeles (japonica); Clematis; Cotoneaster; Forsythia; Fothergilla; Garrya; Gaultheria; Jasminum (jasmine); Kerria (Jew's mallow); Laurus (bay laurel); Lonicera (honeysuckle); Parthenocissus (virginia creeper); Polygonum (knotweed); Pyracantha (firethorn); Rosa (many shrub roses will grow quite well in open shade).

Plants for dappled shade

Bulbs: Cyclamen; Eranthis; Nomocharis.

Flowers: Acanthus (bear's breeches); Aconitum (monkshood); Dicentra; Digitalis (foxglove); Doronicum (leopard's bane); Helleborus; Hosta; Lunaria (honesty); Myosotis (forget-me-not); Primula; Saxifraga (saxifrage).

Ground cover: Ajuga; Bergenia; Geranium; Lysimachia; Polygonum (knotweed); Stachys; Vinca.

Shrubs: Daboecia; Deutzia; Fuchsia; Hamamelis (witch hazel); Kalmia; Leucothoe; Mahonia; Philadelphus (mock orange); Pieris; Rhododendron; Ribes (flowering currant); Senecio; Skimmia; Weigela.

Ferns: Adiantum (maidenhair fern); Athyrium; Matteuccia; Osmunda (royal fern).

Plants for dense shade

There are comparatively few plants that grow reliably in deep shade. However, some of those suggested for dappled shade will also do tolerably well under deciduous trees that are not too densely planted.

Flowers: Brunnera; Convallaria (lily-of-the-valley).

Ground cover: Euonymus (spindle tree); Gaultheria; Viola (pansy).

Shrubs: Aucuba; Buxus (box); Fatsia; Griselinia; Hedera; Ligustrum (privet).

Ferns: Asplenium (spleenwort); Dryopteris (buckler fern); Onoclea; Polystichum.

Coastal gardens

For many people, a house overlooking the sea is the ambition of a lifetime. But, if realized, it may not take long to find out that there is a price to be paid for the view – in gardening terms. High winds make it difficult to establish trees and shrubs, and many species wilt and wither if exposed to the salty and drying winds from the sea.

To protect your plants from the worst effects of the wind, erect a windbreak and/or grow a hedge. Make sure you choose plants that can take the full force of the wind and allow less adaptable types to be planted in their lee.

Plastic windbreak material (see p26) can be used, but a more natural-looking alternative for a seafront garden is wattle hurdles wired to stout stakes hammered well into the ground. Space permitting, guy lines will give additional strength.

When you have fixed an initial barrier in position, continuous hedging or close-growing shrubs can be planted next to the barrier. After a few seasons, when they are fully established, they can take over as the main windbreak.

If preferred, instead of being planted behind a windbreak, the shrubs may be individually staked or tied to wires stretched tightly between posts at either end of the row. However, a year or two's shelter behind a windbreak gives the plants a chance to make a surer start in life.

It is essential to stake any trees very firmly. Use broad ties and check frequently that these are not damaging the trunk. Avoid tall-growing species which, inevitably, will be bent or even broken by the wind as they grow.

Provided that they are protected from the wind, plants in coastal gardens grow exceptionally well, for the light is usually excellent and the air should be very pure.

Surprisingly, many plants thrive on a cliff-top site.

Creating a sun trap

A garden is not only for growing plants; it should also be a place for relaxation. The problem is how to shelter from the wind without losing the view or making the garden feel too enclosed. How difficult the problem is depends upon the garden's aspect.

First, make the most of shelter provided by the house and any adjacent fence or hedge. With luck, this may provide all the protection necessary without detracting from

You can create a sheltered patio without sacrificing the view.

COASTAL GARDENS

Particular problems ● Creating a sun
trap ● Hedges for seaside gardens ●
Plants for seaside gardens

the outlook or feeling of space.
Usually, though, at least one more
side of a patio will need to be
protected. One of the most
satisfactory ways of doing this is to
build a low wall (about 3ft high)
and then top this with a couple of
feet of glass, which should be about
¼in thick and should be either
toughened or laminated.

A 5ft screen of this kind will
ensure a really sheltered sitting
area, yet allow ample light and an
uninterrupted view. This can be
continued along the fourth side of
the area, leaving just enough space
to allow access.

Hedges for seaside gardens

There are a number of shrubs that
thrive in a windy, salt-laden
atmosphere. Some are a little
susceptible to frost but this is
seldom a problem in coastal
gardens. Among the suitable
plants for hedging are escallonias,
any of the shrubby senecios,
euonymus, tamarix, hebe, olearias
and *Hippophae rhamnoides*.

Plants for seaside gardens

Trees: Acer (maple); Arbutus
(strawberry tree); Chamaecyparis
(cypress); Cornus (dogwood); x
Cupressocyparis leylandii (Leyland
cypress); Juniperus (juniper); Pinus
(pine); Sorbus (rowan, whitebeam).

Shrubs: Aucuba; Berberis; Ceanothus;
Cytisus (broom); Elaeagnus; Erica
(heather); Fatsia; *Fuschia magellanica*;
Genista (broom); Griselinia; Hydrangea;
Laurus (laurel); Lavandula (lavender);
Pittosporum; Potentilla (cinquefoil);
Santolina; Senecio; Spartium (Spanish
broom).

Perennials: Achillea; Armeria (thrift);
Chrysanthemum; Dianthus (carnation,
pink); Eryngium (sea holly); Euphorbia;
Geranium (crane's bill); Iris; Kniphofia
(red hot poker); Penstemon; Polygonum
(knotweed); Veronica.

Hebes make attractive hedging plants for coastal gardens.

Euphorbia wulfenii is a species suitable for mild coastal districts.

Town gardens

Many town gardens suffer from lack of sunshine, limited space and access, as well as the damage done by cats and birds. However, the main problem is the thin, sour, worked-out soil so often found in city surroundings. There are several reasons for this, not least that for decades more has been taken out of the soil than has been put into it, and bulky organic material is difficult to obtain. Pollution also affects the soil.

You should first improve the soil before embarking on any planting program. Follow the advice given for sandy soils *(see pp16-17)* and also run a soil test to see whether or not the soil is acid *(see pp20-1)*; if it is, you should treat it with a dressing of lime.

The choice of plants for town gardens is determined mainly by space, the amount of available light and a plant's ability to prosper in somewhat impoverished soil.

If shade is the problem, and it cannot be solved by removing a tree or tall hedge, you will have to settle for shade-loving species *(see p31)*: plants such as camellias, hostas, foxgloves and the hellebores provide a restful green background when not in flower. You should also consider whether a paved area might not be better than a lawn – a lawn will rarely flourish without a fair amount of sunshine.

Find space for wall-mounted containers, such as window boxes, wall pots and hanging baskets. Clad bare walls and fences with colorful climbers, using vertical space to supplement the limited ground area.

Cats and birds are principally a menace to seeds and seedlings. Heavily-twigged branches laid over a seedbed will stop cats from doing much damage; black thread stretched an inch or two above the surface will deter birds, as will, of course, a household cat.

A small town garden, delightfully transformed into a restful oasis.

Patio gardens

Where space is very limited, the best solution is often to pave the whole area, while allowing for rainwater to drain away. One or more raised beds, which will also vary the contours, can be most effective. Pots and tubs can be filled with commercial compost to avoid the limitations of poor soil. They are also easily movable and can be replanted to provide interest throughout the year.

Paving slabs now come in a wide range of colors and finishes. On level ground they are easily laid by tapping each slab on to five fist-sized blobs of mortar. Brick pavers, which are thinner than ordinary bricks, may also be laid on concrete or vibrated into a sand bed.

You may prefer crazy paving, but it is tedious to lay. Cold-applied asphalt, sold in bags for home laying, needs a concrete base and in any case is not a completely satisfactory surface. Gravel also has its drawbacks; it becomes dirty relatively quickly and needs frequent raking and weeding.

Always check that any paving slopes away from the house to ensure that water drains away from the foundations.

A clipped box growing in a stone tub. Other varieties have variegated leaves.

Suitable trees and shrubs

Given the required amount of sun or shade, most plants are quite at home in town gardens. Some easily-grown plants are listed below.

Climbers: Clematis*; Garrya*; Hedera (ivy)*; Humulus (hop)*; Lonicera (honeysuckle)*; Rosa (rose).

Trees: Catalpa; Laburnum; Malus (crab apple)*; Prunus (ornamental almonds, plums and cherries).

Shrubs: Buxus (box)*; Choisya (mexican orange)*; Elaeagnus; Escallonia; Hamamelis (witch hazel)*; Jasminum (jasmine); Kerria*; Viburnum.

Note: * *tolerates some shade.*

The white-painted wall behind this tiny patio garden lightens the whole garden.

Neglected gardens

There may be long-lost treasures in even the most overgrown patch of garden, lovely plants that gave pleasure to some previous gardener and will do the same for you. Therefore, one of the first jobs, when surveying the garden, is to take stock of what is growing and insert a marker by anything promising. If the time of year is right you can move such plants to a temporary "survival" bed.

A convenient design
Start work by opening a path. If the ground is overgrown with tall weeds, hire a powered brushcutter to clear them. A sickle or grass hook will do for a small area. Applying a total weedkiller on part, or all, of the garden will give you a clean start. However, if the weeds are mostly annual they can be removed by hoeing or digging.

Start a compost heap for soft growth; a fire site will be needed for tough, woody material, preferably in the middle of the garden, well away from any fences. If there is rubble or broken paving lying around, pile this separately; it may be useful for a patio base or crazy paving.

Choose a convenient site for a toolshed. Most sheds soon become overcrowded, so choose the largest shed you can afford: a medium-sized shed with, say, 48 square feet of floor space costs only half as much again as one of 24 square feet.

Look at the lawn carefully – if there is any – and decide whether to attempt renovation or to start again from scratch. There is still hope for a lawn if the finer grasses have not been swamped by weeds and coarse grass. Also, consider whether or not you can salvage the flower beds.

Deciding a plan of action
You are now in a position to rough

Restoring a neglected garden is not too daunting if you tackle jobs in the right order.

out an overall plan, either taking in existing features or starting from scratch. Work out a realistic work plan, so that you can decide what to do first and where to begin. Most people prefer to start remaking a garden from nearest the house;

making a path is also a good first step.

Do not fall into the trap of trying to do too much at once. Let your garden evolve naturally rather than forcing it to conform rigidly to your initial plan.

Reminders

On heavy ground, do not start work while the soil is wet and sticky.

Remember that a tree takes only moments to destroy, but many years to grow. Think carefully before felling any trees.

If a tree has to be felled, have this done before laying out the garden.

Wear safety goggles when using a brushcutter.

Only burn dry refuse. Have fires on still days as smoky fires may upset your neighbors.

On a small or shaded plot, consider paving as an alternative to grass.

Try to include evergreen and winter-flowering shrubs in the garden.

Labor-saving gardens

The easiest gardens to manage
have clean, simple lines and not too
many different elements. A lawn,
for instance, is much easier to cut if
there are no island beds or bird
baths to obstruct the mower,
especially if the mower is electric.
One or more edges of the lawn may
be curved, but scalloped edges are
a nuisance.

Avoid a rock garden or a pool as
they both require time and effort.
Avoid planting annuals, too, for
they involve a lot of digging,
planting and clearance, even if the
plants are bought rather than
grown from seed.

Shrubs are the least demanding
of plants. Perennials are also not
too time-consuming, especially if
you choose types that do not need
staking. In the cases of shrubs and
perennials, mulching reduces the
time and effort normally needed for
weeding and watering. Ground-
cover plants are also ideal, needing
little or no attention from one year
to another.

Think carefully when buying
tools. Electric mowers, cultivators,
hedge trimmers and other aids
need less maintenance than their
fuel-powered counterparts; they do
not suffer from starting problems
and are also lighter to handle.
Finances permitting, choose a
mower with a wide cut, as this
reduces mowing time considerably.
Also, choose one that collects the
grass rather than leaves it for you to
rake up afterwards.

Two-wheel barrows are lighter
on the arms than single-wheel
models. If you prefer a single-
wheel model, one with a pneumatic
tire will be easiest to push on
uneven ground. Tools with quick-
change heads that fit on to a single
handle are convenient and save
you carrying whole armfuls of
tools. Nylon-cord trimmers make
light work of grass trimming and
will cut right up to trees and fences.

Evergreen shrubs, dwarf conifers, a paved area and an uncluttered lawn are
features of this labor-saving garden.

Reminders

Level out uneven patches of grass that
make mowing difficult.

Hire a cultivator if annual digging is
taking too much time.

Use weedkiller on paths and drives or
wherever hoeing is too laborious.

Keep tools – especially hoes – really
sharp. They will be easier to use and
much more effective.

Make sure your toolshed has plenty of
shelves, so that everything can be
found at a glance.

Plants in plastic pots require watering
less often than those grown in
earthenware pots.

Annual weeds

The battle against weeds never ends. Even the best-kept soil contains countless ungerminated weed seeds and fresh ones arrive all the time, carried by birds or on the wind. Many kinds of weeds reproduce themselves vegetatively by means of runners, creeping roots, bulbils or even segments that have become detached from the parent plant.

The unsightliness of weeds is not the only reason for destroying them. They take moisture and nourishment from the soil that could otherwise feed cultivated plants, and they also harbor various garden pests. A heavy, blanketing growth of weeds increases the risk of disease.

Broadly, weeds can be divided into annual and perennial types. Although they reproduce and spread rapidly, annual weeds are relatively easy to deal with. They include the annual nettle, chickweed, cleavers (goosegrass), common persicaria, fat hen, hairy bittercress, groundsel, knotgrass, lesser and bird's-foot trefoil, purple deadnettle, shepherd's purse and sow thistle. Most are easily kept under control.

Of course, weeds are also the wild plants of the countryside, but those you find in your garden are successful species and in no danger of becoming scarce. If you decide to cultivate wild plants, set aside a special area for them. Varieties of wild flowers are available from major seed companies.

Chickweed flowers almost throughout the year, producing an exceptional number of seeds.

Bird's-foot trefoil is a common and pretty weed that is not a great problem.

Common persicaria is a relative of wireweed and its tough, branching stems are not dissimilar.

Red deadnettle is not related to the stinging nettle, though the young plants are similar.

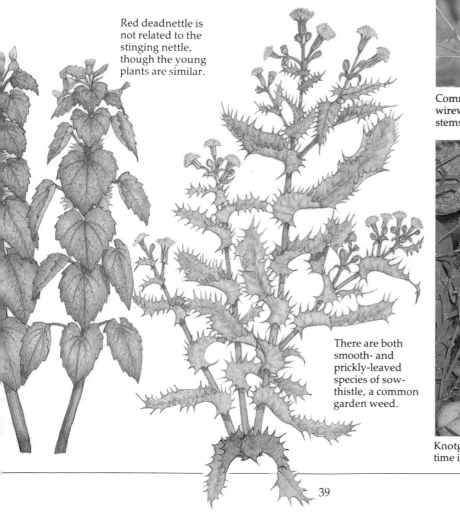

There are both smooth- and prickly-leaved species of sow-thistle, a common garden weed.

Knotgrass's seeds can survive for a long time in the soil.

39

Perennial weeds

There are many perennial weeds which are generally persistent and therefore very difficult to control, and in some cases may have some or even a strong resistance to chemical weedkillers.

Simply severing tops of perennial weeds with a hoe provides only a temporary check to their growth. The roots remain unharmed and will soon grow again. Burying the whole plant while digging is not much use either; the persistent roots produce new shoots and in digging them over you may even have aggravated the problem by dividing the roots into several pieces. Perennial weeds are especially difficult to control on heavy land, which may be too wet to work for months on end, allowing invasive types of weed to become well established.

Perennial weeds are best controlled chemically, especially on land that is to be cultivated for the first time. "Total" weedkillers may be used at any time except late fall and winter to clear uncultivated ground.

Other weedkillers to control the weeds between growing plants in beds and borders are best applied between mid-spring and early summer, when the weeds are growing, but before they seed.

Ribwort belongs to the plantain family and is easy to control.

Coltsfoot grows almost anywhere. Avoid breaking the creeping roots.

Convolvulus twines around cultivated plants. It is best controlled chemically.

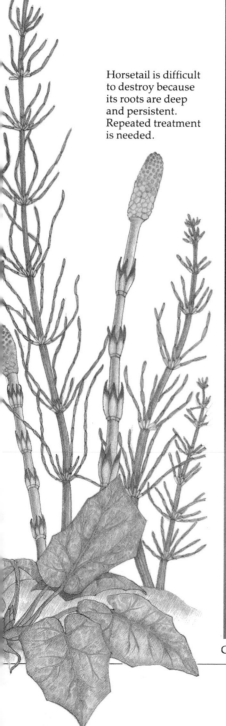

Horsetail is difficult to destroy because its roots are deep and persistent. Repeated treatment is needed.

Creeping thistle is a tough, resistant weed. Both its roots and seeds spread.

Dealing with weeds

There is no one ideal way of dealing with weeds. The treatment they require depends on whether they are perennial or annual weeds, where they are situated, the time of year and the state of the soil. However, for every situation there is a countermeasure, and weeds should seldom prove more than a minor nuisance once an initial clearance has been made.

Destroying weeds need not mean wholesale reliance on chemicals. Although weedkillers can play a useful part, many experienced gardeners use them only sparingly. There are other equally effective methods – more natural and less costly – of keeping most garden weeds under control.

Hand weeding

This is slow, tedious work and should be reserved for weeding between close-growing plants in a rock garden or in any place where there is insufficient space for even a small hoe. Hand weeding is also necessary where weeds are growing right against plant stems, where they have appeared between closely-spaced seedlings, such as hardy annuals, and where individual perennial weeds have to be removed.

On the whole, however, it is much better to leave sufficient space between plants for a hoe. Even the most careful hand weeding, lifting all the roots, will not prevent another crop of annual weeds appearing almost at once, as the soil is full of their seeds.

Hoeing

If annual weeds are severed at ground level on a dry day, they will die almost immediately and their roots will not throw up fresh shoots. Hoeing on damp soil is less effective and is of little value for controlling perennial weeds, which simply grow again from the roots left in the soil.

A Dutch hoe, used with a pushing or prodding action, is the best type of hoe. An onion hoe with a short handle is also effective for close work around small plants. To maintain your hoes in good working condition, keep the blades sharp with a coarse file.

Digging and forking

If it is properly done, digging provides a chance to bury all weed growth. However, well-developed perennial weeds should be removed, as otherwise many of them will simply grow again, possibly in even greater profusion.

For effective burial, keep an open trench in front of you as you dig so that each slab of soil can be inverted completely.

Forking the soil between shrubs and perennials gives you the chance to bury at least some annual weeds, to loosen others for easy removal and to lift deep-rooted perennial weeds. Forking is best done when the soil is neither excessively wet nor dry.

Mulching

Everyone agrees in theory that mulching is good for a garden, yet too few gardeners actually practice it. This is a pity, for as well as providing better growing conditions for the plants, a layer of organic matter spread over the surface is extremely effective in suppressing weeds.

However, for mulching to be effective, you should first remove perennial weeds and hoe the soil to destroy annual weeds. Spread the mulch while the soil is still damp after rain.

Shredded bark, peat, compost, thoroughly-rotted manure or lawn

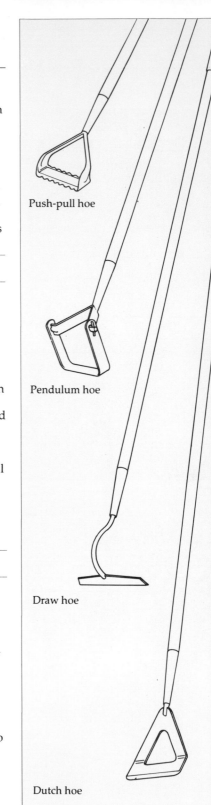

Push-pull hoe

Pendulum hoe

Draw hoe

Dutch hoe

DEALING WITH WEEDS

Hand weeding ● Hoeing ● Forking and
digging ● Mulching ● Weed-
smothering plants ● Weedkillers

Ajuga reptans, known as "bugle", is a favorite ground cover plant.

mowings are some of the materials
suitable for mulching. On rock
gardens, a covering of gravel or
chippings serves the same purpose.

Weed-smothering plants

Just like cultivated plants, weeds
need light and air if they are to
grow well: mulching will slowly kill
weeds by depriving them of both of
these. You can also prevent weeds
from spreading by growing plants
that form dense, spreading cover.
This effectively smothers weeds as
they attempt to grow.

The use of weed-smothering
plants is not standard treatment for
all beds and borders, however.
Many ground cover plants (*see
pp44-5*) are too invasive to mix
satisfactorily with annuals and
herbaceous types, but they can be
used beneath roses and other
shrubs, on banks and verges and to
bring color and interest to tree-
shaded areas.

Chemical weedkillers

Used sensibly, chemical
weedkillers can save much time
and effort and will destroy weeds
without adversely affecting lawns
or cultivated plants. There are
various kinds of weedkiller
developed for different purposes. It
is important to understand how
each type works, so that you know
exactly which type you need to
cope with any particular problem.

To what extent chemical
weedkillers are used depends
entirely on the individual gardener.
Many arrive at a compromise,
using chemicals for the most
stubborn weeds, and for treating
paths and lawns, but continuing
with hoeing, hand weeding,
digging and mulching for many of
their beds and borders. (For details
of the different types of weedkillers
see pp46-7).

Ground cover plants

A considerable and varied range of carpeting plants fall into this category. All of them will suppress weeds, cover the soil, and require very little effort on the part of the gardener. Moreover, many ground cover plants have eye-catching foliage or bear attractive flowers, so they can be the perfect choice for gardeners short of time or energy.

However, although ground cover plants will suppress the spread of weeds, they will not kill established weeds, especially perennials. Therefore, it is important to plant any ground cover plants in relatively "clean" ground to give tham a good start. If they are encouraged to grow rapidly right from the beginning, they will spread and link up more quickly and prevent other weeds from becoming established.

Ground cover plants are also useful for covering steep banks, where regular planting and hoeing, for example, may be difficult. Most spread evenly, but some grow in individual clumps, which eventually meet. A few, not included here, grow so vigorously that they may well begin to invade the rest of the garden if not kept under close control.

Container-grown plants may be put in the soil at any time, except when it is freezing or saturated. Plant those with bare roots during fall or late winter

The New Zealand burr is notable for its spiny, crimson seed cases.

Soil preparation

Annual weeds can simply be dug in and buried. However, perennial weeds – docks, creeping buttercup and other such weeds – must either be dug out individually, complete with roots, or killed by an overall application of weedkiller. If you use a non-selective translocated type (*see pp46-7*), such as one that contains glyphosate, it will kill the roots of the weeds as well as the visible growth.

If the soil is very poor, you should dig in some manure or compost to improve its structure and capacity for holding moisture. All soils benefit from a dressing of balanced fertilizer to give the plants a good start in life.

Planting distance varies, of course, with each individual species. If you are in doubt, plant more plants rather than fewer, so that the bare ground between them is soon covered. If you plant your ground cover plants at the distances suggested, complete cover should be established, on the average, in about two or three years.

Vinca minor is neater and less invasive than *Vinca major*.

Suitable ground cover plants

Acaena microphylla (New Zealand burr)
H 2in, S 12in. Semi-evergreen, with
spiny burrs (late summer). Sun.

Ajuga reptans (bugle) H 4in, S 12in.
Hardy perennial with blue flower
(summer). Shade.

Bergenia cordifolia H 12in, S 14in. Hardy
perennial with pink flowers (mid-
spring). Sun/shade.

Cotoneaster dammeri H 3in, S 24in.
Evergreen with white flower (early
summer). Sun.

Epimedium perralderianum H10in, S 18in.
Evergreen with yellow flowers (early
summer). Shade.

Euonymus fortunei H12in, S 30in.
Evergreen with attractive foliage. Sun/
shade.

Euphorbia robbiae H 18in, S 24in. Hardy
perennial with yellow bracts (summer).
Shade.

Gaultheria procumbens H 6in, S 18in.
Evergreen with pink flowers (summer).
Shade.

Geranium endressii H 12in, S 18in. Hardy
perennial with pink flowers (summer).
Sun/shade.

Hebe pinguifolia H 18in, S 18in.
Evergreen with white flowers
(summer). Sun.

Hedera helix (common ivy) H 12in, S
27in. Evergreen (many variegated
forms). Sun/shade.

Hypericum calycinum (St. John's wort) H
15in, S 15in. Semi-evergreen with
yellow flowers (summer). Sun/shade.

Lamium maculatum (deadnettle) H 12in,
S 15in. Hardy perennial with purple
flowers (spring). Sun/shade.

Lysimachia nummularia (creeping jenny)
H 2in, S 18in. Hardy perennial with
yellow flowers (summer). Sun/shade.

Pachysandra terminalis H 12in, S 16in.
Evergreen with white flowers (spring).
Shade.

Polygonum affine (knotweed) H 6in, S
18in. Hardy perennial with red flowers
(summer). Sun/shade.

Stachys lanata (lamb's tongue) H 15in, S
12in. Hardy perennial with purple
flowers (summer). Sun/shade.

Symphytum grandiflorum (comfrey) H
9in, S 12in. Hardy perennial with white
flowers (spring). Sun/shade.

Tiarella cordifolia (foam flower) H 9in, S
12in. Semi-evergreen with white
flowers (early summer). Shade.

Veronica prostrata (speedwell) H 6in, S
12in. Hardy perennial with blue flowers
(early summer). Sun/shade.

Vinca major H 9in, S 20in and *Vinca
minor* H 3in, S 20in. Blue flowers (early
summer). Sun/shade.

Viola labradorica (pansy) H 4in, S 9in.
Hardy perennial with mauve flowers
(spring). Sun/shade.

Note: H *indicates height*, S *indicates
spacing*.

The white flowers of *Gaultheria procumbens* are followed by crimson berries.

Weedkillers

It is necessary to understand how weedkillers work in order to choose the most effective type for a particular purpose. Do not simply aim for a familiar brand name.

There are three basic kinds of weedkiller: contact, translocated and residual. Each acts differently and has been developed for a specific purpose. Contact weedkillers kill the foliage that they touch, but their action does not extend to the root system and the chemical does not linger in the soil to kill germinating weed seedlings. Some contact weedkillers are selective, which means they kill some plants and not others – for instance, they may kill lawn weeds without harming the grass itself. Other types kill all green tissue.

Translocated weedkillers work through the whole plant – spreading from the leaves to the roots and vice versa. They act fairly slowly, but eventually kill the whole plant even if only part of the foliage is treated. As with contact weedkillers, there are selective and non-selective types, some killing grasses, such as couch or quack, but not broad-leaved plants, others killing plants but not grasses.

Residual weedkillers are applied to the soil in order to kill the germinating seedlings of weeds, and remain active for many months. There are several kinds. Some, notably sodium chlorate, kill all existing plants and prevent new growth for many months afterwards. Other types of residual weedkillers may be used safely between plants and crops to prevent more weed growth.

In addition to ordinary weedkillers, a number of products are available for killing moss and lichen. Some types are selective, which makes them suitable for use on lawns, but others harm grass and so may be used only on paths, fences and roofs, for example.

Spraying with alloxydim sodium kills couch or quack grass but not the polyanthus.

How to apply weedkillers

A spray gives the best overall coverage when the purpose is to drench the foliage. Only spray on still days.

A dribble bar attached to a watering can gives good, tight control when applying a contact weedkiller between or alongside garden plants. A watering can rose is suitable for a residual weedkiller, such as sodium chlorate, when treating a neglected area. When applying a granular weedkiller, mark the area first in measured squares.

A dribble bar gives precise control, slows down the rate of application and prevents spray drift.

Safety first

Weedkillers, along with other garden chemicals, should be kept well out of reach of children. If you do not have a cupboard with a lock, put them on a high shelf in a shed or garage. Safety precautions are printed on every bottle and box of weedkiller. Always follow them very carefully.

Do not use bottles or other temporary containers for weedkillers. Only use a spray or a watering can.

Wash the spray or can very thoroughly after use, but first disposing of any surplus liquid in a place where it cannot cause any harm.

Rinse the container several times, and clear the spray lance and nozzle by pumping clean water through it.

Dispose of surplus or unwanted chemicals immediately rather than allowing them to accumulate. Flush liquids down the toilet; place closed containers in the garbage.

Choosing the right weedkiller

If a sales person cannot help you, study package labels carefully until you find a weedkiller containing the chemical you need. Some manufacturers supply charts and leaflets to make selection easier. The product name, such as "Path Weedkiller", may also help you.

Ammonium sulfamate is a residual weedkiller for clearing neglected ground and kills most weeds. Do not use it where there are tree or shrub roots growing.

Alloxydim sodium is a translocated weedkiller, usually applied as a spray. It kills perennial grasses without harming ornamental plants.

Aminotriazole is a translocated weedkiller that controls most weeds and perennial grasses. It is used in path weedkillers.

Dalapon is a translocated weedkiller that kills perennial grasses and some other plants. Use mainly before sowing or planting, following the instructions exactly.

Dichlorbenil is a residual weedkiller that kills existing weeds and prevents regrowth for several months. Can be used on rose beds and on paths.

Dichlorophen is a selective moss-killer, suitable for paths, walls and fences but also for use on lawns.

Glyphosate is a non-selective translocated weedkiller that kills the whole plant when applied to its leaves. It is essential to avoid contact with garden plants.

Paraquat and diquat are contact weedkillers that kill above-ground growth but do not prevent regrowth of perennials. May be used between ornamental plants.

Propachlor is a residual weedkiller that kills weed seedlings as they germinate. Useful around shrubs, fruit and some vegetables.

Simazine, in concentrated applications, kills all existing weeds; a diluted mixture prevents weed seedlings from emerging.

Sodium chlorate is a "total" residual weedkiller, effective for clearing neglected ground. Do not plant anything on the ground for at least six months afterwards.

2,4,5-T and 2,4-D give good control of brushwood and brambles. Also kills most weeds other than grasses.

Keep the nozzle of the spray low to limit spray drift. Avoid excessive pressure. A still day is essential.

Individual weeds can be killed with a "touch-weeder" that smears plants with a translocated weedkiller gel.

Use a board to protect nearby plants when treating a path with weedkiller, specially formulated for the purpose.

Bird and animal pests

Preventing bird damage

The principal damage done by birds is to fruits and berries; pigeons will also devastate a brassica crop during cold weather in their search for food. In both cases the only permanent solution is to erect a protective cage, using ¾-in mesh netting (wire or plastic) to keep out even the smallest birds. If a fruit cage is also needed to provide winter protection from pigeons, remove the netting from the roof in late fall and replace it with 4-in mesh. (Snow may collect on a smaller mesh, damaging both the netting and the framework of the cage).

A suitable cage can be constructed from tubular metal – sold in ready-made kit form – or timber. If you decide on the latter, any timber that will be in contact with the ground should be pressure-treated first with preservative. If you have difficulty in obtaining ready-treated wood, soak the butts in preservative for 24 hours before using them.

Low-growing crops, such as strawberries, can be protected from birds by netting, draped like a tent over a length of taut wire. Currant bushes can simply have the netting draped over them.

For fruit trees that cannot be netted you can stretch a proprietary "humming line" at about the level where damage usually occurs. The wind causes the line to emit a high-frequency sound that frightens birds, while being inaudible to people.

At ground level, seedbeds and seedlings can be protected by black thread stretched between plastic hoops pushed into the soil at the ends of the rows. You can also hang strips of foil from a line, which dance and flash in the wind and scare away the birds. Another

A permanent fruit cage made from timber and wire netting.

Lightweight plastic netting laid directly over a crop protects it from birds.

Homemade bird scarers can be made with foil baking cases.

A cherry tree encased in plastic netting. This is one way to protect a solitary tree from birds.

should be treated in advance of sowing. The chemicals are equally effective against dogs and may also deter birds.

Animal pests

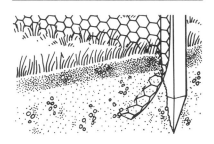

Rabbits can be a problem in rural areas. A cat will deter them, but otherwise wire mesh fencing may be necessary. To be effective, the fence should be of 1½-in-mesh and about 3ft high. Bend the bottom 6in of mesh outwards and bury it a few inches under the turf or soil.

Moles are also a difficult problem. Some cats learn the art of catching tham, but mole "smokes" and chemical fumigants are the usual method of control. Traps are also effective, provided that they are set properly.

Hares, squirrels and deer are other animals that may occasionally cause trouble. Deer, in particular, can do a lot of damage in a short time by ring-barking trees and shrubs. For deer (and for rabbits) there are various chemical substances that serve as deterrents if used strictly in accordance with instructions. A string soaked in one of these liquids and erected at a height of about 3ft around vulnerable plants gives a measure of protection against deer. However, permanent protection by this method is difficult and fencing is advisable in the long term. Alternatively, you can protect the stems of young trees with plastic tree guards.

effective type of scarer is a cut-out shape of a hawk, which can simply be hung over the vulnerable area from a line or long pole.

Pets

Cats will frequently defecate on new seedbeds, attracted by the finely-raked soil, and so are a particular nuisance at sowing and planting time. Therefore, any seedbeds need special protection.

A covering of twiggy branches will often act as a sufficient deterrent to cats. However, a neater alternative is to lay large-mesh plastic netting over the seedbed, removing it only when the plants are large enough to survive by themselves. Black thread used as protection against birds will serve for cats as well, but the strands must be quite close together and tightly stretched.

A different deterrent altogether is offered by the various chemical repellents now available. These do not necessarily have an instant effect, so a potential seedbed

The gardener's friends

Not everything that stirs in the garden is out to sabotage the gardener's efforts. On the contrary – quite a few bugs and insects are effective allies to the gardener, feeding on other creatures that do considerable damage to plants. It pays to know friend from foe before trying to destroy them.

Birds are well in the black on any garden balance sheet. Titmice eat innumerable aphids, while robins, blackbirds and thrushes have an insatiable appetite for grubs of every kind. There may be other occasional visitors to the garden, including frogs and toads. Most of these are on the gardener's "side".

Spiders (**1**) are tremendous hunters, and live on a great variety of insects. None actually damage plants. Unfortunately, however, they too suffer from the widespread use of pesticides.

Both ladybugs (**2**) and their blue-gray larvae have a prodigious appetite for aphids. Avoid spraying when you see them at work. Wasps (**3**), too, kill great numbers of insects to provide food for their grubs. That other familiar garden visitor, the bumble bee (**4**), does not prey on insects but obligingly pollinates flowers and fruit blossom.

Toads (**5**) and birds (**6**) eat slugs, snails, worms and insects and so help protect your garden. Butterflies (**7**), apart from the cabbage white, whose caterpillars can devastate an entire brassica crop, do no harm.

Lacewings (**8**) are yet another predator of aphids on which both adults and larvae feed. Most garden beetles (**9**) are useful, for they live on a variety of soil pests, including slugs.

Parasitic wasps (**10**), such as ichneumons, lay their eggs in adult insects or their larvae. When the eggs hatch, the wasp larvae consume their hosts, destroying great numbers of aphids and caterpillars each year.

Butterflies

Buddleia davidii, the butterfly bush, has an irresistible appeal, its tapering flowerheads being seldom without butterflies in mid- to late summer. Sedums, valerian and veronica also attract butterflies in numbers, as do asters in late summer. If you particularly like butterflies, seeds of wild flowers known to be especially attractive to butterflies can also be bought. Spraying should always be postponed when butterflies are in evidence in the garden.

Birds

The damage done by birds is minimal. Having taken basic precautions (*see pp48-9*), many gardeners prefer to attract birds rather than discourage them. This can be done by providing food during the colder months, water all the year round (water is especially welcome during freezing or hot weather), and nestboxes for the birds that will take to using them (mainly titmice).

Birds also prefer gardens where there is some cover as well as open space. Position any bird table well clear of the ground and away from bushes that may provide protective cover for predatory cats.

Bread, nuts, cheese, fat, grain – all will be eaten readily. Try to provide food little and often. Do not leave food lying around to become saturated or frozen in wet or cold weather, or to attract cats.

Nestboxes can be bought or made. Measurements of 6in by 6in and 9in high are about right for most small birds. An entrance hole with a 1⅛in diameter is needed for titmice and nuthatches. Sparrows may use the box if it is larger. Robins prefer a box with the front partially open. Hang the box on a wall or a smooth tree trunk above head height and in a place where it is shaded from the hottest sun.

Pool life

A garden pool attracts much wild life, including, if in luck, magnificent dragonflies that emerge from the water after spending over a year there as nymphs. The adult dragonflies live for only a month, but during this time they put on fantastic flying displays as they hunt for insects.

Two creatures whose lives are considerably longer, and which may breed in garden pools, are frogs and toads – both with a fancy for slugs, snails, worms and practically any insect that moves. However, toads, especially, are conservative creatures and prefer their ancestral pond to a new one, even if this involves a hazardous return journey in spring after hibernating underground through the winter.

Lawns

54 Assessing your lawn
56 Maintaining your lawn
58 Mowing and trimming
60 Lawn mower care
62 Lawn care around the year
64 Repairing a damaged lawn
66 Planning a new lawn
68 Establishing a new lawn
70 Weeds and moss
72 Lawn pests and diseases

Assessing your lawn

There is no doubt that a well-cared-for lawn sets off the rest of the garden. It is the key to most successful designs, and certainly deserves some thought and effort. Nothing else ever looks quite right when the lawn has an uneven or threadbare appearance.

On very small plots, especially if they are shaded, it might be better to lay paving rather than lawn, for grass needs plenty of light in order to grow well. However, with a certain amount of hard work, it is possible to have a good lawn on almost any soil.

The golden rule to remember is that lawn grasses are plants just like all the others in the garden. They therefore respond to good management, especially feeding and weeding and, if you are fully aware of this, it is possible to transform a poor lawn into lush grass in a single season. This is much easier than starting a lawn again from scratch, provided that there is still a reasonable coverage of lawn-type grasses over most of the area, however submerged or weak-looking they may be.

If it is absolutely necessary, you can dig the site and either lay sods or sow grass seeds (*see pp66-7*). Whether you decide to renovate the lawn, or to begin again from scratch, it is very important to do jobs at the right time of year and in the right order to achieve the best possible results.

A beautiful lawn complements any garden.

Deciding what to do first

Lawn needs general improvement
Rake the surface thoroughly. Apply weed- or moss-killer, if necessary. Repair edges and level humps and hollows. From mid-spring to late summer, apply fertilizer and weedkiller as necessary. Avoid close mowing until the grass is growing strongly. Scarify the lawn surface in early fall.

Lawn needs major renovation
In addition to giving the lawn the general treatment for improving its condition, apply a proprietary top-dressing in early fall. Any bare patches should be reseeded at the same time or, alternatively, in mid-spring. If you are resodding any parts of the lawn, do this between mid-fall and mid-spring when the weather permits.

Lawn needs complete resowing
Clear and level the site. Apply a chemical weedkiller to destroy perennial weeds.

When all the weeds have died, dig over or cultivate the soil. Then break down the surface, and firm and rake it in preparation for sowing or sodding. This should be done, weather permitting, either in mid-fall or in mid-spring.

ASSESSING YOUR LAWN

Lawn problems ● Moss and weeds ●
Bare patches ● Weak growth ● Mower
damage

Lawn problems

Moss and weeds

If weeds are left unchecked, they will gradually swamp the grass and spoil the lawn. Also, if you wait until the weeds have spread over large patches before destroying them with weedkiller, you will have to cope with large bare patches all over the lawn when the weeds are eradicated. Fortunately, weed control is easy with modern chemicals.

Moss can also be treated chemically, but you must first diagnose the cause of the moss – check whether shade or poor drainage is responsible.

Weak growth

A thin lawn may simply be undernourished-and in need of a good feed – after years of producing lush growth, with nothing given in return, a lawn is likely to be exhausted.

The answer to the problem is to feed the lawn with a quick-acting nitrogenous fertilizer during the spring or summer, and with a slower-acting type in fall.

Other causes of poor lawn growth are lack of moisture, a compacted surface, too-close mowing and a build-up of dead grasses and weeds (see pp56-9).

Fairy rings

A mysterious dark green circle on your lawn is the result of a fungal infection – a rather harsh description for the delightfully-named fairy ring. You may also sometimes find toadstools growing within the fairy ring.

Fortunately, fairy rings rarely do the lawn much damage and are not often serious enough to warrant concern. In most cases the grass will come to little harm and is probably best left alone. However,

Unless you take some action, moss can soon invade the grass.

sometimes a circle of grass may be killed, and in such a case chemical treatment is necessary (see p73).

Mower damage

Sometimes, bare patches on a lawn may be caused by mower damage, and incorrect cutting of the grass (see pp58-9). Circular "scalped" areas, in particular, may be caused by the blades of a rotary lawn

mower that has shaved a slightly raised area.

The bare patches will continue to worsen during subsequent mowing unless the blades of the mower are raised or the area made level. It is important, in any case, to adjust the blades of all mowers to suit the time of year and stage of grass growth (see pp58-9), to avoid damaging the lawn.

Fairy rings are rarely harmful.

Mower damage can spoil a lawn.

Maintaining your lawn

Many gardeners lack the time to undertake all the tasks involved in routine lawn maintenance, but some are essential if the lawn is to be kept in good condition. A good deal of extra work will be involved if major renovation is needed as a result of neglect.

The amount of attention a lawn requires depends to a certain extent on the type of soil. Regular feeding and frequent watering are particularly important for lawns on light "hungry" soil. On heavier land, annual spiking or aerating may be needed to improve drainage. Only a lawn on good loam requires a relatively low level of maintenance. Ultimately you will have to base your program on conditions in your own garden.

Watering

Watering should begin before the grass starts to look faded and ceases to grow, as by this time the topsoil will have dried out and it will be difficult to restore it to its normal condition. Lack of water may not permanently damage the grass itself, but it allows drought-resistant weeds to make progress at the grass's expense.

Use a sprinkler for watering (see p28), giving sufficient water to soak right down to the roots. This may be necessary every week during prolonged dry weather, so choose a sprinkler with a throw to match the size of your lawn. A faucet timer, which will turn the water off at a preset time is also useful if you are not always around to keep an eye on the watering.

Feeding

All lawns benefit from an annual feed – for some it is almost essential. The most effective time for feeding is late spring, but fertilizer may also be applied throughout the summer. An all-nitrogen fertilizer, such as sulfate of ammonia, will stimulate growth and make the grass green, but it acts as a tonic rather than giving long-lasting nourishment. If you are likely to feed the lawn only once, it is better to use a compound lawn fertilizer that also contains phosphate and potash or just a general-purpose fertilizer.

Ideally, you should apply fertilizer when the grass is dry but the soil is moist. You should water the lawn after applying a granular fertilizer.

For liquid fertilizers, use a watering can, first marking the lawn in strips to avoid overlapping. This also helps when applying a solid fertilizer by hand. (You can make this job much easier by using a wheeled distributor.)

Top-dressing

Top-dressing will benefit your lawn, but whether or not you apply a top-dressing is a matter of individual judgement. Most gardeners do not bother and are still able to keep a respectable-looking lawn. However, gardeners with light soil will undoubtedly improve the lawn by top-dressing it in the fall.

Top-dressing consists of spreading a thin layer of peat, compost, leaf mould or any other thoroughly-rotted organic material, mixed with some sharp sand, over the lawn. (The lighter the soil, the less sand you need.) A bucketful of the mix should cover 3-4 square yards. Use a broom or the back of a rake for spreading.

Top-dressing also fills small hollows in the lawn and reduces general unevenness. This in turn reduces the risk of the grass being "scalped" when you mow the lawn and improves the lawn's general appearance.

Spread top-dressing with a broom, or the back of a rake.

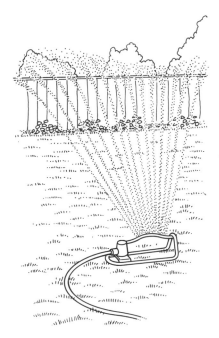

You should water your lawn with a sprinkler.

MAINTAINING YOUR LAWN
Feeding ● Top-dressing ● Watering ●
Raking and scarifying ● Aerating ●
Mistakes to avoid ● Tools

Raking and scarifying

The surface of any lawn acquires a layer of "thatch". This accumulation of dead grass and mowings, which tends to stifle growth, may hardly show until a rake is put to work, but it is remarkable how the extent of the accumulation of thatch then becomes evident.

Fall is the best time for "scarifying", as this vigorous raking is called. A wire-tined rake or, a scarifier with heavier tines should be used. The lawn may look rather shaggy and torn after scarifying but it will soon recover, and will be healthier in the long run.

Lighter raking is needed to remove leaves and twigs in late fall. Raking in spring is necessary for the same reason and prepares the lawn for its first cut of the season.

Aerating

This job is often confused with scarifying, but it serves a completely different purpose. Aerating consists of piercing holes in the top few inches of ground in order to relieve compaction, aid drainage and aerate the soil. It will usually improve any parts of the lawn that tend to become waterlogged and moss-grown, if these problems are due to compaction of the topsoil. However, it cannot actually rectify poor drainage of the lower soil.

Fall is the best time for aerating the lawn as, to be effective, the soil must be moist. If you use a fork, take care not to lever it too much as this will make the surface of the lawn uneven. The holes you make should be about 4in deep. There are also wheeled aerators and special tools available, which remove cores of soil.

Reminders

Rake up leaves in late fall and again in winter. They will harm the grass if left on the lawn.

Lawn thatch will develop very rapidly if your mower does not have a grassbox.

Mixing powdered fertilizer with sand makes it easier to distribute. However, you should adjust the rate of application accordingly.

Rolling, once a regular part of maintenance, is seldom done nowadays, except occasionally in spring to level ground that has become uneven during the winter.

Place stepping stones on areas of lawn which tend to be used too frequently as a path.

Do not apply nitrogenous fertilizers to lawns after late summer.

Lawn sand, applied to damp grass, acts as both a nitrogenous fertilizer and a weedkiller.

Mechanical sweepers are much quicker and easier to use on the lawn than hand rakes.

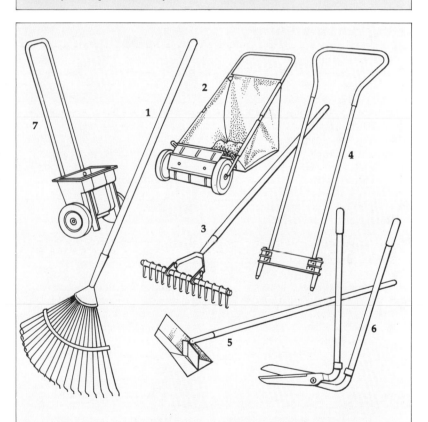

Use a wire rake (**1**) for removing leaves and thatch. A mechanical sweeper (**2**) will clear leaves and other debris. A scarifier (**3**) is a more drastic tool for removing thatch. An aerator (**4**) can be used for piercing holes to relieve compaction. For cutting a lawn edge to shape, use an edging iron (**5**). Edging shears (**6**) are used before mowing to trim lawn edges. Use a distributor (**7**) for distributing fertilizer or grass seed quickly and easily.

Mowing and trimming

Mowing does more than improve the appearance of a lawn – it also encourages the grass to grow more thickly. However, you will achieve a healthy flourishing lawn only if you cut the grass at the right time and in the right way.

The cutting season extends from spring until fall. Within that period, mowing is necessary about once a week – sometimes less frequently in spring and fall but perhaps twice a week at times during the summer. Frequent cutting is the key to a successful lawn, and you should try not to leave the grass uncut for two or three weeks at a time.

The right way to cut a lawn centers on cutting height. So many lawns are virtually shaved, stripping the grasses of the leaves they need for healthy growth. At no time should the blades of a mower be set lower than ¾in, while 1in is better during dry weather in summer.

To measure the height of cut on a cylinder mower, tip it on its side and place a batten across the front and rear rollers. The cutting height is the distance between the fixed blade and the batten. On a rotary mower, place the batten between the front wheel on one side and the rear wheel on the other.

It is better to collect mowings than to leave them on the surface of the lawn. If your mower does not have a grassbox, either sweep up the cuttings afterwards or else cut the grass frequently so that the clippings are fine. Also, cut the lawn when the grass is dry so that the clippings disperse more readily.

Even if your mower has a grassbox it is better to avoid cutting wet grass. If you have an electric mower, position the cable so that you are actually working away from it, drawing it after you. If possible, cut the lawn at right angles on alternate mowings.

This rotary mower has a rear roller to give the lawn a striped finish.

Types of lawn mower

Cylinder mowers have a series of curved, moving blades that shear the grass against a fixed blade beneath them. Many cylinder mowers run on rollers, which facilitates cutting the grass right up to the edges of the lawn and also gives it a striped look. However, some hand-pushed types have wheels instead of a rear roller. Cylinder mowers give a fine finish to the lawn and collect clippings, but most are suitable only for cutting fairly short grass.

Cylinders also have other disadvantages. Because of their shearing action, their blades need adjusting fairly frequently. You will

This damage was done by a rotary lawn mower on an uneven lawn.

MOWING AND TRIMMING
Mistakes to avoid ● Types of
lawn mower ● Trimming lawn edges

Reminders

Rotary lawn mowers collect cuttings less efficiently when the grass is wet.

When choosing a mower, note that it may not be self-propelled even though the blades are power-driven.

Raise the cutting height a little during warm, dry weather.

A hover mower may lose its lift and damage the lawn if it is pushed too far over a lawn edge.

Never wear open-toed sandals when using a rotary lawn mower.

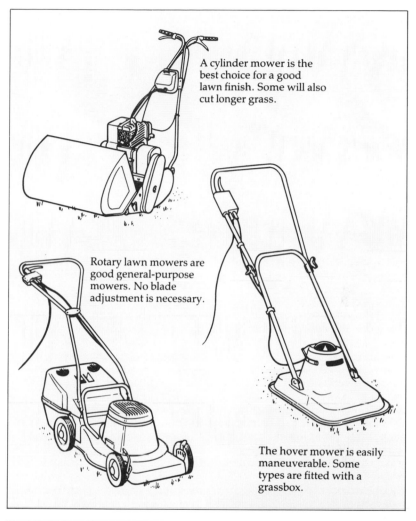

A cylinder mower is the best choice for a good lawn finish. Some will also cut longer grass.

Rotary lawn mowers are good general-purpose mowers. No blade adjustment is necessary.

The hover mower is easily maneuverable. Some types are fitted with a grassbox.

also find it more troublesome to sharpen the blades of cylinder mowers than the blades of their rotary counterparts.

Rotary lawn mowers have two or more blades attached to a power-driven rotor or disk, which is fixed beneath a protective deck. Many rotary cutters designed for lawn use will collect the grass. Most types are better than their cylinder counterparts at cutting fairly long grass, but it can be difficult to give a really close cut without the risk of "scalping" uneven patches. Some also run on rollers to give an attractive striped finish.

Hover, or air-cushion, mowers work on the same principle as rotary lawn mowers but are supported by a down-draft of air instead of wheels. Some will collect the cut grass, although the capacity of the collecting box or bag is usually limited. They are excellent for use on uneven ground, or for cutting banks; and on ordinary lawns they are lighter to push than other types of mower. However, the finish tends not to be as good as that produced by most other types of mower, especially if the machine does not have a box or bag for collecting the grass clippings when the lawn is cut.

Trimming lawn edges

You should cut a vertical edge with a half-moon edging iron when you lay a new lawn, and occasionally recut the edges in subsequent years to maintain neat edges. The grass overhanging the edge should also be trimmed every time you mow the lawn (long-handled shears save stooping). Plastic edging strip can be hammered in flush with the lawn surface to reduce the amount of trimming necessary.

Plastic edging strip is unobtrusive and saves work.

Lawn mower care

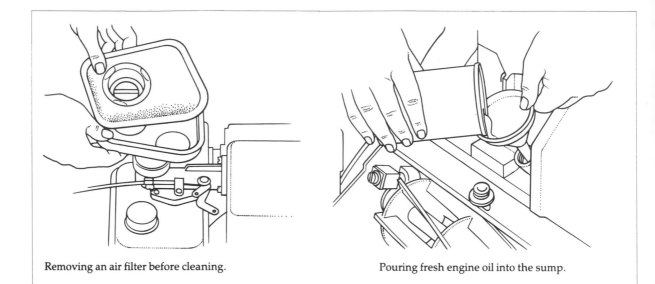

Removing an air filter before cleaning.   Pouring fresh engine oil into the sump.

Mower maintenance

If your mower has a four-stroke engine, change the engine oil annually at either the beginning or the end of the season. Before doing this you must run the engine to warm the oil and then drain the sump. With the sump and fuel tank empty, the machine can be tilted, or even turned upside down, for a thorough cleaning. Special attention should be paid to the underside of rotary lawn mowers, where cut grass accumulates. Two-stroke mowers may be turned over at any time for cleaning, provided that the fuel tank is empty.

The tension of belt or chain drives on cylinder mowers should be checked (see the instruction manual for details) and lubricated as advised. Use an oil can to lubricate all external moving parts of the mower, such as the throttle linkages, height adjusters and wheel bearings.

If the engine has a sponge air filter (fitted inside a metal container), remove it and wash it in warm detergent. After drying, squeeze a little light oil into it before replacing it. Remove the spark plug and scrape any black carbon off the end. With a feeler gauge, check the gap between the points as advised in the engine handbook (usually about 0.025in).

Refill the sump with the correct grade of oil. For some, SAE 30 is recommended; others require multigrade oil. If the machine has a two-stroke engine, use special two-stroke oil, mixing it with the gas, in the exact proportions advised, before filling the tank.

If you have an electric mower, check that the ventilation slots in the motor cowling are not clogged. Once or twice a year examine the cable for physical damage, cutting out any damaged section or replacing it altogether – never repair it with tape. Always fit connectors with the socket section on the mains lead, and the pins on the lead fitted to the mower. Check that the wires are securely fastened and clamped in the plug.

For a first-time start

Check that there is fuel in the tank and that the fuel supply is on.

If the fuel has been in the tank for several months, drain the tank and refill it with fresh fuel – the mower will not run on old fuel.

Operate the manual choke (if your mower has one) or put the throttle slide in the "start" position. Do not choke a warm engine.

Pull the starter cord firmly, bracing one foot against the machine. Do not pull the cord to quite its full length.

If starting is difficult, remove the plug, close the throttle and pull the cord several times. Replace the plug and repeat the starting procedure.

Stale fuel apart, the most likely causes of starting difficulties are a dirty or incorrectly adjusted plug or a failure in the fuel supply.

Sharpening a cylinder mower

With the spark plug and or the electricity disconnected, check the sharpness and adjustment of the blades by tilting the machine backwards and then seeing whether paper can be sheared between the fixed and moving blades. If this is not possible, even after adjusting the cutting cylinder, the blades are definitely blunt.

Professional regrinding is the best way to sharpen blades but is relatively expensive. The alternative is to buy an inexpensive sharpening kit, consisting of abrasive strips stuck on to a metal plate. In turn, the plates are secured to the fixed blade of the mower. When the cylinder is turned, the moving blades are reground on strip. This method is simple and works quite well, but it does not grind the fixed blade. This must be must be reground separately, or replaced, if it is in poor condition.

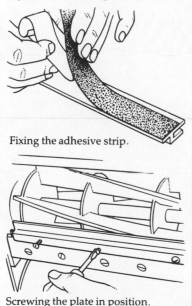

Fixing the adhesive strip.

Screwing the plate in position.

Safe winter storage

After the final cutting in the fall, clean the lawn mower thoroughly. Remembering to clean the grassbox, especially the ventilation holes, on rotary lawn mower boxes is very important.

Other routine maintenance can be carried out during the winter or left until later. However, oiling the external moving parts and spraying the mower with a rust-inhibiting aerosol will prevent corrosion during the winter. Drain the fuel tank, remove the spark plug, and pour a teaspoonful of oil into the hole. Turn the engine to distribute the oil over the cylinder walls, then replace the plug. Turn the engine again until you feel compression. Store the mower in a dry place. Stand the machine on battens, covered with plastic, if there is a risk of the floor becoming damp.

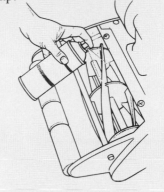

Spraying with rust inhibitor.

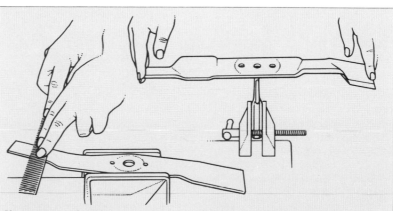

Sharpening with a file.

Balancing the blade after sharpening.

Rotary and hover mowers

With the spark plug or electricity disconnected, remove the blade bar by undoing the central securing nut. Place the bar in a vise and sharpen each cutting edge in turn with a broad, coarse file.

After sharpening, check the balance of the bar by inserting a pencil through the bolt hole or resting the center of the blade on a sharp edge. File off more metal from the heavier end until an even balance is achieved. If the blade is not balanced properly, it may vibrate when the mower is used, which may damage the engine bearings. After re-sharpening the blade, always check that you have replaced it the right way up, and that the nut is securely tightened.

Lawn care around the year

Early winter

Sweep off any remaining leaves, twigs and other debris, together with worm casts. A wire rake will do the task very well, although a wheeled sweeper saves time. Check that the mower and lawn-care tools are kept dry during winter storage. Sod may be laid if the soil is not too wet.

Use a wire rake to collect fallen leaves and twigs.

Early spring

Now the soil is starting to dry out, it is a good time to complete seedbed preparation for a new lawn. You can begin sowing when the weather – and the soil – become noticeably warmer.

Mowing established lawns can begin when the grass is 2-3in high, but rake the lawn first to remove any twigs and to raise grass blades flattened during the winter. The first cut should remove only the top from the blades of grass. If the grass is wet, delay the first cut until the grass is dry.

Early spring is also a good time to repair broken lawn edges and to level any hollows or bumps. Apply moss killer – either lawn sand or proprietary moss killer – if necesssary.

Mid-winter

Sod may still be laid provided that it is not too cold and wet. However, if the soil is heavy, this is seldom possible. Do not work on established lawns on any type of soil during wet or frosty weather.

Leaves may have been blown on to the lawn from beneath shrubs or a hedge. Sweep them off if the surface is not too wet.

To avoid the spring rush, have your mower sharpened professionally, or do it yourself. Spray the blades and other bare metal on the mower with a moisture-repellent aerosol as a precaution against rust. Start gas engine mowers once or twice during the winter and run them until they are warm. It is best to use fresh gasoline.

Mid-spring

The lawn needs frequent mowing now and the blades of the mower can be lowered as the grass grows faster. With a cylinder mower, the grass can be cut as low as ½in, but if you cut this low with a rotary mower you run the risk of "scalping" any slightly raised areas of the lawn.

This is the ideal time for spring sowing, because seeds will germinate rapidly in the warmer soil and the young plants make rapid growth. Fertilizers and weedkillers may be applied, provided that the grass is growing noticeably. The soil should be moist at the time of application, but the grass itself should be dry.

This is a good time to reseed bare patches, as well as to sow new lawns. Loosen the surface with a fork and rake, sow the seeds, then cover them thinly with sifted soil. Protect the surface from the birds with strands of thread.

Late winter

Sod may still be laid if it is not too cold or wet, but laying should be completed before spring. If you plan to sow a new lawn, continue with seedbed preparation as soon as the soil is dry enough; that is, as soon as it does not stick to your boots. The preparation should include leveling, feeding, raking the soil to a tilth and firming. However, do not sow grass seed until early or mid-spring. If there are a lot of worm casts on the lawn, scatter them with a broom or rake, and collect any leaves.

Service your mower. If it is gas-powered, change the engine oil and lubricate the moving parts, unless this was done before the winter. If the mower is electric, check that the wiring and all the connections are safe.

Late spring

Though occasional light raking is good for a lawn, this is not a suitable time of year for vigorous scarifying. If you have a powered lawn rake or scarifier, it should be used only on a high setting, unless you are trying to remove an area of moss from the lawn.

This is the perfect time for application of selective weedkillers and lawn fertilizers, together or separately. Apply weedkillers when there is plenty of leaf growth – usually a week after the previous cut is a suitable time.

It is generally too late to establish a new lawn from seed but, if the weather is damp, or you are prepared to irrigate the area, it is worth taking a chance.

A lawn in good condition may now need mowing twice weekly during damp weather. This is better than removing larger amounts of grass less frequently.

Early summer

Sowing and turfing must now wait until fall. Summer is the time to keep established lawns growing healthily. Watering is necessary during a prolonged dry spell; this should be done before the soil has become too parched and there should always be enough water to soak right down to the grass roots and below.

Do not cut the lawn lower than about 1in during a prolonged spell of dry weather.

Apply a lawn fertilizer if this was not done earlier, together with a selective weedkiller if needed. Even if fertilizer was applied earlier, an application of one of the nitrogen-rich lawn tonics may still be necessary if your lawn is not in the best condition, and you wish to restore its color.

Mid-summer

During prolonged dry weather, the mower blades should be raised a little, so that the grass is not cut too short. However, you should continue cutting the lawn weekly rather than at longer intervals. During warm, damp weather, when the grass grows particularly rapidly, you may find that twice-weekly cutting is necessary.

Continue watering the lawn if the ground shows signs of drying out, always bearing in mind that generous waterings at intervals are better than frequent moistening of just the surface.

You may still feed and weed the lawn. Local applications of a weedkiller – perhaps with a paint-on touch-weeder – may also be necessary, even if overall treatment was given earlier.

Late summer

Preparations can now begin for sowing a lawn during the first half of fall. Having dug, leveled and firmed the soil, leave the plot for two or three weeks for weeds to germinate. Before sowing, hoe these off, apply fertilizer and give the soil a final raking.

There is still time for fertilizer and weedkiller treatment, but make sure that the soil is thoroughly moist, and the grass dry, before applying either.

Hoeing before you sow a lawn will destroy weed seedlings.

Early fall

This is the best period for establishing lawns from seed. The soil is warmer than in spring and both germination and seedling development are rapid. If the preparations were not started earlier, follow the late summer procedure already described, but omit the short interval allowed for weeds to grow.

Fall is also a good time to repair your lawn and reseed bare patches. There is also no better season for scarifying established lawn, loosening and pulling out the "thatch" of dead and prostrate grasses and weeds. Compacted ground should be aerated to admit air and assist drainage.

After scarifying, and removing all the material raked out from the lawn, top-dress it with a mix of sand and either compost or peat. Also, a slow-acting fall lawn feed is beneficial.

Mid-fall

As the weather turns colder, the grass's growth will slow down and you may be able to stop mowing and trimming the edges of the lawn. Aerating, top-dressing and fall feeding can still proceed as already described, and you can also continue with preparations for laying sod, and the laying itself.

Mid-fall is one of the best times for aerating a lawn.

Late fall

Use a wire rake to collect leaves and scatter worm casts. Sod may be laid from this time onwards whenever conditions are suitable. Aerate and top-dress the soil if this has not already been done. Give the lawn a final trim, if necessary.

When you have finished using the lawnmower, clean it thoroughly, and lubricate all moving and bare metal parts. Store it under cover for the winter.

Repairing a damaged lawn

Fall and spring are the best times for eradicating the blemishes from which so many lawns suffer – broken edges, an uneven surface, bare patches and so on. These problems may arise for a number of reasons; the lawn may have been badly laid in the first place, or the harm may have been done by subsequent mistreatment. In addition to repairing the damage, consider how it might be prevented in the future. This often involves nothing more dramatic than raising the mower blades a little to avoid shaving the grass too closely, or discouraging the use of a damaged part of the lawn as a path.

Repairing broken edges

Lawn edges are particularly likely to crumble on light soil. Children playing in the garden are often responsible for broken edges, and damage is most likely to occur if clear, sharply-defined edges are not cut in the first place where the lawn adjoins a border or an island bed. Repairing edges is simple but you will need to keep people and animals off the affected patch for a few weeks. To repair the damage you will need a half-moon edging iron, which has a curved blade and is much better than a spade. You will also need a small amount of grass seed.

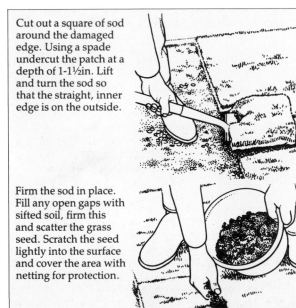

Cut out a square of sod around the damaged edge. Using a spade undercut the patch at a depth of 1-1½in. Lift and turn the sod so that the straight, inner edge is on the outside.

Firm the sod in place. Fill any open gaps with sifted soil, firm this and scatter the grass seed. Scratch the seed lightly into the surface and cover the area with netting for protection.

Leveling bumps and hollows

An uneven surface is generally due to faulty preparation before the lawn was laid. If the ground was not dug, prepared and firmed properly, the soil will settle unevenly and remain so permanently. Bumps may also result from mole workings or from undue movement of the fork when you aerate the lawn. Hollows may occur in places that receive more than average wear. Apart from being unsightly, hollows and bumps should be put right because an uneven surface may suffer mower damage. The repair stages are much the same for both faults.

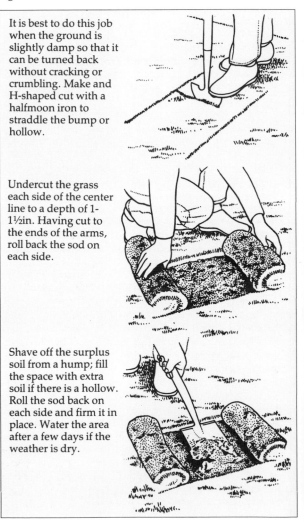

It is best to do this job when the ground is slightly damp so that it can be turned back without cracking or crumbling. Make and H-shaped cut with a halfmoon iron to straddle the bump or hollow.

Undercut the grass each side of the center line to a depth of 1-1½in. Having cut to the ends of the arms, roll back the sod on each side.

Shave off the surplus soil from a hump; fill the space with extra soil if there is a hollow. Roll the sod back on each side and firm it in place. Water the area after a few days if the weather is dry.

REPAIRING A DAMAGED LAWN

Repairing broken edges ● Repairing
bumps and hollows ● Making good
bare patches ● How to prevent damage

Restoring bare patches

A bare patch may be large, perhaps due to excessive wear from children playing or from ball games; or it may be just a small area caused by fuel spillage. The remedy is either to resod or reseed the area. New sod can be laid at any time during the fall and winter; seed is best sown in spring or late summer.

If the bare patch is due to a more serious and persistent problem, such as waterlogging or drip from trees, it is not worth renovating the area unless steps are taken to remove the primary cause.

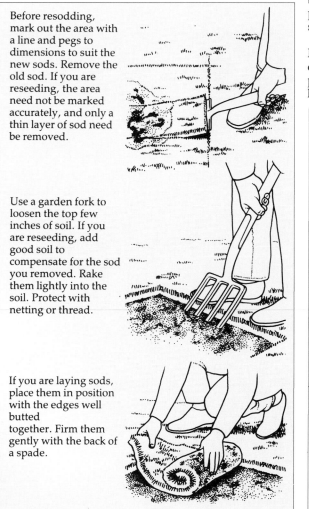

Before resodding, mark out the area with a line and pegs to dimensions to suit the new sods. Remove the old sod. If you are reseeding, the area need not be marked accurately, and only a thin layer of sod need be removed.

Use a garden fork to loosen the top few inches of soil. If you are reseeding, add good soil to compensate for the sod you removed. Rake them lightly into the soil. Protect with netting or thread.

If you are laying sods, place them in position with the edges well butted together. Firm them gently with the back of a spade.

How to prevent damage

Grass seldom grows well beneath a tree that casts deep shade or drips heavily. Consider planting ground cover instead (see pp44-5), or perhaps covering the area with gravel or paving (see pp34-5).

If the lawn is often used as a path, you can either discourage this by blocking the route with trellis or a shrub, or minimize the damage by setting stepping stones in the lawn. Lawn edges that suffer frequent damage can be replaced by a row of bricks set flush with the lawn.

Grass paths lose their visual appeal when they become worn. If this happens, either widen the path to spread the wear more evenly or lay a hard surface instead.

Make sure you cut the lawn correctly (see pp58-9). Irregular mowing and cutting grass too closely cause serious damage when continued over long periods. If this is combined with hot weather or heavy wear, bare patches may develop.

Bricks laid along the lawn edge, flush with the ground, prevent it from crumbling. Use paving bricks for edging; ordinary building bricks will themselves crumble as a result of frost action.

Circular paving stones are very attractive. Put them in position, cut around them with a heavy knife and remove the sod. Take out enough soil for the stone to rest flush with the surface.

Before laying gravel, remove the top inch or two of soil. Then fix an edging strip and spread the gravel. Shade-tolerant plants can be grown here.

Planning a new lawn

Before establishing a lawn you should be clear about its likely use and how much time you are prepared to spend looking after it. Do you need and ordinary, family-type lawn for children's games and barbeques? Or do you want an immaculately-groomed lawn, even though it will need cosseting right through the year?

The point is that different grasses are needed for each purpose – hard-wearing, tolerant types for the family lawn; fine, sometimes finicky grasses for a showpiece lawn. For most gardeners the best choice, without doubt, is a utility-type lawn. With a reasonable amount of care this can look very presentable and is more likely to withstand occasional lapses in management. A perfectly-groomed lawn, on the other hand, involves hard work (and extra expense) from beginning to end.

You must also decide whether you would rather lay sods or sow seeds. Both methods have their separate advantages.

Sods are more expensive than grass seed and involve extra work. The quality is often variable and you risk disappointment unless you buy your sod from a specialist supplier. On the other hand, sods may be laid at any time of the year between fall and spring, and even a little beyond these seasons if you are prepared to water them repeatedly in hot and dry weather. They also provide a serviceable lawn in a shorter time than seeding, although you should not use the grass for some weeks after claying.

A seeded lawn is cheaper than buying sods, while its quality is less variable. A seeds mixture can also be chosen specifically to suit your purpose. However, it will take longer to become established and sowing is restricted to spring and late summer.

Hard-wearing grasses

These are some of the types that may be included in "family-lawn" type mixtures. Most are tolerant of a variety of conditions and will stand up to a fair amount of hard wear. They may also be present in sods, but unfortunately, when you buy the sods, you can rarely be certain about the types of grass they contain.

Timothy (*Phleum pratense*) is especially good on heavy soil. It is suitable for cold, exposed gardens but is best avoided on dry, sandy soil.

Smooth-stalked meadow grass (*Poa pratensis*) has a spreading habit and is drought-resistant. It dislikes being cut too closely.

Annual meadow grass (*Poa annua*) self-seeds in many lawns. It grows well in shade and thrives on close cutting but dislikes excessive dryness.

Perennial ryegrass (*Lolium perenne*) is hard-wearing and found in most utility mixtures. It is considered coarse, but the newer, named strains are finer.

Crested dog's tail (*Cynosurus cristatus*) is a tough, slow-growing grass with a compact habit. It grows well on most soils. Avoid cutting it closely.

PLANNING A NEW LAWN

Choosing grasses ● Fine grasses ●
Hard-wearing grasses ● Popular lawn
mixtures

Fine grasses

Although these are used to create top-quality lawns, some are also found in a few everyday mixtures. Before buying, check whether the grasses in your chosen mixture are the ones most likely to suit your particular requirements. Some of these finer grasses may also be found in the better grades of sod. Try to check a sample first.

Velvet bent *(Agrostis canina canina)* is a fine, soft grass which prefers a rather damp soil and also likes shade. It benefits from regular scarifying.

Chewing's fescue *(Festuca rubra commutata)* is fine-leaved, with a tufted habit. It grows almost anywhere and withstands drought and close mowing.

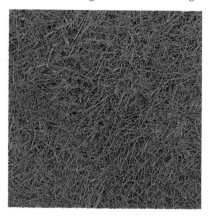

Browntop *(Agrostis tenuis)* is a hard-wearing grass but with fine, dense leaves. It grows in almost any soil and is found in most "luxury" mixtures.

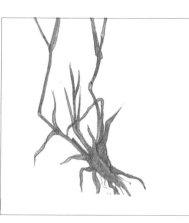

Creeping red fescue *(Festuca rubra rubra)* is suitable for most lawns, being fine yet quite hard wearing. It grows on most soils but dislikes close cutting.

Hard fescue *(Festuca longifolia)* is a tufted grass, which is occasionally included in mixtures. It grows anywhere and withstands drought well.

Seeds mixtures

There is little point in making up your own mixture of grass seeds. Commercial suppliers offer carefully-balanced mixes, indicating in each case whether they are for a utility type-lawn or a higher-quality one. There are also mixtures available for shaded areas.

In many cases, two or more named strains of the same species are used in a mixture, providing a balance that the amateur is unlikely to achieve by him or herself. However, it is important to buy from a reputable supplier, bearing in mind that a lawn should last for many years.

If you want an average, everyday lawn, the main question is whether or not to buy a mixture containing perennial ryegrass. Provided that the ryegrass is one of the slower-growing, finer-leaved strains, it is usually an advantage to do so, because of the hard-wearing qualities of this type of grass.

Buying sod

For top quality sod you should go to a reputable supplier to see what is available. Quality sod has to be grown for the purpose or else stripped from an area, such as parkland, where the grass has been carefully maintained.

Each sod usually measures 3ft x 1ft, but check the size with the supplier before ordering a particular quantity. Allow for some wastage around the edges.

As your lawn will be a centerpiece in your garden, there is no point in skimping at this stage. It is possible to buy cheaper quality sod, but you will find that this is not worth it in the long run, because the sod is likely to include any combination of grasses or weeds.

Establishing a new lawn

Whether you plan to sow a lawn or lay sod, the soil should be prepared in the same way. Complete the main digging or cultivating of the soil at least a month – or preferably longer – before you plan to sow or sod. This will give the soil time to settle before you give it a final leveling and raking. Always prepare an area slightly larger than the intended lawn, so that the new grass can be trimmed to shape afterwards.

Fork over the site to loosen the soil. If you need to save time, hire a cultivator. Remove perennial weeds, complete with their roots, together with any large stones and other debris. Fork in some compost, rotted manure or peat (unless the soil is already in first-class condition) and break it down as finely as you can, rather than leaving large lumps. Make the surface as even as possible – a gentle slope will not affect the surface, but you should eliminate any obvious high or low spots.

Leave the site untouched until just before you plan to sow or sod. it. Then, if many annual weeds have germinated, treat them with a contact weedkiller (see pp46-7).

A few days later, break up the surface with a cultivator or a fork, then compact the soil by treading over the surface, shuffling from side to side across the plot to achieve an even level of compaction.

Now the soil is ready for a final leveling. First, remove your footmarks with the pronged cultivator, without penetrating the soil too deeply. Then work right across the plot with a garden rake in one direction – and then across it again at right angles to the first raking. This serves the dual purpose of creating a fine tilth and leveling the surface. Check for any unevenness by looking at the surface from a low level at several standpoints around the edge.

Laying sod

This should be done in fall or spring. Lay the sods as soon as possible after delivery, since they soon deteriorate.

When laying, stand on a broad plank to avoid walking on the sods. You will need sufficient planks to take you from the edge to at least the middle of the plot.

Start by laying a row of sods along one edge – slightly overlapping the edge to allow for trimming. If necessary, adjust the soil beneath the sods to achieve a level surface. Butt the sods tightly

The joints between sods in adjacent rows should be staggered. Work from a plank rather than standing on the prepared site or the sods.

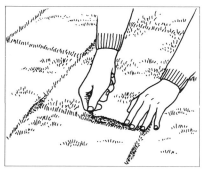

Use sifted soil, with some peat added to fill any small gaps between sods. Firm this with your fingers. The grass roots will soon grow into the soil.

together and gently firm them with the head of a rake or with a spade. Fill the gaps with fine soil.

Lay the next row with staggered joints, like brickwork. Butt each sod firmly against the first row. Continue working across the lawn, standing on planks laid across the new sods.

When sodding is complete, trim the edges of the lawn to shape with a half-moon edging iron. If you want a straight edge, use pegs and a line – or boards – as a guideline. If you want a curved edge, you can use a hose. Experiment first with different shapes and sizes of curves before cutting the edge.

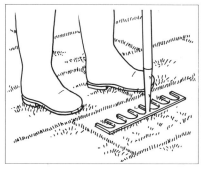

Firm thumping with a rake head, or a spade, will press the underside of the sods against the garden soil, but avoid being too heavy-handed.

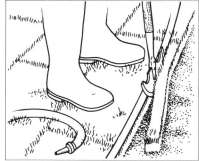

A hose can be laid in a gentle curve as a guide when trimming the lawn edge, but first try various curves to see which you prefer.

Sowing lawn seed

The best time to sow grass seed is late summer. They will germinate rapidly, giving the lawn time to become established before winter sets in. Spring sowing is also satisfactory but germination is slower and the young lawn will need prompt watering if a dry spell follows. Apply a balanced fertilizer before the final raking.

The sowing rate is 1-1½oz per square yard – the larger amount is for fine grasses. Accurate sowing is easiest with a distributor, but it can be done by hand. To do this, first mark a yard-wide strip down one side of the plot with pegs and string. Measure the length and weigh out the required amount of seeds. Scatter them evenly along the strip, then rake them lightly into the surface. Move the first length of string over the second to mark out another yard-wide strip, and continue sowing.

Work backwards, strip by strip, across the unseeded area. If the soil is soft, lay planks across it, on which to stand, to avoid making deep footmarks. After sowing, protect the area against birds and cats with a covering net of black thread (*see pp48-9*).

Lawn aftercare

Sod laid during the fall or winter should require little attention until the spring. Only during a very dry fall will it need watering. However, spring-laid sod should be watered without delay if a dry spell follows. It should not be necessary to roll the lawn during damp weather but you may find rolling helps to establish the grass if conditions are dry.

Seeded lawns need watering if the weather turns dry after they have germinated, but only use a fine spray – a perforated hose is ideal. A coarse spray, with large droplets, will pan the surface soil and harm the young grasses. Do not water the area if the seeds have not germinated.

Allow both sod and seeded lawns to make planty of growth – about 2in – before cutting. Then only cut the tips of the grasses, preferably with a rotary mower or hover mower. Reduce the cutting height gradually, especially for seeded lawns, until the grass is fully established.

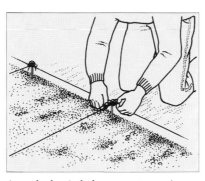

A dressing of balanced fertilizer gives the lawn a good start. Granular fertilizers take some time to dissolve, so their effect is long-lasting.

A marked strip helps accurate sowing. Strings can be fixed crossways at yard intervals for greater accuracy, but this is not strictly necessary.

Until you are experienced, sow rather thinly at first and then go back over the strip with whatever remains of the measured amount.

Only a light raking is necessary after sowing to mix the seed with the surface soil. A proportion of seeds will still be visible afterwards.

Weeds and moss

Weeds do more than just make a lawn look untidy; if left unchecked, they will gradually take over the area, swamping the finer grasses and making the lawn look patchy and uneven. Belated control of the problem with weedkiller also results in bare patches, which then have to be reseeded.

Fortunately, regular mowing disposes of most weeds, especially the dense crop that springs up after a new lawn is sown. Unlike grasses, which thicken and spread as a result of mowing, weeds are weakened by being regularly cut. The ones that do survive are those with a prostrate habit, such as plantains, or with a creeping form of growth, such as buttercups.

The gardener's first line of defense against weeds is to keep the grass growing strongly by good all-around management. This means feeding the lawn at least once a year, watering it when necessary and always mowing it to the right height – ¾-1in. Healthy, dense grass leaves little space for weeds to germinate and develop.

In spite of this, some weeds will inevitably appear, as their seeds are carried everywhere by the wind or birds. Isolated weeds are best dealt with by a touch-weeder or spot-weeder. These are devices consisting of a sponge or wick saturated with weedkiller which can then be dabbed or smeared on leaves. This method is particularly useful for dealing with deep-rooted weeds, such as dandelions.

Where weeds are widespread, it is necessary to treat the whole lawn with a selective weedkiller, which destroys weeds but not the grass.

Alternatively, lawn sand may be applied. This will kill most annual weeds (and moss as well) and act as a tonic to the grass. However, unfortunately it does not control the more difficult and deep-rooted perennial weeds (see pp42-3).

Treated and untreated – a striking example of weed control.

Moss

Excessive damp and shade are common causes of moss appearing in lawns, but there are others. Certain types of moss will grow where the ground is unusually dry. Most types of moss are encouraged by acid soil.

Dampness and waterlogging may be due to compaction of the soil. If this is the case, the solution is to aerate the lawn (see pp56-7). If the garden as a whole suffers from waterlogging, try to improve overall drainage (see pp14-15).

Shade can sometimes be lessened by felling a tree or thinning out the branches. However, if this is impractical, or a building is the cause of the shade, it may be better to lay paving or gravel over the affected area, or to establish a bed of shade-tolerant plants.

Lime discourages moss but should be applied only if a soil test shows an unusually low pH reading. Use ground limestone. Vigorous scarifying in the fall also helps to eliminate moss and the conditions in which it thrives.

It is only worth applying a commercial moss-killer when you have dealt with the underlying

WEEDS AND MOSS

How moss and weeds spoil a lawn ●
How and when to destroy them ●
Weedkillers ● Moss-killers

causes of the problem. Although moss-killers are based on a number of different chemicals, in each case the most effective time for application is spring or early fall when the moss is growing actively. Lawn sand should be applied in spring or early summer.

Weedkillers

Selective weedkillers intended for lawn use are hormone substances that overstimulate and distort weed growth, but have little or no effect on the grass. The weeds die soon after treatment.

There are many selective weedkillers, some formulated to kill all common lawn weeds and others that are designed to destroy difficult types, such as clover and speedwell. Most are intended for use on established lawns, but there are types suitable for treating newly-sown lawns.

Liquid weedkillers are easy to apply, but there are also some granular and powder forms available. Some contain a balanced fertilizer, so a single application both weeds and feeds the lawn.

Selective weedkillers are also available as spot-weeders for smearing on individual weeds and in aerosol form. Early treatment with one of these prevents isolated weeds from spreading.

Although it is not a hormone-type product, lawn sand has a selective weedkilling – and moss-killing – action and also stimulates lawn growth. It must be applied while the ground is damp. The lawn sand may scorch the grass slightly, so the lawn should be watered two or three days after application.

Applying weedkillers

It is best to apply weedkillers in spring and early summer, but

The weeds in this newly-sown lawn will be destroyed when the lawn is cut.

treatment remains reasonably effective until late summer. If possible, apply a lawn fertilizer a couple of weeks before the weedkiller but, if you do this, you should not use a combined weedkiller-fertilizer.

Do not mow the grass for a few days before applying the weedkiller. Ideally, the grass should be dry but the ground damp at the time of application. After using the weedkiller, leave the lawn uncut for at least another three days. Do not use the lawn cuttings as a mulch until the lawn has been mown several

times. Any compost made from the cuttings should not be used for at least six months.

It is safest to apply the weedkiller with a watering can fitted with a fine rose. If you use a spray, choose a calm day and make sure that the spray does not drift on to nearby plants. Always divide the lawn with a line and pegs to avoid gaps or overlapping in your application. This also applies if you spread granules or powder by hand, but a small wheeled distributor usually makes marks that are clear enough for guidance.

Lawn pests and diseases

The most dramatic lawn damage, by far, is caused by an invasion of moles. Leatherjackets are another likely source of trouble.

Moles
Smoke cartridges, used when the moles are active in spring or fall are reasonably effective. A lighted cartridge should be placed in a tunnel, some 6-12in beneath a recently formed molehill. The smoke should then penetrate the whole underground system.

Leatherjackets
These mud-colored grubs are the larvae of craneflies, which lay their eggs in late summer. They feed on grass roots – and on numerous garden plants as well – causing extensive yellow patches. Water the affected area with a product containing carbaryl.

Earthworms
Although worm casts are unsightly and, when flattened by walking or with a mower, may smother the grass, worms are not a serious problem. Commercial worm-killers based on carbaryl are available, but the casts can easily be swept away.

Chafers
Like leatherjackets, these gray-white grubs are sometimes the cause of discolored patches on the grass. By the time these patches appear, the damage has alraedy been done. However, fall treatment with a carbaryl-based compound will prevent the problem recurring in subsequent years.

Ants
These are only a minor problem, although they may do a certain amount of damage on light soil during a hot summer. If necessary, dust the lawn with a commercial ant-killer or water with a carbaryl-based product.

Fusarium patch causes patches of grass to turn yellow and then die.

Worm casts are most evident during mild weather in autumn.

Red thread is unlikely to occur on lawns that are fed regularly.

Excessive damp and poor management may result in algae developing.

Moles often invade gardens close to agricultural land.

Diseases

These may stem from mismanagement or unfavorable conditions. If your lawn is in poor condition, you should treat it before any disease can take hold.

Red thread

This is a fungal disease that attacks lawns in poor condition. In fall, patches of dead lawn will have a reddish tinge. Treat the lawn with a commercial lawn fungicide, such as one containing benomyl or dichlorophen. You should also aerate the lawn and apply a lawn fertilizer in the spring.

Fusarium patch

This is a fairly common fungal disease, which causes patches of grass to turn yellow and die. The patches will be covered with white mold in damp weather, and will often be seen when snow melts. Fusarium patch may be triggered by use of nitrogeneous fertilizer during the fall. Treat the affected patches with a fungicide, as for red thread.

Algae

The grass may become covered with a slippery, slimy layer of algae on badly-drained ground, especially if it has been cut carelessly or fed insufficiently. Lawn sand or moss-killer will destroy algae, but you should also aerate and feed the lawn.

Fairy rings

A circle of dark lawn, accompanied by toadstools, is evidence of a fungal infection. If the ring is not greatly disfiguring it is best not to treat it, as the only reliable cure involves removing a broad band of grass and soil to a depth of 9-12in and then re-filling the hole with fresh soil.

Flowers

76 The garden in bloom
78 Annuals
80 Half-hardy annuals
82 Easy half-hardy annuals
84 Biennials
86 Herbaceous perennials
88 Dividing perennials
89 Annual and perennial climbers
90 Dahlias
91 Chrysanthemums
92 Easy-to-grow perennials
96 Bulbs, corms and tubers
98 Caring for bulbs
100 Irises
101 Lilies
102 Easy bulbs and corms
104 Container plants
106 Rock gardens and plants
108 Other sites for rock plants
110 Caring for rock plants
111 Easy-to-grow rock plants
114 Preventing plant problems
116 Flower pests and diseases

The garden in bloom

For most people flowers are the crowning glory of the garden, the enchanting and exciting reward for all our efforts. The pity is that beginners may feel inhibited by the very diversity of the plants from which they have to choose. However, the confusion can be reduced considerably if we divide flowers into their broad botanical categories. The flowers within each category share common characteristics, so the category to which a flower belongs will determine how, where and when it should be grown.

Annuals

These are plants that grow, flower and die in a single season. Hardy annuals are capable of withstanding frost and are generally sown outdoors in the place where they are intended to flower. Half-hardy annuals (sold as bedding plants) are raised in warmth and not moved outdoors until the danger of frost is over.

Petunias are among the best-known half-hardy annuals.

Biennials

These are plants that flower and die the year after they have been sown. Foxgloves, for instance, are sown in early summer, planted out during the fall and flower the following spring. Usually they die after their seeds have formed.

However, the accuracy of the term "biennial" depends to some extent on how the plants are grown. Some biennials will flower in the first year if raised under glass in the same way as half-hardy annuals.

Foxgloves are usually biennial, but sometimes live for several seasons.

Herbaceous plants

Plants that live for a number of years, their growth dying down each fall, are called herbaceous perennials. They are also termed "hardy" plants, as they can withstand severe winters in their dormant state. Some hardy types can go through the winter without losing their stems or foliage.

Bulbs and corms

Botanically, bulbs are underground buds and corms are underground stems. These flowering plants, many of which may be left undisturbed for years on end, come in many different varieties. They are by no means confined to spring flowering. There are species to bloom in summer, fall and even winter.

 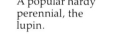

A popular hardy perennial, the lupin.

The gladiolus has magnificent blooms.

Climbers

Most garden climbing plants are shrubs, but there are also some other types worth considering. In particular, plants such as the nasturtium (climbing varieties), will cover a fence or an arch very rapidly and provide a mass of color during the summer months. Some climbers are half-hardy and need to be raised in a greenhouse at first, and planted out later.

Nasturtiums are just as happy climbing over a trellis as on the ground.

Rock plants

These are also called alpines, and originally come from hills and mountain areas. Rock plants include some of the brightest and daintiest of all garden plants. There are perennial rock plants, both evergreen and deciduous, as well as some shrubby types.

Most rock plants are perfectly hardy but tend to dislike damp conditions. If you do not have a suitable site for a rock garden, or do not wish to build a dry stone wall, they will grow just a happily in a well-drained trough or raised bed.

Lithospermum – a marvelous and compact summer-flowering alpine.

Tubers

Certain plants, including dahlias and some begonias, have fleshy underground stems or roots which carry buds for the following year's growth. Called tubers, they have been singled out here and elsewhere in this chapter, not because they demand a particular site or growing conditions, but because their care and propagation differs a little from other plants. Tuberous plants use their swollen roots to store nourishment during the winter and ensure a good start the following spring.

Mesembryanthemums will give your rock garden brilliant colour.

Annuals

Setting the garden ablaze from early summer until fall, annuals earn their keep many times over during their brief lives. They may only live for one year, but they are not difficult plants. As long as they are sown and planted at the right time, they are undemanding plants, asking only a place in the sun and water in dry weather.

Hardy annuals are generally sown where they are to flower. Even so, most will transplant quite well, so surplus seedlings from an overliberal sowing can be moved to new sites.

Half-hardy annuals must be protected until the risk of late spring frosts is over. They should then be hardened off gradually by being covered only at night for the week or two before planting.

Both hardy and half-hardy annuals are best grown in beds where they can be reached easily for hoeing and removing dead blooms. They can be grown in separate beds; alternatively, they can be used to fill spaces between herbaceous plants.

Hardy annuals

Hardy annuals should be sown in mid-spring. Before you begin, make sure that the soil will crumble to give a tilth – this indicates that it is ready for sowing seeds.

Sowing hardy annuals in late spring will provide late-summer flowers after many annuals are over. Exceptionally early flowers will result from sowing some of the hardiest sorts in the early fall of the previous year. However, you should be prepared for the fact that the cold may kill some of the flowers.

Rake a general fertilizer into the surface when preparing the seedbed, then use the corner of a hoe to mark out the areas for each type of plant. These may be

Linum grandiflorum 'Rubrum' flowers abundantly all summer long.

irregular interlocking shapes, with repeats of the same plants at intervals rather than large, solitary blocks. Rake each patch lightly in one direction to leave parallel lines. Scatter the seeds thinly along the furrows left by the rake, then draw the rake over the ground at right-angles to the original furrows to cover the seeds.

Push in sticks or pegs around the edge of the bed at regular intervals and create a net over the bed by crisscrossing black thread between the pegs to keep off the birds. Later, thin overcrowded seedlings.

Sow sweet peas individually, first soaking the seeds for 24 hours. When the seedlings begin to grow, support them with net or sticks.

Though eschscholzia flowers are similar to poppies, the plants are not related.

Easy-to-grow hardy annuals

Species names are given where there is a chance of confusion. Most plants are available in a range of colors and shades. Average heights (H) and spacings (S) are given.

Calendula (pot marigold) H 12in, S 9in. Cream, yellow, orange flowers. Sun.
Centaurea (cornflower) H 2ft, S 12in. Sprays of pink, red or white flowers. Sun/light shade.
Chrysanthemum carinatum H 18in, S 12in. Color-banded daisies. Sun.
Clarkia H 2ft, S 9in. White, pink or red spikes. Sun.
Coreopsis tinctoria H 2ft, S 12in. Yellow and red daisy-like flowers. Sun.
Delphinium ajacis (larkspur) H 30in, S 12in. Graceful spires. Sun.

Eschscholzia (Californian poppy) H 12in, S 6in. Bright yellow and orange flowers. Sun.
Godetia H 12in, S 6in. Bushy, brightly-colored flowers. Sun.
Gypsophila elegans H 18in, S 9in. Pink and white cascades. Sun.
Iberis (candytuft) H 12in, S 6in. White, pink or crimson flowers. Sun.
Lathyrus (sweet pea) H 3-6ft, S 6in. Numerous pastel shades of flowers. Sun.
Lavatera trimestris (mallow) H 30in, S 18in. White or rosy pink flowers. Sun.
Limnanthes (poached egg flower) H 9in, S 4in. Massed white and yellow blooms. Sun.
Linum grandiflorum (flax) H 18in, S 9in. White, blue, and red, long-lasting flowers. Sun.
Matthiola bicornis (night-scented stock) H 12in, S 9in. Strongly-scented lilac flowers. Sun.
Nemophila H 6in, S 4in. White-centered blue flowers. Sun/light shade.
Nigella (love-in-a-mist) H 12in, S 9in. White, pink or blue flowers. Sun.
Papaver rhoeas (poppy) H 2ft, S 12in. Cup-shaped, pink and red flowers. Sun.
Tropaeolum (nasturtium) H 12in, S 12in. Red, orange or yellow. Sun/shade.
Viscaria H 12in, S 4in. White, blue, pink and purple flowers. Sun.

Nemophila is a spreading plant, often used as an edging for borders.

Reminders

Support floppy plants, such as cornflowers and larkspurs, with twiggy sticks.

Use twigged branches to keep cats off the seedbed.

When thinning, avoid disturbing nearby seedlings.

Remove dead blooms every day or two to encourage further flowers.

If weeds are kept down in the early stages the plants will then tend to smother them.

Summer annuals

Growing summer annuals

Bedding plants, as half-hardy annuals are called, are often on sale well before it is safe to plant them. If you buy them at this time, place them in a cold frame and cover them at night until the risk of frost is over. Whether you buy early or later in the season, always buy compact, bushy plants and avoid those that are already in flower.

Planting out

Plant half-hardy annuals in soil that has been dug and broken down fairly finely. Scatter a dressing of general fertilizer before giving the soil a final raking.

Water the trays of plants an hour or so before setting them out. Using a trowel, set the plants in groups of between six and twelve (or in

The massed flowers of *Phlox drummondii* continue until late summer.

Raising plants

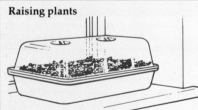

With a covered propagator, half-hardy annuals can be raised on a windowsill.

The roots should extend to their full length when placed in the compost.

A cold frame provides the intermediate stage between greenhouse and garden.

Half-hardy annuals can be sown in a greenhouse and planted out as soon as the weather is suitable. They need only a little warmth.

Plants can also be raised on an indoor windowsill, but they may become lanky and overgrown when they pass the seedling stage. To minimize this, avoid very early sowing and place the boxes of half-grown plants in a sunny, sheltered spot outdoors for part of the day during warm weather.

Sow the seeds in labeled pans of seed compost, covered plastic to prevent drying out; then put them in a warm place to germinate. Remove the plastic as soon as the seedlings appear. "Prick out" (plant) the seedlings individually in trays of potting compost, just over 1in apart. Hold the seedlings by their leaves, make the planting holes with a pencil and put the

seedlings in firmly.

Put the seedlings in a warm and light place, away from drafts and keep the compost slightly moist by watering it with a fine rosed can. About two weeks before planting, move the trays to a cold frame. Keep this open during the day unless the weather is cold, and at nighttime as well during the second week provided that there is no risk of frost.

straight rows if you prefer) with approximately the right spacing between plants. Remember to place the tall varieties behind the shorter ones and try to avoid obvious color clashes.

Firm the soil around each plant. Water them in afterwards, and again whenever the soil shows signs of drying out during the next few weeks.

Aftercare

Pinch out the tips of plants that have a central stem – this makes them produce many more flowering side-shoots.

If the weather remains damp after planting, scatter slug pellets around the plants, as their tender young leaves act as a magnet to slugs. Keep the soil watered during dry spells, or growth will be checked and flowering will suffer. Always give sufficient water to reach the roots. Remove dead flowers as often as possible. This can become an overwhelming task in mid-summer, but it does help to prolong flowering. A liquid fertilizer watered on to the bed every week or two will also help to keep the plants blooming.

Reminders

Allow plants to harden off gradually before you plant them out, and provide nighttime protection if there is a risk of frost.

Moist soil is essential for newly-planted half-hardy annuals to encourage root growth beyond the ball of compost with which they were planted.

Watch for aphids clustering on young shoots. Spray them if necessary.

In town gardens, protect plants against birds and cats (*see pp48-9*) until they are well established.

Ivy-leaved geraniums add depth to a window box.

Geraniums

Today's F_1 hybrid varieties of geraniums (correctly called pelargoniums) are quite easy to raise from seeds. However, early sowing is necessary (during winter or early spring) and a compost temperature of at least 70°F is recommended.

Alternatively, geraniums may be grown from cuttings of existing plants taken during mid- to late summer. Simply cut off 3in from the ends of the shoots and insert them in a tray or large pot of seed compost. When the cuttings make fresh growth (showing that they have rooted), transfer them individually to small pots containing potting compost. The young plants will flourish best in a greenhouse, with a minimum winter temperature of around 45°F, or in a cool room indoors.

In spring, geraniums should be planted out when the risk of frost has passed. They may be mixed with other bedding plants in the open garden or planted in containers. If you wish to keep mature plants for another year, lift them in late fall, trim the stems, then pot them individually and keep them free from frost during the winter.

Hybrid geraniums are a fairly recent introduction, derived from the zonal pelargoniums that have been favorite bedding plants for many years. There are plenty of different varieties, some in single colors but others mixed.

Zonal pelargoniums derive their name from the dark, rounded markings found on the leaves of most varieties. Some have single flowers, others double. There is another group with scented leaves and the so-called ivy-leaved geraniums.

Easy half-hardy annuals

Most half-hardy annuals will grow in any well-drained soil. Heights (H) and spacings (S) given here are average.

Ageratum H 6in, S 6in. Rounded pink or blue heads. Sun.
Antirrhinum (snapdragon) H 6in-3ft, S 6-12in. Single and mixed colors. Sun.
Begonia semperflorens H 8in, S 8in. White, pink, salmon or scarlet flowers (long-flowering). Sun/light shade.
Calceolaria H 10in, S 10in. Pouch-like yellow, orange or red flowers. Sun/shelter.
Callistephus chinensis (china aster) H 1-2ft, S 9-18in. Single or double blooms in many colors (late summer). Sun.
Celosia argentea cristata (cockscomb) H 9in, S 9in. Crests of red or yellow flowers. Sun.
Cosmos H up to 3ft, S 12in. Single, dahlia-like white, pink or red flowers. Sun.
Dahlia H 18in-4ft, S 12-18in. Single or double blooms in numerous shades. Sun.
Dianthus caryophyllus H 1-2ft, S 6-9in. Fragrant white, pink, yellow or scarlet flowers. Sun.
Felicia bergeriana (kingfisher daisy) H & S 6in. Yellow-centered blue flowers. Sun.
Gaillardia pulchella (blanket flower) H 18in, S 1ft. 'Lollipops', a favorite variety, has double flowers of cream, yellow or crimson. Sun.
Gazania H 9-15in, S 1ft. Daisy-like flowers in brilliant colors. Sun.
Lobelia erinus H 6in, S 4in (also trailing varieties). Blue, carmine, red, white flowers; long-flowering. Sun/light shade.
Matthiola incana H 1-2ft, S 9-12in. Fragrant spikes of white, pink, yellow or magenta flowers. Sun/light shade.
Mesembryanthemum criniflorum (Livingstone daisy) Carpeting, daisy-like flowers in many colors. Sun.
Nemesia H 12in, S 6in. Funnel-shaped flowers, many brilliant colors and mixtures. Sun.
Nicotiana (tobacco plant) H 1-3ft, S 1ft. Colorful flowers, scented in evening. Sun.
Penstemon H 2ft, S 1ft. Bell-shaped flowers of pink, red, mauve or white. Sun.
Petunia H 9-12in, S 9-12in. Trumpet-shaped blooms in many bright colors. Sun.

Phlox drummondii H 6-15in, S 9in. Clusters of blue, pink or scarlet flowers. Sun.
Rudbeckia hirta H 1-3ft, S 12-18in. Daisy-like flowers, mostly gold or bronze (late summer). Sun.
Salvia H 1ft, S 1ft. Spikes of brilliant scarlet flowers. Sun.
Sanvitalia procumbens H 6in, S 3in. Spreading plant with black-centered yellow flowers. Sun.
Tagetes (African and French marigolds) H 6in-3ft, S 6-12in. African marigolds have large, rounded flowers of yellow, orange or gold. French marigolds are more compact, with smaller, bi-colored flowers. Sun.
Thunbergia alata (black-eyed Susan) H to 10ft. A tender climber with orange, yellow or white flowers, each with a black "eye". Sun/shelter (warm gardens only).
Verbena H 6-12in, S 6-12in. Fragrant, variously-colored flower clusters. Sun.
Zinnia H 4-30in, S 6-12in. Scarlet, pink, gold or purple dahlia-like flowers. Sun.

Sanvitalia makes good ground cover for a dry, sunny place.

Antirrhinums flower right through summer and early fall.

The china aster, a peony-flowered form of callistephus.

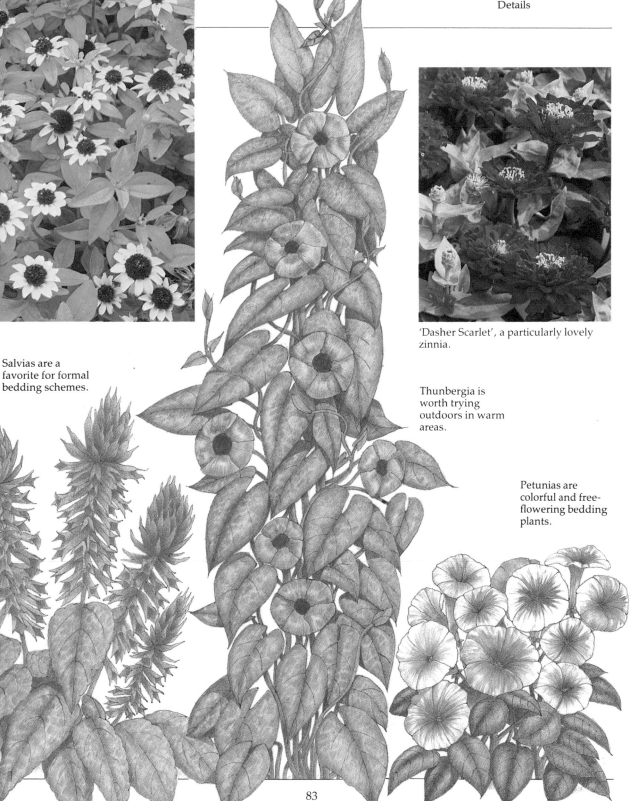

'Dasher Scarlet', a particularly lovely zinnia.

Salvias are a favorite for formal bedding schemes.

Thunbergia is worth trying outdoors in warm areas.

Petunias are colorful and free-flowering bedding plants.

Biennials

Because they need two seasons to complete their life cycle, most biennials are sown in early summer for flowering from mid-spring onwards the following year. They are particularly useful for bringing color into the garden well before the main summer display.

Some of the plants usually grown as biennials are really perennials. They are treated as biennials because they tend to be short-lived or because they rarely flourish very well after their first flowering season. Examples of such perennials are foxgloves, wallflowers and sweet williams.

Although they have a longer growing cycle than annuals, biennials need not occupy border space until the bedding season is over. Instead, you can raise them in a separate nursery bed where they will not interfere with the summer display in the flower garden. The bed can be situated in either a sunny or partly shaded spot, but the soil should contain plenty of humus to keep young plants growing even in a dry summer.

Raising from seed

Most biennials should be sown in early summer, but leave forget-me-nots, Brompton stocks and evening primroses until mid-summer. Fork peat or compost into the seedbed if it lacks humus. Rake a light sprinkling of Growmore into the surface. Check the pH level of the soil before sowing wallflowers as they will not thrive in an acid soil. Sow the seeds thinly in shallow drills, watering them afterwards if the soil is dry.

Transplant the seedlings several inches apart in a fresh row when they start to crowd one another. Water them, if necessary, to keep the plants growing steadily throughout the summer.

'Orange Bedder' is one of many varieties of the popular wallflower.

Planting and aftercare

Lift biennials from their nursery
bed at the beginning of fall and
replant them in the garden in the
following spring. If they are
planted later, they will not have
time to root properly before the soil
starts to get cold.
be transplanted to the garden when
they are 5-7cm high.

Make sure that the soil is well-
drained – biennials will not grow in
waterlogged ground. Next, prepare
the ground for planting. If you
intend to put your biennials in a
bed where annuals were formerly
grown, fork the soil over and add
plenty of compost. Add lime if the
soil is acid – especially if you are
planting wallflowers.
may be loose if it has just been dug.
If you plant the biennials early, it
may be necessary to water them.
The tips of wallflowers should be
pinched out to encourage more
flowering shoots.

In an exposed garden, erect a
windbreak of plastic netting
alongside the windward side of the
bed. This can be removed in spring
before flowering.

The flowers of lunaria (honesty) are
followed by flat, pearly seedpods.

Canterbury bells are lovely flowers with
a cottage-garden appeal.

Easy-to-grow biennials

Only average heights (H) and spreads
(S) are given here, but there are many
variations.

Bellis perennis (double daisy) H 5in, S
5in. White, pink or red flowers. Sun/
shade.
Campanula medium (Canterbury bell) H
30in, S 12in. Bell-shaped white or blue
flowers. Sun.
Cheiranthus (wallflower) H 12-18in, S
12in. (See **Reminders** panel). Sun.
Digitalis (foxglove) H 4ft, S 15in. Tall
and dwarf, pastel flowers. Shade.
Dianthus barbatus (sweet william) H
18in, S 9in. Mainly pink or red flowers.
Sun.
Lunaria (honesty) H 2ft, S 9in. Mauve
flowers, silvery seedpods. Light shade.
Matthiola incana (Brompton stocks) H
18in, S 9in. White, pink or mauve
clusters. Sun.
Myosotis (forget-me-not) H 9in, S 6in.
Mostly blue, but also pink and white
flowers. Sun/shade.
Oenothera biennis (evening primrose) H
2ft, S 12in. Saucer-shaped yellow
flowers. Sun.
Papaver nudicaule (Iceland poppy) H
30in, S 9in. Tissue-paper white, pink
and orange blooms. Sun.

Although they are really perennials, primroses and primulas are grown for their
spring flowers and are often mixed with biennials and spring bulbs.

Reminders

Low-growing biennials are excellent
plants for window boxes and other
containers.

The most widely-grown wallflower
(*Cheiranthus cheiri*) comes in a range of
yellow, gold, scarlet and crimson
flowers.

Foxgloves are one of the very few
biennials that grow best in moderate
shade.

Lay down slug pellets or gel as a
precaution against damage during the

Herbaceous perennials

Stately delphiniums, sumptuous peonies, spires of lupins – these are the very essence of a traditional flower garden in high summer. Along with other herbaceous perennials they form the rewarding, reliable backdrop for bedding displays and more temporary features. A mixed bed of perennials and shrubs can look very attractive, the latter providing out-of-season color.

Perennials save time, for there is no annual cycle of mass propagation and planting. Sensibly planted, with the taller varieties set behind the shorter ones, they add height and depth to a summer display and provide a pleasing contrast to the carpeting effect of many annuals. Also, if you choose species and varieties carefully, perennials will provide color throughout the summer.

If possible, plant perennials in a bed where they can be reached – and seen – from both sides. If the borders are set against walls and fences, the plants at the back get insufficient light and air for healthy, sturdy growth. A bed about 4ft wide in the sunniest position available is ideal.

When choosing plants, plan their arrangement so that you have a variety of colors. Unless you have a particular affection for a certain perennial, avoid the tallest varieties; short plants need less staking and look more at home in the average garden. Provided that the soil is well prepared, you can be confident of a stunning display for years to come.

Buying perennials

Most garden centers have a reasonable selection of perennials, but generally a greater range of varieties will be found at specialized hardy plant nurseries. Perennials grown in plastic containers may be bought and planted at any time of year, subject to weather and soil conditions. Otherwise, they should be planted in late fall if the soil is light or in early spring if the soil is heavy.

Raising from seed

It saves money to grow perennials from seed but you will have to wait a year after planting for them to flower. It is not necessary to sow them in a greenhouse – perennials may be sown in a cold frame or even in an outdoor seedbed.

Sow the seeds in late spring or early summer. Thin out overcrowded seedlings, and then prick them out individually so that they continue growing during the summer. Plant the seedlings during the fall.

Soil preparation

Having chosen your site, fork out perennial weeds or destroy them with herbicide. Dig the soil well in advance of planting to give it time to settle, adding manure or compost and afterwards sprinkling with lime if the soil is acid.

Before planting, mark the intended position of your plants with twigs. Use a trowel or a spade, depending on the size of the roots or container. Set plants in groups of three or four rather than individually. Do not be tempted to plant them too closely together.

Supporting perennials

Tall perennials, notably delphiniums, will flop without support. Commercial support systems can be bought, but three or four stakes with string tied between them remains a simple, reliable method. Set the supports in place when the plants are only half grown, with the stakes angled slightly outwards, and they will soon be hidden. Thin out some of the weaker shoots, to give the stronger ones a better chance to develop than they would have otherwise.

Feeding

Early spring is the time to give established perennials a balanced fertilizer. After loosening the soil with a pronged cultivator, sprinkle the fertilizer evenly at a rate of about 2oz per square yard and rake it into the surface. If this is the first application on a newly-planted bed, you can give a little more.

Watering

Perennials need a constantly moist soil, which is not always easy to maintain during long dry spells. In dry weather, water the plants before the soil becomes too dry. You should then give the plants enough water at regular intervals to soak right down to the roots: light watering may do more harm than good to the plants.

Sprinklers that throw the water over the foliage may cause stems to bend or break, and you should aim to wet the soil rather than the leaves. One of the best ways to water a herbaceous bed is with a perforated plastic hose. Mulching in late spring (first watering the soil if it is dry) will help to conserve moisture.

Removing dead blooms

Cutting off the stems of dead flowers serves two purposes. In some cases it encourages the plant to produce a second crop of blooms – as with lupins, heleniums and pyrethrums, for instance.

With every kind of perennial it helps to maintain the plant's strength by preventing it from

HERBACEOUS PERENNIALS

Buying perennials • Soil preparation
and planting • Avoiding problems •
Aftercare

A delightful herbaceous border.

Removing dead flowers encourages
strong, healthy growth in perennials.

setting seeds.

Remove dead flowers as soon as
they have died or the flower spikes
look unattractive.

Cutting back

During the fall, cut back the
remaining dead stems to ground
level. For the most part they will be
too dry for the compost heap and
should be burned. When the bed
has been cleared and the remaining
supporting stakes removed, fork
around the plants and remove any
perennial weeds; annual weeds
may be buried. If available, add
rotted manure or compost at the

same time. Afterwards, sprinkle
bonemeal at a rate of about 2oz per
square yard and work it into the
surface with the tips of the tines.

Protecting

A few common perennials are not
completely hardy and may
succumb during a hard winter in
cold areas. Examples are such
plants as agapanthus, morina,
penstemon, phygelius, romneya
and schizostylis.

As a precaution, protect such
plants during the winter with a
layer of straw or bracken, enclosing
or securing this with netting.

Dividing perennials

Dividing perennials

Most hardy perennials can be propagated by dividing their roots. Apart from increasing the stock, this is actually good for the plants. Fall is usually the best time to do this, when all the growth has died down, but on sticky soil you should postpone the job until near the end of the winter.

How plants should be divided depends on the type of root. After lifting, many roots can simply be sliced into fist-sized pieces with a large knife or sharp spade. Check that each piece has plenty of roots before replanting it. If there is a clump of fibrous roots bound together in a single mass, insert a pair of garden forks, back to back, and lever the roots gently apart. In each case, cut away any old, dead material from the roots before replanting. When dealing with plants such as irises, with rhizomes (thick stems at, or below, soil level), cut the newest growths into finger-length pieces, each with buds and roots, and replant them. (Irises are best divided in summer after they have flowered.)

When you lift and divide perennials, take the opportunity to fork some manure or compost into the border and to replan its layout. The plants are more likely to flourish if they are moved around and not just put back in the same spot. It may be possible to exchange some of your perennials for different types with friends.

Taking cuttings

Although seeds and division are the most common ways of propagating perennials, quite a few can be increased by taking cuttings. When and how this is done depends on the type of plant.

Root cuttings, taken while the

Fibrous roots can be split more easily by levering them first with forks.

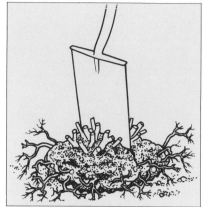

Woody crowns should be divided by cutting them.

plant is dormant, are suitable for althaea (hollyhock), anchusa, brunnera, gaillardia, papaver (poppy), phlox and verbascum. After lifting, 2in sections of root should be sliced off, with a slanting cut at the base of each, and inserted in compost in a cold frame. The slanting cut ensures that they are placed the right way up. Cover the root sections thinly with coarse sand. If the plant has very thin roots, place the sections horizontally instead of vertically.

Basal cuttings are shoots taken from the plant near soil level during early to mid-spring. They provide an easy way of propagating a

number of perennials, including delphiniums and lupins. The shoots will root readily if inserted into pots or trays of compost and placed in a cold frame. To prevent the cuttings wilting, keep the frame shaded and closed. Spray them frequently in warm weather.

A few perennials may also be propagated by removing the 3in end of side-shoots in early fall and inserting them in compost. Place the cuttings in a shaded cold frame, keeping the atmosphere humid until they have rooted. This method is especially useful for preserving stocks of plants that are not reliably hardy.

Basal cuttings, taken in spring, root particularly easily.

Root cuttings are useful for plants that cannot be divided.

Climbers

Most garden climbers are shrubs, but there are also some non-shrubby climbers. Some of these are perennial and some annual, although on the whole the former are treated in the same way as annuals. All grow quickly and are useful for providing an "instant" screen. Those mentioned here have eye-catching flowers. These short-lived climbers also make good container plants, as a large pot or tub will provide ample root space for a single growing season.

The outstanding climbers are eccremocarpus, ipomoea (morning glory), lathyrus (sweet pea) and two species of tropaeolum – nasturtiums and canary creeper. Although strictly a perennial, eccremocarpus is usually grown as an annual because it is only half hardy and needs a sheltered position. It will climb to 10ft.

The most popular sweet peas are hardy annuals. They are scented, grow to 8-10ft and are available in numerous lovely colors. There are also perennial sweet peas, which are less colorful but also less demanding.

Climbing varieties of nasturtium (*Tropaeolum majus*) will scramble 8ft or more and provide a dazzling show of color throughout the summer. This plant is a hardy annual. Canary creeper (*Tropaeolum peregrinum*) is a perennial but almost always grown as an annual. It carries a mass of yellow flowers throughout the second half of summer.

Propagation and after-care

When treating eccremocarpus as a half-hardy annual, sow it in a

Each morning glory bloom lasts for only a day.

Nasturtiums flower best in relatively poor soil.

If left, eccremocarpus may survive a mild winter.

Sweet peas combine colour and exquisite scent.

greenhouse in gentle warmth in early spring and plant the seedlings out when the risk of frost is over. Choose a sheltered, sunny spot and provide netting or trellis up which the plant can scramble.

The same treatment is suitable for ipomoea, although this plant needs plenty of warmth for successful germination and the seeds should be soaked for 24 hours before sowing. Sweet pea seeds should also be soaked. If they are sown in a cold frame or greenhouse in early spring they

will bloom earlier than seeds sown in the garden in mid-spring. Provide twigged sticks to help them climb up to the main support. Both nasturtiums and canary creeper are usually sown in mid-spring in the place where they are to flower, but can also be sown a little earlier under glass for transplanting.

All these climbers need liberal watering during dry weather. Liquid fertilizer may be given every two weeks, although this is best omitted for nasturtiums. Removing dead blooms helps flowering.

Dahlias and chrysanthemums

Because they are not hardy, dahlias need different treatment from most other perennials. They grow from tubers that will be killed by frost if left in the ground during all but the mildest winters. In the spring, young shoots are equally at risk.

The standard routine is to lift the tubers during the fall, after the first frosts. After removing the top growth, store them in dry peat in a well-ventilated but frost-free place. The following spring, the tubers may either be divided and replanted in mid-spring or set in trays of compost to encourage shoots to develop. This should be done in early spring and the trays placed in a greenhouse or conservatory. The shoots should be treated as cuttings and potted individually when they are about 3in long. Plant them out when the risk of frost has passed.

Tubers and rooted cuttings are sold by nurseries and garden centers in spring. There are a number of different groups of dahlias, based on the shape and formation of the flowers. Simplest and smallest are "single-flowered" types, which grow about 2ft high and have blooms about 4in wide. At the other end of the scale are "decorative" and "cactus" types, growing to 4-5ft, with massive blooms. A specialist grower's catalog will help you to choose.

Dahlias may also be raised from seed, but these are relatively short-stemmed bedding varieties, grown as half-hardy annuals. They are valuable for brightening the garden long after most other annuals have finished flowering.

Planting and aftercare

Dahlias are "hungry" plants so, before planting, prepare the soil by digging in manure or compost the previous fall or winter. Apply bonemeal or a general fertilizer in spring. Push in supporting stakes before planting, so that you do not damage the tubers. Tall plants with large blooms require stout stakes, but bamboos are sufficient to support smaller ones. Tie the plants regularly as they grow.

Plant tubers so that the crowns are 2-3in below the surface. Planting distance is 1-3ft, depending on the plants' eventual height. Plenty of water is needed during dry weather, otherwise growth will be checked. A mulch applied fairly early in the season will help the soil to retain moisture. Give the plants regular applications of liquid fertilizer from mid-summer onwards.

Pinching out the main growing points of plants in early summer encourages bushier growth and extra flowers. Removing dead flowers will keep the plants in flower longer, usually into mid-to-late fall, when the first frosts can be expected.

> **Reminders**
>
> **Before planting,** harden off rooted cuttings in a cold frame that can be closed for the first few nights.
>
> **In damp weather,** scatter slug pellets around newly-planted cuttings. Spray as necessary against pests.
>
> **Tubers lifted** in fall dry more rapidly if laid upside down for a week before being stored in peat.

'Glow' is a miniature ball dahlia. It flowers from late summer onwards.

Chrysanthemums, such as 'Nobleman', are popular flowers of late summer.

Chrysanthemums

Annual and herbaceous perennial chrysanthemums (shasta daisies) are described on *p79* and *p92* respectively. This page deals with the early-flowering varieties of so-called florists' chrysanthemums – plants that are raised from cuttings each year and then grown outdoors to bloom by early fall. Their name distinguishes them from varieties that do not flower until mid-fall or later, and need greenhouse protection from frost.

The annual cycle of these chrysanthemums has some similarities with that of dahlias. The plants are lifted during mid-fall, their stems cut back to 6in or so, and then placed in boxes with compost spread around the stools (as these root clumps are called). The boxes are then placed in a cold frame or unheated greenhouse and kept just moist. Any excessively long shoots that develop during the winter should be removed.

If you have a greenhouse, very gentle warmth from mid-winter onwards will encourage shoot development. Even without this there should be suitable growths to form cuttings by early spring. The shoots growing from the foot of the stem should be removed. After pulling off the lower leaves and trimming beneath a leaf joint, root them in John Innes No 1 compost, or an equivalent soilless type. Then plant them in individual pots.

The rooted cuttings may be planted outdoors in late spring. Provided they have been hardened off gradually, they will not be harmed by late frosts.

There are many different forms, with blooms of widely-differing sizes and shapes. These can be studied in nursery catalogs and much will be learned, too, from a visit to a specialist grower.

Planting and aftercare

Chrysanthemums need soil that is well-prepared with manure or compost dug in during the fall or winter, and a dressing of general fertilizer at 2oz per square yard, given just before planting. Special chrysanthemum fertilizers can also be used. A sunny or slightly shaded spot is suitable.

Plant the chrysanthemums so that the soil ball is only just covered, first pushing in a stake to match the eventual height of the plant. Summer management consists principally of keeping the plants tied to the supports, watering during dry spells and applying a liquid fertilizer every two weeks until late summer.

The plants must be stopped – that is, their main growing point nipped off – in early summer. Later, some of the sideshoots growing from leaf joints can be pinched out in order to limit the number of blooms and improve their size. However, although this and other refinements are practiced by exhibitors, they are not essential for a colorful garden display.

As an alternative to planting in the garden, early-flowering chrysanthemums are good plants for growing in large pots or other containers. These can be placed in a spare corner of the garden during the summer and then brought on to the patio or into a conservatory when they flower in late summer.

Easy-to-grow perennials/1

The perennials listed here are reliable, easily-obtained types. There are many hybrids and varieties, so heights (H) and spacings (S) are only approximate.

Acanthus (bear's breeches) H 5ft, S 3ft. White or purple spikes (late summer). Sun/light shade.
Achillea H 2-5ft, S 18in. Flat yellow or white heads (summer). Sun.
Aconitum (monkshood) H 2-3 ft, S 18in. Blue or white spires (mid-summer). Sun/shade.
Agapanthus H 3ft, S 30in. Lily-like blue flowers (summer). Sun.
Althaea (hollyhock) H to 8ft, S 30in. Tall spikes (late summer). Sun.
Anchusa H 3-5ft, S 2ft. Brilliant blue flowers (summer). Sun.
Anemone (windflower) H 2-4ft, S 18in. Saucer-shaped pink or white flowers (late summer). Sun/shade.
Aquilegia (columbine) H 2ft, S 12in. Spurred flowers in many colors (early summer). Sun/shade.
Artemisia H 4ft, S 2ft. White plumes (late summer). Sun/light shade.
Aster (Michaelmas daisy) H up to 5ft, S 1-2ft. White, pink, red or blue flowers (late summer, autumn). Sun.
Astilbe H 3ft, S 2ft. White, pink or red plumes (summer). Sun/shade.
Brunnera H 18in, S 18in. "Forget-me-not" flowers (late spring). Shade.
Campanula persicifolia (bellflower) H 2-5ft, S 12-24in. White, blue or pink bells (summer). Sun.
Centaurea (cornflower) H to 5ft, S 18in. Blue, yellow or pink flowers (early to late summer). Sun/shade.
Chrysanthemum maximum (Shasta daisy) H 3ft, S 18in. White, daisy-like flowers (summer). Sun.
Convallaria (lily-of-the-valley) H 6in, S 2ft. White or pink bells (spring). Sun/shade.
Coreopsis H 18in, S 18in. Yellow daisy-like flowers (late summer). Sun.
Cortaderia (Pampas grass) H 8ft, S 6ft. Creamy-white plumes (late summer). Sun.
Delphinium H up to 6ft, S 3ft. Blue, pink, yellow or white spires (summer). Sun.
Dianthus (border carnations and pinks) H 9-12in, S 12-18in. White, pink, yellow or crimson flowers (summer). Sun.
Dicentra (bleeding heart) H 1-2ft, S 18in. Pendulous red and white flowers (late

spring). Sun/light shade.
Doronicum (leopard's bane) H 2-3ft, S 18in. Yellow daisy-like flowers (early summer). Sun/light shade.
Echinops (globe thistle) H 3ft, S 2ft. Spiky blue heads (summer). Sun.
Erigeron (fleabane) H 2ft, S 18in. Many-colored daisy-type flowers (summer). Sun.
Eryngium (sea holly) H 18in-3ft, S 12-18in. Spiky blue flowers (summer). Sun.
Euphorbia wulfenii (spurge) H 3-4ft, S 3-4ft. Yellowish bracts (late spring). Sun.
Gaillardia (blanket flower) H 18in-3ft, S 12in. Red or orange daisies (summer). Sun.
Geranium (crane's bill) H 12in, S 18in. Saucer-shaped, pink and other color flowers (summer). Sun/shade.
Geum H 18in-2ft, S 18in-2ft. Red, pink or yellow flowers (summer). Sun/shade.
Gypsophila paniculata (baby's breath) H 4ft, S to 4ft. Masses of tiny pink or white blooms (summer). Sun.
Helenium H 30in, S 18in. Red and yellow daisies (late summer). Sun.
Helianthus (sunflower) H 5ft or more, S 18in. Golden, single or double flowers

(summer). Sun.
Helleborus (Christmas rose) H 18in, S 12in. White or purple flowers (winter and spring). Light shade.
Hemerocallis (day lily) H 30in, S 18in. Lily-like flowers, many colors (late summer). Sun/shade.
Hosta (plantain lily) H 1-3ft, S 2-3ft. Striking foliage. Light shade/sun.
Iris *(see p108)*
Kniphofia (red hot poker) H 2-4ft, S 18in. Pink, yellow or scarlet spikes (summer). Sun.
Linaria (toad flax) H 30in, S 12in. Pink or purple spikes (late summer). Sun.
Linum narbonense (flax) H 18in, S 12in. Small, rich blue flowers (summer). Sun.
Lupinus (lupin) H 3-5ft, S 18in-2ft. Spires in many shades (early summer). Sun.
Malva (mallow) H 4ft, S 18in. Long-lasting pink or blue flowers (summer). Sun.
Meconopsis H to 3ft, S 9-18in. Blue or yellow poppies (late spring and summer). Light shade.
Nepeta (catnip) H 1-3ft, S 1-2ft. Blue spikes (summer). Sun.

Oriental poppies – brilliant flowers in June.

Verbascum 'Pink Domino'.

Geum 'Lady Stratheden'.

Rudbeckia 'Marmalade' is in bloom from August onwards.

Helenium 'Coppelia'.

Easy-to-grow perennials/2

Paeonia (peony) H 30in, S 2ft. White, pink, yellow or crimson flowers (early summer). Sun.

Papaver orientale (poppy) H up to 3ft, S up to 3ft. Bowl-shaped red, pink or white (early summer). Sun.

Penstemon H 3ft, S 18in. Pink, red or purple spikes (summer). Sun.

Phlox H 2-4ft, S 18in. Large clusters in many colors (late summer). Sun/shade.

Polygonum H 1-3ft, S 2ft. Pink and red spikes (summer). Sun/shade.

Primula denticulata (polyanthus) H 12in, S 12in. Large heads, many colors (spring). Sun/shade.

Primula vulgaris (primrose) H 6in, S 9in. Yellow flowers (spring). Sun/shade.

Pyrethrum (feverfew) H 2-3ft, S 18in. White, pink or crimson flowers (early summer). Sun.

Rudbeckia H 30in, S 2ft. Star-like yellow flowers (summer). Sun/shade.

Salvia x superba H 3ft, S 2ft. Purple spikes (summer). Sun.

Sedum (stonecrop) H 18in, S 18in. Flat pink flowers (late summer). Sun.

Sidalcea H 3ft, S 2ft. Pink or red spires (summer). Sun.

Solidago (goldenrod) H up to 6ft, S 2ft. Massed golden heads (late summer). Sun/shade.

Stachys H 15in, S 12in. Silvery foliage, purple flowers (summer). Sun/shade.

Trollius (globe flower) H 18in-3ft, S 18in. Orange buttercup-like flowers (summer). Sun/shade.

Verbascum (mallow) H 3-6ft, S 2ft. White, pink or yellow spires (summer). Sun.

Veronica (speedwell) H 2ft, S 18in. Blue spires (summer). Sun/shade.

Aster frikartii blooms two months earlier than its relative, the Michaelmas daisy.

There are white, pink and red varieties, both single and double, of pyrethrum.

Kniphofias come in many shades of
pink, yellow and red.

Aquilegia will grow happily in sun or shade.

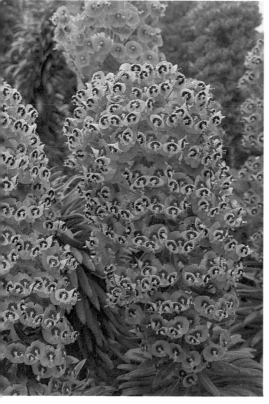

The bracts of euphorbias are extremely striking.

'White Wings' is one of the many varieties of *Paeonia lactiflora*.

Bulbs, corms and tubers

For reward without effort, bulbs surely take first prize. Many of them will grow in either sun or shade and in practically any soil that is not waterlogged. They will go on producing lovely flowers for year after year with the minimum of attention.

There are the inevitable exceptions. Some bulbs and corms, including tulips and gladioli, have to be lifted after they have flowered, and then dried off and stored before being replanted; other bulbs are more fussy about where they are planted. However, there are plenty of trouble-free bulbs for any gardener looking for results with a minimum of effort.

Bulbs are also very versatile. Spring bulbs may be grown in borders to brighten them up long before herbaceous plants are in flower. Alternatively, they can be grown in separate beds to make a massed display, or intermixed with spring-flowering biennials, such as wallflowers and double daisies. Miniature varieties look delightful in rock gardens and there are sizes to suit containers of every kind. Bulbs can be naturalized both in grass or in the uncultivated ground beneath trees.

The term "bulb" is used here loosely to cover corms and tubers as well, all having fleshy, below-ground storage organs as well as root systems (see pp76-7).

Bulbs in containers

Fall is the time to plant tubs, pots and window boxes with bulbs for a cheerful spring display. Crocuses, scillas, hyacinths and dwarf varieties of narcissi and tulips are especially suitable. Fill the containers with John Innes No 2 compost, first checking that drainage holes in the base are unobstructed, then covering the bottom with curved pieces of

pottery to prevent the compost falling through.

After flowering, and before the foliage dies down, the bulbs may be lifted and planted elsewhere to build up their reserves for the following year. This allows containers to be planted with summer-flowering plants.

Buying bulbs

The best way to buy bulbs is to place a summer order with one of the specialist suppliers. You can then choose at leisure from illustrated catalogs, which offer a much wider range than most stores. You can also be assured that the bulbs will be in good, fresh condition when they are delivered at planting time.

However, at the height of summer it is not always easy to plan for the following spring. Garden centers and stores will have bulbs in stock from late summer onwards and it is then a matter of choosing plump, good-sized specimens that have not started to dry out. Do not buy until you are ready to plant.

Planting bulbs

Late summer/early fall is the time to plant spring-flowering bulbs. Plant summer-flowering bulbs in spring.

Bulbs flourish best in soil that is well drained and contains a reasonable amount of organic matter, but any manure dug in before planting must be completely rotted. Organic fertilizers are best. Rake about 4oz of bonemeal dressing per square yard into the soil if its fertility is in doubt.

The usual rule is to plant bulbs in holes three times deeper than their height – that is, a 6-in hole for a bulb 2-in high. Plant with a trowel. Suggested spacings should be

taken as a rough guide, for irregular planting gives a more pleasing effect than plants grown in precisely-spaced rows. Just bear the average figure in mind when placing the bulbs on the ground in random order before planting.

Small groups of bulbs always look better than single plants when grown in vacant patches in a border or rock garden. Clear the ground of weeds first so that the soil will not have to be disturbed again after planting. Where bulbs and spring bedding are grown together, plant the biennials first, leaving the spaces for groups of bulbs to be planted afterwards.

Naturalizing bulbs

The term "naturalizing" means planting bulbs in grass or under trees where they can be left

A massed planting of spring bulbs – grape hyacinths in front of stately crown imperials, with dense clumps of narcissi and tulips beside them.

A mixed planting of chamomile (anthemis) and 'Red Shine' tulips.

undisturbed for a number of years. Narcissi and crocuses are favorite plants for the purpose, while snowdrops look particularly delightful beside a hedge or under deciduous shrubs. Although bulbs can be naturalized in lawns, a rougher area is better as the grass will have to be left uncut until the bulb foliage dies down – as long as five or six weeks after flowering.

Aim for a natural, informal effect. To do this, scatter the bulbs at random over the area to be planted, mixing different sorts if you like, and then plant them where they fall. Avoid the temptation to even out the spacings.

For planting, there are special bulb planters that take out neat cores of soil. Alternatively, lift flaps of lawn, loosen the soil beneath with a hand fork and then replace the sod after planting.

Before planting bulbs in beds, place them on the ground at about the right spacings but in no set pattern.

Using a trowel, make holes deep enough for the bulbs to be covered by twice their own depth of soil.

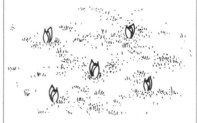

A scattering of bulbs looks best when naturalizing them in grass or other uncultivated parts of the garden.

A bulb planter removes a plug of soil. This is replaced after the bulb has been put in the soil.

Caring for bulbs

Looking after bulbs

Most bulbs need little aftercare. Planted in free-draining soil, they will reappear and increase year by year. However, even with the least demanding bulbs, there are a few points to watch, while others do need more careful attention.

With the popular spring-flowering bulbs, such as crocuses and daffodils, it is essential to leave the foliage intact (and unknotted, in the case of daffodils) until it has died down naturally. During the period after flowering the bulb is building up its reserves for the following year's blooms – a process for which the leaves are vital. It even pays to go a step further and, as the bulbs finish flowering, to feed them with a liquid or soluble fertilizer watered on to the soil or lawn. Alternatively, a granular fertilizer may be used if it is raked into the topsoil.

If the bulbs are in a bed that is urgently needed for other plants, they can be lifted with a fork before the foliage has died and moved to another part of the garden. To do this, dig a trench and lay the plants in this with about half their stems below soil level. Replace the soil and leave the bulbs until the foliage has died down. Then lift them again and store them under cover until planting time in the fall.

Whether or not you move the bulbs, remove the dead flowers as soon as they fade so that the plant does not divert its energies into forming seeds. Remove a few inches of stem with the dead flowers, but leave the remainder. Do not remove the dead flowers of small bulbs such as crocuses, snowdrops and scillas if you would like them to spread by self-seeding.

Early-flowering bulbs need watering during an exceptionally dry spring. You should also bear in mind that the roots require moisture until the foliage has died away. Summer bulbs should be watered if the ground shows signs of drying out between the time the bulbs emerge to the time their foliage withers.

Lifting and drying bulbs

Tulips are usually planted in beds for a spring display, and lifted after they have flowered to make way for summer flowering plants. They are then dried off and stored until planting time comes round again.

Lift the tulips from the beds or from the temporary trench when the foliage has died down before preparing them for storage. The same treatment may be given to narcissi grown as bedding.

Gladioli, which flower in summer and often form part of a mixed border, must also usually be lifted and stored after their foliage has died down, because they are not completely hardy and are liable to be killed by frost. In particularly mild districts, where hard frosts do not occur, this is not always necessary, and it may be worth taking a chance and leaving them where they are.

Three other bulbs that are not reliably hardy, and therefore need storing during the winter, are acidanthera, canna and ixia. Tuberous begonias must be brought indoors before the first fall frosts. Keep them in a greenhouse or a cold frame until the foliage has died.

Several forms of fungi cause bulbs and corms to rot. Dry rot (1) affects gladioli and crocuses; tulip fire (2) is confined to tulips, and smoulder (3) to narcissi. Grubs of the narcissus fly (4) eat away the insides of bulbs. Basal rot (5) may attack a number of plants, including lilies and crocuses.

CARING FOR BULBS

Aftercare ● Lifting and drying ● Storing
● Dividing and replanting ● Avoiding
problems

Storing bulbs

To prepare tulip bulbs for storing, leave them to dry off for a few days, then remove the dead leaves, remnants of soil, flaking skins and any small bulbs. Place the bulbs in an open box or on a netting "hammock" so the air can circulate; then store them in a cool, dry palce until the fall.

With gladioli and other tender bulbs, cut off the stem and remove the old corm from the base of the new one. Place the corms in a tray and store them where they are safe from frost but not too warm. When the foliage of tuberous begonias has died down, store the tubers in a box of very slightly moist peat and keep them in a frost-free place during the winter.

Remove dead leaves and skin before storing bulbs. Burn any bulbs that show signs of disease.

A slatted box, allowing a free passage of air, is ideal for storing bulbs or corms during the winter.

Dividing and replanting

Bulbs that are left in the ground from one year to the next will gradually form congested and overcrowded clumps. In order to flourish, these clumps should be lifted every few years, divided and the bulbs then replanted at the original spacings. Of course, dividing and replanting can also be used as a way of increasing your stocks of bulbs.

Bulbs should be divided and replanted after they have flowered. This also applies to plants, such as crocuses, that grow from corms. This may be done between mid- and late summer. Mark exactly where the bulbs are if the job has to be left until after the plants' leaves have withered.

While dividing the bulbs, remove the new small bulbs that will have formed around their bases. If you wish to increase your stock still further, plant the biggest of the new bulbs in a new bed, marking the row carefully, and leave them to develop undisturbed for a couple of years before moving them to their final quarters.

Tulips and gladioli, which are usually lifted every year, will not have a chance to become overcrowded in this way but can nevertheless be propagated from the small offsets which form on their bulbs. Newly-formed corms on gladioli bulbs should be stored in the same way as the parent corms before being planted out the following spring.

Many small bulbs are best replanted immediately after they have been lifted and the clumps separated. However, some, including crocuses and daffodils, can be kept out of the ground until replanted in the usual way in the fall. In this case they must first be allowed to dry and then stored in a cool shed during the rest of the summer.

Reminders

Although bulbs can be propagated from seeds, this is a slow process and the plants may not grow true to type.

Species tulips, as opposed to the hybrid varieties that are used for bedding, should not be lifted and stored after flowering.

Mark the places where bulbs are grown in a border so that you can easily avoid them when digging.

Bulbs grown as pot plants may be planted in the garden, complete with compost, when flowering is over.

Earth or foliage left on bulbs or corms lifted in fall may cause them to rot.

Irises and lilies

Irises

There are two different sorts of iris
– those that grow from rhizomes
(horizontal, ground-level stems)
and others that are bulbous. The
former group includes the familiar
flag iris, a popular choice for
herbaceous borders. For the most
part they are quite tall plants,
although there are dwarf species as
well. Some are more suited to
growing in or around garden pools
(see pp176-7).

Many of the bulbous irises are
smaller, daintier plants than the
rhizomatous sorts. The smallest are
a natural choice for rock gardens;
others can be placed in beds or
borders where they will not be
submerged by larger plants.

Planting and aftercare

Most widely grown of the
rhizomatous irises are the tall,
bearded varieties, so called because
each flower has a tongue-like tuft of
hairs at the base of the petals. But
there are also many beardless
types. Their basic needs are sun
and good drainage, while some
prefer a non-acid soil.

After preparing the ground with
manure or compost, and a
sprinkling of lime if necessary,
plant the rhizomes in late summer,
barely covering them with soil.
Every three or four years, lift and
divide the clumps of rhizomes in
late summer, after flowering. The
ones to retain are the most recent
growths nearest the outside of the
clump. Replant them at once,
cutting the fan of leaves in half to
reduce moisture loss and lessen the
risk of wind damage.

The tall irises, which grow up to
5ft high, should be planted about
18in apart. Smaller types, 2-3ft
high, need a space of around 12-
15in left between them, while

dwarf kinds, such as hybrids
derived from *Iris pumila*, may be
planted as close together as 9in.

The right time to plant bulbous
irises is early fall. They , too, need
well-drained soil, preferably
containing lime, and a sunny
position. Some, notably the dwarf
Iris danfordiae and *Iris reticulata*,
flower in late winter or early
spring. Others, including the much
taller Dutch, Spanish and English
xiphium hybrids, flower in early to
mid-summer.

Given well-drained soil, these
bulbous types are reasonably
hardy, but Dutch hybrids are best
lifted in late summer and stored
during the winter if there are any
doubts about the soil or site. To
propagate them, divide the clumps
of bulbs when they become dense.
Wait until the foliage has withered
before lifting, and allow them to
dry off before splitting the clumps.
Replant the large bulbs in early
fall in a permanent bed, but plant
the bulblets in a nursery bed.

Iris sibirica is a rhizomatous beardless iris. It flourishes best in damp soil.

Lilium auratum bears massive bowl- shaped flowers in late summer.

Reminders

Sprinkle slug pellets around young growth in spring.

Mottling of the leaves and general deterioration are signs of virus. Lift and burn the plants.

It is best to support even small lilies when they are growing in tubs or other containers.

A sprinkling of coarse sand in the planting holes aids drainage.

Choosing lilies

Unsurpassed for sheer elegance, lilies are not the easiest flowers to grow. Some, indeed, are most exacting. However, if you have suitable soil and choose one of the less demanding types, there is every hope of success. It is important to find out from a specialist supplier the particular needs of the plants you buy, for these will vary from species to species.

One basic distinction is between stem-rooting and base-rooting types of lily, the former needing to be planted deeper than the others. Flowers are bowl-shaped, with wide-spread petals, trumpet-shaped or "turk's cap", the last with petals that curl backwards.

One of the easiest lilies with which to start is *Lilium regale*, which bears trumpet-shaped white blooms in summer and grows up to about 5ft high. It should be planted in mid-fall, setting the bulbs 6in deep in soil that is really well drained but also contains plenty of humus to prevent it drying out in summer. The soil should be neutral or slightly acid and in a sheltered, sunny spot.

Lilium candidum, the Madonna lily, is another relatively undemanding species. Growing up to 4ft, it carries trumpet-shaped flowers in early summer. This base-rooting species, planted in summer, prefers an alkaline soil and the bulbs should be set no deeper than about 1in.

"Backhouse Hybrids" are base-rooting turk's cap lilies, which flower in early summer and grow up to 5ft high. "Mid-Century Hybrids", including the very popular 'Enchantment', with speckled red flowers, are stem-rooting lilies bearing trumpet-shaped flowers in early summer. Plant bulbs of both groups in the fall, in soil similar to that for *Lilium regale*. Plant stem-rooting kinds 6in deep and others 2in deep.

Aftercare

Stake tall lilies if they are exposed to wind. It is important to keep the soil watered in dry weather during the summer, and mulching is particularly beneficial. Feed the soil with a high-potash, low-nitrogen fertilizer. When clumps become overcrowded, lift, separate and replant them at once at their normal planting time.

Easy bulbs and corms

Allium moly (golden garlic) H 10in, S 4in. Yellow sprays (early summer). Sun. Plant fall.

Amaryllis belladonna H 2ft, S 12in. Pink flowers (late summer). Sun and shelter. Plant summer.

Anemone coronaria H 9in, S 5in. Single ('de Caen') and double ('St Brigid') strains in bright colors (spring to fall, depending on time of planting). Sun/shade. Plant in the fall or in the spring.

Colchicum autumnale (autumn crocus) H 6-9in, S 9in. Pink, crocus-like flowers (fall). Sun/shade. Plant summer.

Crinum x powellii H 30in, S 18in. Pink or white lily-like flowers (late summer). Sun/shelter. Plant spring.

Crocus H 4-5in, S 4-5in. Numerous varieties, some fall-flowering. Some spring-flowering types bear white, yellow, blue or purple flowers. Sun. Plant late summer.

Cyclamen coum H 3in, S 5in. Pink or white flowers (winter). Shade. Plant early fall.

Eranthis hyemalis (winter aconite) H 4in, S 3in. Glossy yellow flowers (late winter). Sun/shade. Plant late summer.

Fritillaria meleagris (snake's head fritillary) H 12in, S 6in. Checkered bell-like flowers (spring). Sun/shade. Plant fall.

Gladiolus (sword lily) H 18in-4ft, S 4-6in. Many hybrid types, including miniatures (summer). Lift and store corms in fall, plant spring.

Hyacinthus (hyacinth) H 9in, S 6in. Fragrant pink, blue, white or yellow flowers (spring). Sun/light shade. Plant fall.

Leucojum aestivum (summer snowflake) H 2ft, S 6in. Green-tipped white flowers (spring). Sun/shade. Plant late summer.

Muscari armeniacum (grape hyacinth) H 8in, S 3-4in. Blue or white spikes (spring). Sun. Plant early fall.

Narcissus (daffodil) H 3in-2ft, S 2-8in. A remarkable range of species and varieties, with gold, red, apricot and white the dominant colors (spring). Sun/light shade. Plant early fall.

Ranunculus asiaticus H 12in, S 6in. A mixture of red, yellow, pink and white blooms (summer). Sun. Plant spring. Lift and store in fall.

Scilla nonscripta (bluebell) H 9in, S 4in. Pink, white or blue flowers. Sun/shade. Plant late summer.

Scilla sibirica H 6in, S 4in. Bright blue flowers (spring). Sun/shade. Plant late summer.

Tulipa (tulip) H 8-30in, S 4-8in. Like narcissi, a great range of colors, flower shapes and sizes (spring). Sun/shelter. Plant fall.

Note: H *indicates height*, S *indicates spacing.*

The brightly-coloured ranunculus is not fully hardy.

Bluebells can easily be naturalized in dappled shade.

Leucojums look like snowdrops, but flower later.

Tulips are one of
the most popular
plants for spring
bedding.

The large types of
daffodils can either
be grown in beds or
naturalized.

Allium moly

Muscari armeniacum

Fritillaries have distinctive
checkered markings.

Container plants

Tubs, flowerpots and other containers are particularly popular now that patios are so much a part of gardens today. An area of gray paving can be transformed by containers of flowers or shrubs, which bring color and the scent of the garden right to the spot where you will be spending much of your leisure.

Containers also have a part to play elsewhere in the garden, and a colorful focal point can be created throughout the year: a well-placed tub can conceal a manhole cover or compost heap.

The house itself can be made immeasurably brighter with the aid of window boxes and hanging baskets. Suspended pots transform a featureless brick wall, and tubs full of flowering plants on either side of the front door can provide a particularly warm and attractive welcome to visitors.

Foliage plants, evergreen shrubs and dwarf conifers all have their part to play. Among the many long-term plants worth considering are azaleas, camellias, heathers, *Rosmarinus officinalis*, buxus, *Choisya ternata* and skimmia. If you do not have a sunny position, consider planting hostas, ferns, bergenias, aucubas and mahonias.

Spring bulbs can begin the year's flowering display, with preference given to those that flower early (narcissi, scillas, crocuses, chionodoxas, *Iris reticulata*), which will have finished before bedding plants are set out in late spring. Spring color can also be provided by such plants as wallflowers, forget-me-nots, polyanthus and Brompton stocks. These can all be wintered in their containers following planting in fall.

The choice in half-hardy annuals for the year's main display is enormous. However, avoid tall, floppy varieties that are vulnerable to wind and may look out of

An unusual container complements this display of petunias and geraniums.

proportion to the rest of the garden. Include one or two trailing plants, which will double the height of the display and also conceal the container. Lobelias, nasturtiums, fuchsias, ivy-leaved geraniums and lysimachia are suitable plants.

Container points

Wooden tubs and troughs need occasional treatment with a non-toxic preservative. Keep their bases well clear of the ground to prevent the wood from rotting.

Small earthenware pots (less

than 9in in diameter) dry out very rapidly and are best avoided. Use plastic instead.

Although stone pots are heavy, this can be an advantage in exposed, windy areas. For safety, always secure window boxes to the wall with a hook and eye at each end. If hanging baskets are lined with black plastic instead of moss, pierce holes for inserting trailing plants to hide the plastic.

Buying compost

Either John Innes No 2 or a soilless (peat-based) compost may be used

CONTAINER PLANTS

Choosing plants ● Buying and mixing
compost ● Planting and aftercare ●
Avoiding problems

for containers. The former is the
better choice, especially for long-
term plants, but soilless types are
lighter. (Weight may well be an
important consideration for
window boxes or for large
containers on balconies.) Do not
use ordinary garden soil unless you
are fortunate enough to have a rich
but free-draining loam.

Stone troughs are ideal containers for rock plants and dwarf conifers.

Blocks support this tub to help drainage
and preserve the timber.

Trailing plants hide the hanging basket
containing this summer display.

Planting and aftercare

Check that the container has
drainage holes in the base. Spread a
layer of broken pots, tiles, pieces of
brick or stones over the base to
make a free-draining layer. Raise
the container clear of a smooth
surface by placing it on bricks or
strips of wood.

Fill the container with compost,
leaving a little space at the top. For
large-rooted shrubs, empty
compost on to the base, then firm
the rest of the compost well around
the roots of the shrub.

Water the container regularly,
letting the compost dry out
partially before moistening it again:
plants will not grow in waterlogged
compost. Daily watering is usually
needed during the summer. The
weight of a container is a good
guide to its moisture content.

Give the container a liquid feed
every two weeks or so, following
the instructions on the bottle or
box. The fertilizer in the compost
will have been exhausted by the
time any plants are in full flower.

Perennials need fresh compost
every spring. Move small plants to
a slightly larger container, with
new compost placed around the
root mass. Replace the top 2-3in of
compost around plants growing in
large containers.

Rock gardens and plants

For brilliant color, profuse flowers, and tiny but exquisite blooms, there is nothing to rival the miniature world of rock plants. True alpines, gathered from the world's high places, can bring a touch of romance to the humblest garden, and cultivating such plants may become a passion. However, the term "rock plant" embraces just about any herbaceous perennial that is small enough to exist in company with other ground-hugging, crevice-rooting plants. Many are easy to grow and some may even become invasive.

A conventional rock garden is not necessarily the best choice for a small, flat garden. It requires considerable skill to make a rock garden look uncontrived – a place where such plants would grow naturally – whereas a raised bed with walled edges has no such pretensions.

The reward for success is a garden feature second to none. A sunny spot is vital – light shade for a small part of the day does little harm, but heavy shade is almost bound to result in failure. The construction of a rock garden is always much easier where there is a slope on which to build.

A rock garden should be positioned where it can be seen to advantage from the house. Its slope should face south or southwest for maximum warmth and sun. It is vital that the ground beneath it should be well drained.

A rock garden should not be a pile of soil with rocks pressed into the surface. Besides looking wrong, it will not provide good growing conditions. Instead it should be a fair imitation of an outcrop of rock jutting from a hillside. This means you will have to buy some large pieces of stone from a garden center if there is no local quarry.

Sandy or loamy garden soil can be used to construct a rock garden,

A marvelous example of a rock garden on a massive scale.

with peat added to improve the soil's moisture retention and also either grit or coarse sand, if necessary, to ensure good drainage. However, clay or heavy soil is not suitable for rock gardens, and you will have to buy in good loam if you have this type of soil. Mix in peat and/or sharp sand, according to the soil's texture.

Reminders

A low, broad rock garden looks best on a flat site.

Remove all perennial weeds before you begin work.

Ram rocks firmly in place, so that they will not move.

Building a rock garden

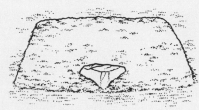

1 If the site is poorly drained, remove the topsoil and replace it with a good layer of hardcore. Top this with small rocks and cover the area with a layer of inverted sods. Replace most of the topsoil.

2 Take a large and roughly triangular stone. Dig a slightly oversized hole and place the stone inside, point outwards and sloping backward. Firm the soil around the stone.

3 Set more stones in the same way on each side of the first one – all sloping gently backward so that water drains toward the plant roots – to create an "outcrop". Butt them together as closely as possible.

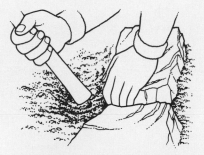

4 Position the stones in your rock garden so that the result imitates a single large outcrop of rock in which cracks have occurred.

5 Fill in the holes behind the rocks as you progress, using a free-draining but moisture-retentive mixture. Firm the soil around each rock.

6 Plant the crevices between the stones in turn as you progress. Set the plants firmly in the soil and then water them.

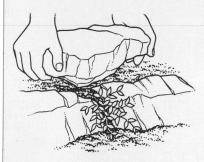

7 Place a second tier of rocks above the first tier, laying some stones across the crevices of the first row to prevent soil erosion.

8 The completed rock garden – a miniature outcrop containing many more species than would naturally be found in the wild in such a small area.

Other sites for rock plants

A rock garden is not the only suitable site for rock plants. A dry wall – one with the joints between stones filled with soil, not mortar – is ideal. Set in the crevices, the plants' roots are assured of good drainage, while their foliage will be well clear of the damp soil. When building such a wall, set it at a slightly backward-sloping angle so that some rainwater drains naturally into the joints. A dry wall may also be used to form one or more sides of a raised bed (*see opposite*). Among suitable plants for a sunny dry wall are aethionema, alyssum, arabis, aubrieta, erinus, helianthemum, iberis, lewisia, origanum, saponaria, sedum, sempervivum and saxifraga.

Spaces may be left between paving stones or bricks for growing prostrate plants – a most effective way to relieve an otherwise flat area. Some suitable choices for this purpose are acaena, androsace, arabis, aubrieta, dryas, helianthemum, lychnis, origanum, saxifraga, sedum and thymus.

A scree bed is a rather specialized site for alpines, consisting of a layer of mixed chippings, loam and peat (use more chippings than loam or peat) placed over a free-draining base. A scree bed can be made separately or as part of a larger rock garden, its purpose being to provide really sharp drainage for plants that appreciate it. Such plants include aethionema, androsace, armeria, erigeron, lychnis, origanum, and thymus.

Old stone sinks are excellent places for growing alpines, though unfortunately they are no longer easy to obtain. If you are lucky enough to have one, or decide to cover a glazed sink to make it look like stone, you should prepare it by first placing drainage material over the base and then filling it with potting compost to which grit or gravel has been added.

A dry wall almost concealed by iberis, aubrieta and alyssum.

Covering a glazed sink

Many old glazed sinks are thrown away, but they can be covered to give an imitation of stone. Mix two parts of well-dampened peat with one part sharp sand and one part cement in a large bucket. Add sufficient water to all the ingredients to make a smooth and stiff mixture.

Score the glaze on the outside of the sink with a coarse

Building a raised bed

A raised bed provides excellent growing conditions for rock plants if some drainage material, in the form of rubble or stones, is placed in the base. Such a bed is particularly useful in a garden where the soil is too heavy to be really suitable for a rock garden. The bed's extra height also makes it easier to weed and look after.

The bed may be built to any convenient height, from a few inches upwards. If the sides are formed from stones, pack the joints with soil instead of mortar. If bricks are used, leave gaps at random intervals to provide sufficient space for planting.

Fill the bed with a loamy, free-draining mix, as for a rock garden. Buy in some good soil for the purpose if your own garden soil is too heavy. Some pieces of stone may be partially buried in the surface, both to give the garden a good appearance and to provide planting crevices.

A raised bed, suitable for rock plants, need only be a few inches high.

hacksaw blade and coat it with a PVA adhesive. When this is almost dry, apply the mixture with a trowel, leaving a rough surface. Smooth the mixture over the top of the sink and a couple of inches down the inside, making a layer about ½in thick.

Cover the sink with plastic to prevent it from drying too rapidly. It will be ready for planting in two weeks.

Planting rock plants

Before planting a newly-made rock garden, give the soil time to settle. If possible discuss your requirements with a specialist nurseryman, who can recommend suitable plants for a beginner, and ones that will provide a succession of interest. Tell him if there are any difficulties concerning the soil or site.

Plants that are grown and supplied in plastic pots can be put in their permanent positions from early spring onwards. Use a trowel to make the planting holes. These should be deep enough for the top of the soil ball to be level with the ground surface.

In most cases, pairs or small groups of plants look more effective than isolated specimens. Allow for each plant's eventual spread and do not place slow-growing types close to vigorous, invasive ones.

Position plants according to their growth habit. When planted at the top of a low wall, for instance, aubrieta will form a tumbling mass of colour and conceal the stonework. An upright conifer, such as *Juniperus communis* 'Compressa', looks best on the lower ground. Lewisias prefer to grow in a wall or crevice, where they are unlikely to remain damp for long periods.

Reminders

Do not plant alpines in frozen soil.

Cover the ground with gravel or chippings after planting.

If planting in summer, keep the soil moist until the plants are well established.

Place sink gardens, which are heavy, in their final positions before filling them with compost.

Caring for rock plants

Planting and aftercare

Pot-grown alpines may be planted at practically any time of the year, the main exception being during freezing weather in winter. However, a newly-made rock garden should be given a few weeks in which to settle first. Use a trowel to dig a hole large enough for the root ball, firm the soil around it, then water around the plant if dry.

After planting the rock plants, cover the exposed soil right up to the stems with a ½in layer of gravel or stone chippings. This stops the plants from becoming mud-splashed and keeps the soil moist. Occasional topping-up the gravel will be necessary.

Take the precaution of scattering slug pellets during damp spells. Keep weeds under control by careful hoeing with an onion hoe, hand-weeding or with a chemical touch-weeder.

Rock plants are not heavy feeders, but an annual spring dressing of an organic fertilizer, such as bonemeal, will keep them growing. Water the plants during dry weather, giving sufficient water to soak to the roots and below.

Winter protection

Some alpines need winter protection – from the damp rather than the cold. Among plants particularly at risk are androsace, cerastium, lewisia and origanum.

Cover the plants with glass or plastic – either will shield them from rain, while allowing plenty of light and air to reach them. A miniature, open-ended cloche, made from two sheets of glass and a patent cloche clip, will be perfectly adequate. Alternatively, tack a small sheet of semirigid plastic to pegs to form a flat roof.

Aubretia will trail over a stone wall or rock garden.

Remove the shield in spring when the weather becomes drier and daylight lasts longer.

Reminders

Spring is the main flowering season, but remember to include some summer-flowering species of rock plants as well.

Do not forget to include some dwarf bulbs for early color.

Avoid using limestone chippings for dressing the soil around such "lime-haters" as lychnis and shortia.

Remove fallen leaves from around rock plants in fall and winter.

Propagation

In common with other herbaceous perennials, many rock plants can be divided (see p88). Others can be increased by taking cuttings. Most seed suppliers sell seeds of basic and easily-grown types of plants suitable for rock gardens. Sow these in spring or early summer, in pots rather than in the soil.

CARING FOR ROCK PLANTS

Winter protection ● Avoiding problems
● Propagation ● Easy-to-grow rock
plants

Dampiera likes a moist, open position with well-drained, light soil.

Easy-to-grow rock plants

In addition to the plants listed below, some dwarf bulbs are described on *pp102-3* and dwarf conifers on *pp160-1*.

Acaena microphylla (see Ground cover plants, *pp44-5*.)
Aethionema 'Warley Rose' H 6in, S 15in. Pink flowers (late spring). Sun.
Alyssum saxatile (gold dust) H 10in, S 15in. Bright yellow flowers (spring). Sun.
Androsace H 2in, S to 12in (depending on variety). White or pink flowers (spring or early summer). Sun.
Arabis albida (rock cress) H 6in, S 24in. Cascades of white flowers (spring). Sun.
Armeria (thrift) H 6in, S 9in. Massed pink heads (late spring). Sun.
Aubrieta (rock cress) H 4in, S 18in. Purple, pink or white flowers (spring). Sun. Lime.
Campanula carpatica H 9in, S 12in. Cup-shaped flowers, white or blue (summer). Sun. Other species with bell-shaped or starry flowers.
Cerastium (snow-in-summer) H 6in, S 2-4ft. Invasive, massed white flowers (late spring). Sun.
Dianthus (pink) H 4-8in, S 6-24in. D.

alpinus has pink flowers (summer). *D. deltoides*, with a carpeting habit, starts and finishes a little later. Sun.
Dryas octopetala (mountain avens) H 4in, S 2-3ft. White and gold flowers (summer). Sun. Lime.
Erigeron macranthus (fleabane) H 9in, S 18in. Daisy-like white or pink flowers (summer). Sun.
Erinus H 3in, S 6in. Small white or pink flowers (spring). Sun.
Gentiana septemfida H 9in, S 12in. Blue trumpets (summer). Sun/light shade.
Geranium (crane's bill) H 6in, S 12in average. Several species and varieties, mostly with pink or crimson flowers (summer). Sun.

Easy-to-grow rock plants

The pasque flower's cup-shaped blooms are followed by silky seedheads.

Helianthemum nummularium (rock rose) H 6in, S to 2ft. White, yellow, pink or scarlet flowers (early summer). Sun. Lime.

Iberis sempervirens (perennial candytuft) H 9in, S 2ft. Massed white flowers (spring). Sun.

Lewisia cotyledon H 12in, S 9in. White, pink, yellow or red flowers (late spring). Sun. Plant in a crevice; protect from wet in winter.

Lithospermum diffusum H 3-6in, S 24in. Deep blue flowers (summer). Sun. Moist soil.

Lychnis H 4in, S 4in. Clusters of pink or white flowers (early summer). Sun.

Origanum amanum H 3in, S 6in. Tiny pink flowers (summer). Sun.

Oxalis adenophylla H 3in, S 6-9in. Pinkish, veined flowers (early summer). Sun.

Phlox subulata H 3in, S 18in. Massed pink, white or violet flowers (spring). Sun.

Polygonum affine (see Ground cover plants, pp44-5).

Pulsatilla vulgaris (pasque flower) H 9in, S 12in. Large purple and gold flowers (spring). Sun.

Saponaria ocymoides (soapwort) H 3in, S 12in. Starry pink flowers (summer). Sun.

Saxifraga (saxifrage) H 2-18in, S 9-18in. Many species, mostly forming rosettes with white or pink flowers (spring). Sun/shade.

Sedum spathulifolium (stonecrop) H 3in, S 12in. Yellow flowers (summer). Sun/shade.

Sempervivum (houseleek) H 2in, S 12in. Attractive rosettes, rosy flowers (summer). Sun.

Shortia galacifolia H 6in, S 12in. White flowers, turning pink (spring). Shade. Acid soil.

Silene acaulis (moss campion) H 2in, S 12-18in. Mat-forming, pink flowers (late spring). Sun.

Thymus serpyllum (thyme) H 3in, S 2ft. Carpeting, with white, pink or red flowers (summer). Sun.

Trillium grandiflorum H 12in, S 12in. White three-petalled flowers (spring). Light shade. Plant late summer.

Note: H *indicates height,* S *indicates spacing.*

Armeria caespitosa is a compact and attractive form of thrift.

Erinus alpinus – an undemanding alpine.

Sempervivums are grown for their striking rosettes as much as for their flowers.

Preventing plant problems

Site

It is asking for trouble to grow sun-loving plants in shade, and vice versa. Even if such plants survive, they will not grow robustly and are more likely to fall prey to diseases or insect pests. There are also plants, such as amaryllis or passiflora, that need a sheltered site to help them survive the winter. Bear these basic needs in mind when choosing plants: it is the surest way to prevent disappointment and avoid needless work and expense.

Soil

Plants are amazingly tolerant of different soil conditions, but few will grow in waterlogged ground. Improving poor drainage is therefore a garden priority.

Remarkably, sandy soils and heavy clay can be improved by identical treatment – digging in plenty of manure, compost or other organic material. Providing humus-rich conditions is a way to assist plant health and help prevent disease. The structure of the soil will also be improved, making it easier to work and more congenial for seedlings and young plants.

pH level

For most plants the degree of soil acidity or alkalinity is not that critical. Even so, all plants will grow best when the right balance is struck – usually a little on the acid side of neutral. For some plants, however, it is vital that the soil is right – especially for plants that cannot tolerate lime. It is a good idea to buy a simple soil-test kit which will provide a reliable indication of the pH level (the measurement of soil acidity) in various parts of the garden.

Timing

Wild plants respond closely to the seasons, and garden plants should be given the same opportunity. By following the recommended dates for sowing and planting you can make the most of the seasonal climate and ensure that plants flower at the expected time. Ignoring the calendar means, at best, poor results, and often failure.

Buying plants

Plants seldom recover after a really poor start in life, so be careful when you buy them. Reject spindly, wilted or diseased stock when buying at stores or garden centers. Mail-order buying is satisfactory, provided that you deal with reputable nurseries; they have too much to lose by sending out poor plants. However, avoid the cut-price suppliers who sell small, sometimes weedy, specimens and are less concerned about their long-term reputation.

Spacing

Setting out plants at more than the recommended spacings will only detract from the overall effect of your garden display. At the other extreme, planting too closely results in weak growth and reduces the flow of air between plants. This, in turn, may foster disease. Although suggested spacings can only be approximate (for growth inevitably depends to some extent on site and soil), they are well worth following if you want the best all-around results.

Planting

Good soil preparation before planting provides the best possible conditions for healthy root development. This involves loosening the soil by digging or forking it, and then adding organic matter. If you are short of compost, bags of commercial "planting mixture" are a sound substitute and will give shrubs, in particular, a good start in life.

Most plants appreciate firm planting, and you should ensure that the soil makes good contact with the roots. Insert stakes before rather than after planting to avoid damaging the roots; protection from strong winds is a sensible precaution in exposed gardens.

Feeding

We expect a lot from our garden plants – robust growth, large and plentiful blooms, and a long flowering period. This can be achieved only if the soil contains sufficient chemical nutrients, as well as plenty of humus. Starved soil will never pay real dividends, even if the plants survive.

A balanced fertilizer raked into the surface at planting time will give your plants a good start in life. As they grow, and the fertilizer becomes exhausted, many plants will benefit from liquid feeding, which has a rapid effect. This applies especially to annuals, which have to grow and flower in a single season. Border perennials will also benefit from an annual feed in spring.

Foliar feeding – a spray of diluted fertilizer applied directly to the leaves – creates an almost instant response and is particularly valuable when plants are not doing quite as well as expected.

Watering

The right time to water your garden is before the soil dries out, not when plants start to wilt. You should always give sufficient water

Flowering plants, such as rudbeckia, respond to well-nourished soil.

they will distort and weaken plant growth and will damage the flower buds.

Take action before harm is done, spraying whenever you see clusters of these insects. A systemic spray, which penetrates the plants' sap flow, gives the longest-lasting protection.

Slugs and soil pests

The trouble in both cases is that serious damage is often done before you are aware of anything being wrong; slugs may decimate a row of seedlings almost overnight. Leatherjackets and cutworms can cause fatal damage to plants before they show serious signs of distress.

Prevention is better than cure; spread slug pellets or gel around vulnerable plants, or treat the soil against underground pests when setting them out, especially on heavy soil, where leatherjackets are a particular pest.

Weeds

Gardeners tend to think of weeds as "untidy" rather than as actually harmful. However, weeds are in fact very real competitors to cultivated plants, vying with them for nutrients, moisture, light, and even air, and adversely affecting their growth. Dense weed growth can also encourage fungal diseases, such as mildew, by impeding the flow of air around foliage and creating damp conditions.

Regular use of a sharp hoe while weeds are still at the seedling stage is probably the best means of keeping them under control. Working closely with a hoe among plants also gives you the opportunity for noting any other troubles at an early stage. If you use weedkillers extensively, you can easily miss the signs of trouble until a lot of damage has been done.

to soak the soil right down to the plant's root level. Frequent, light watering may actually do more harm than good by encouraging the roots towards the ground surface, where the amount of moisture is less constant.

It is worth spending a little money on watering equipment. Hand-watering takes up a lot of time and it is easy not to give the plants sufficient water.

Aphids

From spring onward, sap-sucking insects – especially aphids – congregate on the tender young shoots of numerous plants, notably roses. Left to their own devices

Flower pests and diseases/1

Often, it is physical damage or a plant's distress that will draw your attention rather than the pest itself. However, if you look at the plant more closely, you should be able to find the culprit.

Aphids
The greenfly is the commonest garden pest. There are many commercial sprays for controlling aphids, including systematic types.

Ants
A particular nuisance on rock gardens, ants are also found with aphids. Not a major pest, but they may damage roots. Control with purpose-made preparations containing pyrethrum.

Blackflies
Blackflies are especially common on beans, and a flower pest. Treat with a commercial aphid killer.

Beetles
There are thousands of types of beetles and their larvae in Australia, which feed on living and dead plant material. Some damage roots, flowers or bulbs. Use a specific pesticide in severe cases.

Bulb flies
The larvae of bulb flies feed principally on stored bulbs. Any affected bulbs should be dusted with a commercial aphid killer.

Bugs
Many of these insects suck sap. Some have toxic saliva that withers young shoots; others can eject a caustic fluid. Most do a limited amount of damage. Pick off . harmless types, or spray with maldison, carbaryl or dimethoate.

Caterpillars
There are many different types, all leaf-eaters. Control with permethrin, maldison, carbaryl, rotenone or quassia. Pick off small numbers by hand.

Cutworms
These soil-living moth caterpillars do the greatest damage near ground level. Spray the soil surface with carbaryl or endosulfan.

Earwigs
Earwigs damage plant leaves and flowers, especially those of chrysanthemums and dahlias. Trap them under pots of straw or spray them with carbaryl.

Flea beetles
One of the best-known is the hibiscus flea beetle, which chews holes in the leaves of hibiscus and abutilon. It also eats flower parts, malforming them. Control it with endosulfan.

Froghoppers
"Cuckoo spit" indicates the presence of froghoppers (**11**), pests that damage plant growth. They can be controlled with dimethoate, gamma-HCH or derris.

Leaf miners
Familiar signs of leaf miners are the pale lines in the leaves of chrysanthemums and cinerarias. Spray with a systemic pesticide, such as dimethoate or maldison.

Millipedes
These slow-moving, multilegged creatures damage roots and bulbs. Control them with carbaryl or methiocarb.

Slaters
These feed mainly on decaying plant material, but may damage soft plants nearby. Remove damp, dark hiding places, such as leaf litter. If necessary, use methiocarb snail bait, or spray with maldison.

Slugs and snails
Young growth close to the ground is especially at risk from slugs and snails. Remove leaves or any other cover and sprinkle pellets or apply spray containing metaldehyde or methiocarb.

Soil grubs
These soil grubs damage lawns and destroy plants by attacking their roots. Dust or sprinkle affected plants with products based on diazinon or methiocarb, if control becomes necessary.

Thrips
These tiny sap-sucking insects distort leaves and buds. Spray with derris, maldison, dimethoate, permethrin or rotenone, or quassia. Spray again a fortnight later if necessary.

Whitefly
These are small sap-sucking white insects, which live on the undersides of leaves. Control with permethrin, dimethoate or maldison, or white oil.

Wireworms
These shiny brown larvae of the click beetle damage roots and tubers. Chemical control is difficult but rotation of plants can help.

Weevils
The small white grubs of some weevils feed on plant roots and leaves. For example, the vegetable weevil attacks stocks and calendulas. Various adult weevils feed on flowers or shoots of certain shrubs. Spray affected plants and nearby ground with carbaryl.

Flower pests and diseases/2

Bulb scale mites
These minute pests are especially troublesome on narcissi. They breed inside the bulbs, causing stunting and distortion of visible growth. Stored bulbs feel light and soft. Destroy infected bulbs.

Mealybugs
Mainly pests of greenhouse and house plants, these form wool-covered colonies around the buds and leaf axils of many species. Spray with malathion or a systemic insecticide. Repeat after two weeks.

Stem and bulb eelworm
These microscopic pests attack bulbs – narcissi in particular. The inside of the bulb becomes discolored and rotten, while top growth is stunted and distorted, with yellow swellings. Destroy affected bulbs and plant new ones in fresh ground.

Spraying tips

It is best to spray plants with insecticides in the evening, when the bees have finished working.

Many pests live on the undersides of leaves, so direct the spray upwards. Hold the nozzle about 18in from the plant.

Change pesticides occasionally, rather than using a single product throughout the season, so the pests will not develop resistance.

Follow the instructions on the container exactly. Do not be tempted to use more chemical than recommended.

After use, empty the spray and rinse with clean water, pumping some through the lance and nozzle.

Flower diseases

Black root rot
Discolored foliage and blackened roots are signs of this fairly common disease. Destroy affected plants and do not replant with the same type.

Club root
Swollen roots on stocks and wallflowers, together with poor above-ground growth, are symptoms of club root. Lime the soil; sprinkle calomel dust in the planting holes.

Downy mildew
Damp conditions cause this fungus disease, which forms grayish patches on the leaves of some ornamental plants. Powdery mildew shows as a white coating. Spray with zineb for former, and benomyl for latter type of mildew.

Mealybugs have a wooly covering.

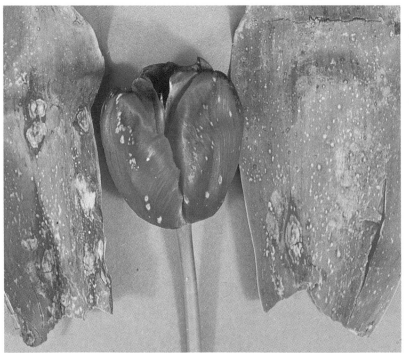

Tulip fire occurs most frequently in damp, cold weather.

Downy mildew on the stems and blooms of anemones.

A chrysanthemum attacked by mildew.

Foot rot

An apt name to describe the discolored, rotted area that may develop at ground level on bedding and herbaceous plants. The disease may persist in the soil throughout the winter. After removing affected plants, water the remainder with copper sulphate and ammonium carbonate (Cheshunt compound).

Leaf spot

Both circular and irregular spots and blotches are symptoms of a number of diseases affecting irises, dahlias, sweet williams and many others. Pick off affected leaves, spray with a copper fungicide and remove fallen leaves.

Peony blight

This causes the stems of herbaceous peonies to become discolored and collapse; the buds of tree peonies become covered in gray mold. Remove and burn affected growth; spray new growth with captan or thiram.

Rust

Visible as rust-colored spots and swellings on the leaves of many plants. Remove affected leaves and spray plants with mancozeb.

Tulip fire

This is a fungus that causes both bulbs and shoots to rot. Leaves and flowers are streaked. Burn affected plants and do not replant in the same soil. Elsewhere, spray young shoots with thiophanate-methyl benomyl.

Virus

Many plants may be attacked. Symptoms include yellow, mottled, striped or distorted leaves and stunted growth. Burn affected plants. Control aphids, which spread the disease.

Roses

122 A bed of roses
124 Where to grow roses
126 Caring for roses
130 Pruning and rose problems
132 Rose pests and diseases

A bed of roses

Roses bring fragrance, color and beauty to the most modest gardens, some continuing to flower for months on end. Within reason, they will tolerate quite a wide variety of soils and treatment, so successful rose-growing is within every gardener's reach.

Roses, however, are nothing if not diverse. Their sizes and habits, their flowering seasons, the shapes of their blooms and their pruning needs all vary. Fortunately, they are divided into fairly clear-cut groups, which provides a basis both for making your choice and for subsequent management. For this reason, you should be clear in your own mind about the type of rose you want before comparing and choosing individual varieties, as their requirements differ so widely.

As a broad rule, roses grow best in a reasonably sunny position that is neither tightly enclosed nor exposed to frequent, strong winds. They will grow in most kinds of soil, provided it contains plenty of organic matter – manure, compost and the like – and is well drained.

Hybrid tea roses have large blooms, often opening from conical buds and carried in twos or threes. Many are scented. Flowering continues at intervals from early summer onwards. Above is 'Silver Jubilee'.

Shrub roses include many original species and also hybrids and varieties derived from them. Flowering tends to be brief. 'Prestige', above, is classified as a modern shrub rose.

Miniature roses, such as 'Sweet Fairy', grow between about 6in and 18in high. They are a good choice for containers, as well as for edging and rock gardens.

Bourbons, such as 'Louise Odier', are a group of scented shrub roses that flower continually from early summer until the fall. With a typical height and spread of 5ft, they make fine specimen bushes.

Climbers have long, sturdy stems that can be trained against a wall or trellis. Some flower only briefly, so look for a repeat-flowering variety such as 'Bantry Bay'. Ramblers make fresh growth from near the base each year and carry only a single flush of flowers. They are better trained on a pillar or arch than against a wall.

Floribundas, or cluster-flowered roses, are in bloom right through the summer and are rather less trouble-prone than hybrid teas. Many, like 'Pink Parfait', lack fragrance, but they provide a display of color second to none.

Where to grow roses

To make the most of your roses, grow them in beds by themselves rather than mixed with border plants and shrubs. In fact, it pays to go even further, planting them in blocks of a single variety rather than in an assortment of heights and colors. Either hybrid teas or floribundas are the ones to choose for this treatment. The drawback, of course, is that there will be nothing much to catch the eye in the months between fall and early summer, when the roses first begin to flower.

If you prefer a mixed planting, using your roses as just another flowering plant, shrub roses are a good choice. However, allow for the plants' eventual size, since many are far larger than ordinary bush roses. Although a single shrub rose can look stunning, make sure that it is a repeat-flowering variety, such as 'Roseraie de l'Hay'.

Rose hedges are practical, provided you choose a suitable variety. Hybrid sweet briars, including 'Lady Penzance' and 'Meg Merrilees', make particularly dense hedges. 'The Queen Elizabeth' and 'Iceberg', both floribundas, are also favorite hedging roses; the climber 'Golden Showers' is also suitable.

Most roses need plenty of sunshine, but climbers that will grow on a wall away from the sun include 'Danse du Feu', 'Madame Alfred Carrière', 'Parkdirektor Riggers' and 'Pink Perpetue'. All are repeat-flowering.

Besides being attractive container plants, miniature roses look delightful on rock gardens. Remember, when choosing a variety, that height varies from around 8in to as much as 18in.

Some roses with a spreading habit also make attractive ground cover. Examples are 'Red Blanket', 'Smarty' (salmon-pink) and 'Snow Carpet' (white).

Varieties of hybrid teas arranged in groups for maximum impact.

Some favorite varieties

Of the new varieties introduced each year, some capture the public's imagination while others soon fade from the scene. The following short selection includes some older favorites as well as more recent introductions.

Hybrid teas: 'Bettina' (salmon); 'Blue Moon' (lilac); 'Deep Secret' (red); 'E.H. Morse' (red); 'Fragrant Cloud' (red); 'Golden Times' (yellow); 'Grandpa Dickson' (soft yellow); 'John Waterer' (red); 'Julia's Rose' (creamy copper); 'Mischief' (pink); 'Pascali' (white); 'Papa Meilland' (red); 'Peace' (yellow); 'Piccadilly' (scarlet); 'Prima Ballerina' (pink); 'Silver Jubilee' (pink); 'Super Star' (vermilion); 'Whisky Mac' (amber).

Floribundas: 'Allgold' (yellow); 'Anna Wheatcroft (vermilion); 'Elizabeth of Glamis' (salmon pink); 'Frensham' (red); 'Fragrant Delight' (orange); 'Iceberg' (white); 'Lilac Charm' (lilac); 'Lilli Marlene' (red); 'Mountbatten' (yellow); 'Orange Sensation' (vermilion); 'Pink Parfait' (pink); 'Rosemary Rose' (red); 'Southampton' (orange); 'The Queen Elizabeth' (pink); 'Topsi' (scarlet).

Shrub roses: 'Ballerina' (pink)*; 'Blanc Double de Coubert' (white)*; 'Constance Spry' (pink)*; 'Fantin Latour' (pink); 'Frau Dagmar Hastrup' (pink)*; 'Fruhlingsgold' (yellow); 'Lady Penzance' (pink); 'Max Graff' (pink); 'Meg Merrilees' (crimson); 'Nevada' (white); *Rosa rubrifolia* (pink); 'Roseraie de l'Hay' (crimson)*.

A mixed planting of climber 'Zephirine Drouhin' and rambler 'Albertine'.

WHERE TO GROW ROSES
Where to grow roses ● Easy-to-grow
varieties ● Buying roses

Ramblers: 'Albertine' (salmon-pink); 'Excelsa' (red); 'Maigold' (yellow); *Rosa filipes* (white); 'The New Dawn' (pink).

Miniatures: 'Angela Rippon' (pink); 'Baby Masquerade' (yellow); 'Coralin' (orange and red); 'Little Flirt' (red and yellow); 'Pour Toi' (white); 'Rosina' (yellow); 'Scarlet Gem' (scarlet).

Climbers*: 'Aloha' (pink); 'Casino' (yellow); 'Danse du Feu' (orange-red); 'Golden Showers' (yellow); 'Guinée' (red); 'Madame Alfred Carrière' (white); 'Mermaid' (yellow); 'Parkdirektor Riggers' (red); 'Pink Perpetue' (pink); 'Schoolgirl' (salmon); 'Zéphirine Drouhin' (carmine-pink).

Note: * repeat-flowering

Buying roses

If you go to a garden center to buy your roses, you will probably find them growing in black plastic containers. If this is the case they may be bought and planted at any time of year provided that the soil is neither soggy nor freezing. However, such plants are quite expensive and only the most popular and widely-grown varieties may be available.

Specialist growers send out bare-rooted plants during the dormant season. Besides being less expensive on the whole, nurseries carry a much greater range of varieties than stores and garden centers. Choose plants from their catalogs, many of which have colored photographs.

Barerooted roses may also be bought in plastic packs at stores and supermarkets. They are competitively priced, although the range of varieties is limited. Make sure you buy your plants from a store with a rapid turnover and check that the stems are neither shriveled nor sprouting.

Miniature roses look effective in a raised bed. Note the variations in height.

Caring for roses/1

Roses are most likely to flourish in a sunny, fairly open position that is sheltered from excessive exposure. Try to avoid planting them under trees.

Although the type of soil is not critical, for the best results it should be reasonably free-draining, yet capable of retaining moisture during the summer. Roses also prefer a rather acid soil with a pH level of 5.5-6.5.

Before planting, dig the bed thoroughly, working in plenty of rotted manure or compost to provide the humus needed for vigorous root growth. Leave the ground unplanted for a month or two to give it time to settle – loose, open soil dries out rapidly and discourages development of healthy fibrous roots.

If you are buying bare-rooted roses, select plants that have plenty of fibrous roots. The stems should be sturdy and green, not brown or whiplike. The quality of container-grown plants is easiest to judge if they are bought between spring and fall. This will allow you to see what the flowers look like and also whether the leaves and shoots are healthy.

Plant barerooted roses as soon as possible after you have bought them. If the weather or soil is unsuitable, store the plants in a cool but frostfree place and ensure that the roots do not dry out. Container plants can be left unplanted longer, but remember to keep the soil just moist.

Preparing for planting

Spread a dressing of general fertilizer over the bed just before planting, working this lightly into the surface with the tips of a garden fork. If the roses are barerooted, cut off any roots that are excessively long, broken or dead. Above the crown (the point where the stems join the rootstock) cut off thin or dead stems, together with any remaining flower buds or leaves. Always cut just above the outward-pointing growth buds, where new shoots will develop.

Container-grown plants should require little preparation before planting, but you should shorten or cut off any stems that have been broken in transit.

Planting roses

Like other shrubs, roses will grow more successfully if some carefully-prepared soil, or a commercial planting mixture, is spread around the roots. If mixing your own planting mixture, use equal parts of soil and peat, with a generous sprinkling of bonemeal. Leaf mold or thoroughly-rotted compost can be substituted for peat.

When planting barerooted roses, dig a hole wide enough for the roots to spread out naturally, by placing a stake across the hole). crown to rest just a little below the surface. (This can easily be checked by placing a cane across the hole.)

Hold the plant in place and shovel in a little planting mixture over the roots. Shake the rose so that the soil settles between the roots, then add some more mixture. Firm the mixture gently. Continue this process of filling and firming until the hole is filled.

For container-grown roses, dig a hole in the ground that is somewhat wider and deeper than the container. Place some planting mixture in the bottom of the hole, then remove the plastic from the plant roots and put the soil ball in the hole. Check that the top of the ball is level with the top of the hole and fill in with well-firmed planting mixture. When planting a climbing rose against a wall, the base of the stems should be 12-15in away from the brickwork.

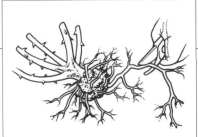

Roots are often broken at lifting time. Remove them before replanting.

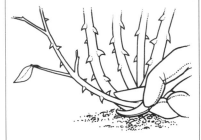

Prune spindly stems at the base. Cut off any that are broken.

The crown should be about 1in below the stake.

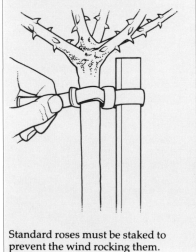

Standard roses must be staked to prevent the wind rocking them.

Plant climbing roses at least 30cm from the foot of the wall.

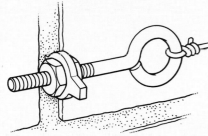

The straining bolt at one end of the wire enables the line to be tightened.

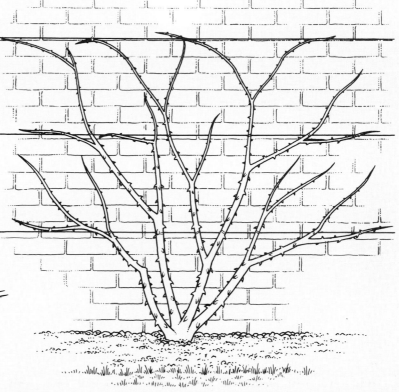

The main stems of a climbing rose should be trained to grow horizontally along the wires. The flowering shoots will emerge from these stems.

Supporting climbers and standards

Climbers grown against a wall must be supported and trained from an early stage in order to establish a more or less permanent framework of arched, horizontally-trained branches. A series of tightly-strained wires should be fastened at 15-18in intervals along the wall, passed through vine eyes (either hammered or screwed into the wall) with a straining bolt at one end of each wire to take up the slack. Use plastic-coated wire to secure the plant stems to the wires.

The same system of wires can be used for a rambler, but this type of rose is not as suitable as a climber for wall training. In addition to being prone to mildew, ramblers require fairly drastic pruning each year and flourish better on arches or pillars.

If standard roses are grown (a standard rose has a tall, bare stem, with a head of flowering shoots on top) they must be supported from planting time onward with a stake that extends to just beneath the branches. Hammer the stake in before planting the rose, or you may damage the roots. Secure the stem to the stake with commercial ties, and examine them at intervals to check they are firm but not tight.

Planting distances

Space hybrid teas and floribundas according to the eventual size of the variety being planted. A gap of about 18in is sufficient for the smallest types, which may be only 2ft high, but 30-36in is necessary for the more vigorous varieties, which may eventually grow to 4ft or more in height.

The usual spacing for standard roses is 3-4ft, while 4-5ft is necessary for most shrub roses. Leave a space of 8ft between adjacent climbers.

Caring for roses/2

Roses are hungry plants and need regular feeding if they are to grow well. Spindly stems, lack of new shoots and pale leaves are all signs of undernourishment.

Additional feeding should not be necessary during the first year if the soil has been prepared as advised on *p126*, and bonemeal has been added to the planting mixture. After the first year, an annual program is essential, and should start with a dressing of general fertilizer, or a commercial rose fertilzer, forked into the top inch or two of soil during the spring. This also gives you an opportunity to loosen the surface crust, but avoid disturbing the roots.

Towards the end of spring a surface mulch should be applied, but wait until a time when the soil is damp after rain. Almost any well-rotted organic material will provide a satisfactory mulch, but use peat or bark if you do not have sufficient manure or compost.

In early summer apply another dressing of fertilizer – preferably a commercial rose fertilizer. Hoe this in through the mulch and then water the bed thoroughly if the weather is dry, since the fertilizer will not become available to the plants until it has dissolved.

Some gardeners apply a foliar feed about every two weeks throughout the summer. This should not really be necessary if the soil has already been fed and mulched, but it will certainly help if any of these previous stages have been omitted. Foliar feeding – that is, spraying dilute liquid fertilizer directly on the leaves – has an almost instant effect and is useful if plants do not seem to be growing or flowering as expected.

If you decide to top up the mulch during the summer or fall, you should first remove any fallen leaves if any of the roses have shown signs of disease.

'Allgold' is a particularly fine yellow floribunda.

Removing suckers

When you buy a rose you are really buying two plants in one – the roots of a wild rose and the stems and flowers of a cultivated variety budded on to it. (Budding is a form of grafting.) As a result of this, an unwanted shoot or sucker will occasionally grow from the roots.

The sucker emerges through the soil and so is easily distinguishable from the other stems. First scrape back the soil to see where it starts, then pull it away from the roots. You should not cut the sucker off at ground level.

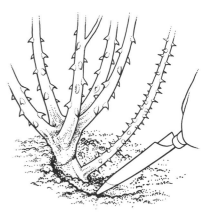

Scrape back the soil to reveal the base of the sucker.

Removing dead blooms

Disbudding

Wall-trained climbers need plenty of
water

Removing dead blooms

Hybrid teas and floribundas can be
encouraged to continue flowering if
the blooms are removed as soon as
they start dying. This diverts the
energies of the bush away from
seed production and into forming
new shoots, as well as making the
bush look more presentable.
Remove the whole truss, cutting
back to a shoot or bud lower down.
You may remove dead blooms on
repeat-flowering climbers, but you
will have to leave the dead blooms
on roses grown for their hips.

Watering

Recently-planted roses must
always be watered before the soil
dries out during their first growing
season, as they will not yet have
formed deep roots. Give sufficient
water to soak down to the roots,
and continue watering as necessary
if dry weather is prolonged. Roses
planted by walls need generous
watering throughout their lives.
Established bushes are less at risk
in dry weather, but will need
watering during periods of low
rainfall, as a lack of water restricts
growth and flowering.

Killing weeds

A Dutch hoe should be used
regularly between rose bushes to
keep weeds under control. A
spring mulch is helpful, too,
provided that the ground is free
from weeds when it is applied.
Alternatively, a chemical
weedkiller may be used. Because
roses are planted at well-spaced
intervals, it is easy to apply a
contact weedkiller between the
bushes simply using a dribble bar
attached to a watering can. A
residual weedkiller based on
simazine will kill germinating weed
seedlings for a whole season.

Disbudding

This is mainly for the benefit of the
enthusiast who exhibits hybrid tea
roses. However, any gardener who
would like some extra-large blooms
may care to try disbudding, which
involves pinching off the small side
buds that appear beneath the main
bud at the end of a shoot. The latter
will grow larger as a result.
   Disbudding has little effect on
the overall beauty of a rose garden.
However, it can help to provide
some spectacular and lovely
blooms for flower arrangements.

Pruning and preventing problems

Pruning cuts

Roses need pruning in order to dispose of old, weak or poorly-placed shoots and to encourage new, healthy growth with a good potential for flowering. The method of prunning varies with the type of rose, but all prunning cuts should be made with sharp secateurs, just above a bud facing in the desired direction (usually outwards). The bud will respond by growing into a shoot. However, if a whole stem is dead, it should be pruned at the base.

Pruning after planting

All newly-planted roses should have any spindly or dead-looking stems removed. However, if the roses are planted in fall, you should wait until early spring before you do this.

Cut back each stem of a hybrid tea to within 4in of the ground (6in for floribundas), to promote a strong framework of new branches. Cut back the weaker shoots of climbers and ramblers to about 4in, other shoots to 12in. Remove any flowered shoots from shrub roses.

Avoiding problems

Waterlogged soil will not produce good roses, since the development of the fibrous root system will be halted and eventually the plant will die. Double digging (see pp14-15), which breaks up the subsoil, is an aid to drainage. Dryness at the roots is also harmful. Dig plenty of organic material into light soil before planting, and apply a deep mulch annually. This can be forked into the top few inches of soil during the fall. When watering climbers, remember that a brick wall absorbs a great deal of water from the soil.

Lime is needed only on very acid soil. Yellowing of rose leaves may be a sign that the plants are suffering from iron deficiency, a condition that is caused by excessive lime in the soil. Apply sequestered iron if necessary (see pp18-19).

Rose sickness may develop in soil where roses have been grown for a long time. It is better not to replant an old rose bed, even if the previous roses appeared to be healthy. If you wish to replant the bed, the soil should be replaced with fresh earth taken from another part of the garden.

Roses grown in containers flourish best in soil-based compost. If you use one made from peat, add grit or sharp sand to provide a more open texture. Miniature roses are ideal for containers, but smaller floribundas and hybrid teas may also be planted. Place the containers in a sunny position, which is sheltered from the wind.

Dense shade is unsuitable for roses, but most will tolerate being in the shade for perhaps half the day. Even so, they should not be planted under trees. Climbing roses that grow surprisingly well against a sunless north wall

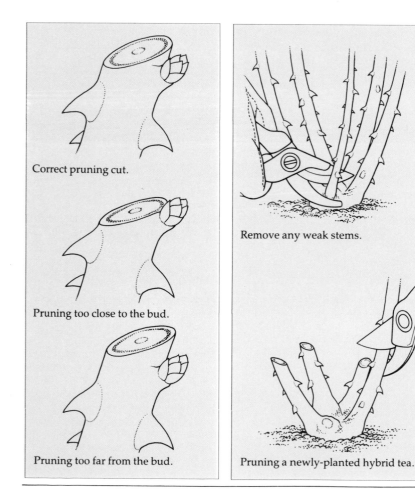

Correct pruning cut.

Pruning too close to the bud.

Pruning too far from the bud.

Remove any weak stems.

Pruning a newly-planted hybrid tea.

PRUNING AND PROBLEMS

How to prune ● Pruning newly-planted
roses ● Routine pruning ● Avoiding
problems

Routine pruning

The best time to prune most roses is in early spring, although the task should be left until a little later in very cold areas. Ramblers are best pruned in late summer after they have flowered.

Regardless of the type of rose, first cut out any dead or diseased growth. Then cut back or remove weak, spindly stems, any stems that are growing in the wrong direction, or ones that are rubbing against one another. You should bear in mind that the harder you prune, the more vigorous the growth that will follow. With rose bushes, the aim is to maintain an open center, so prune them to the outward-pointing buds.

Cut back hybrid teas annually by between a third and a half, removing the greatest amount from the weakest stems. For floribundas, use the same basic pruning method as for hybrid teas, but do not shorten the stems quite as drastically. As standards are either hybrid teas or floribundas budded on to the stem, prune them in the same way as bush roses, but take special care to maintain the shape of the head.

Miniatures need little or no pruning, except for the removal of dead stems or diseased growth.

Leave the main framework of climbing roses alone, although you should remove the ends of any dead shoots. Cut back the laterals (sideshoots) that have flowered to about 3-4in.

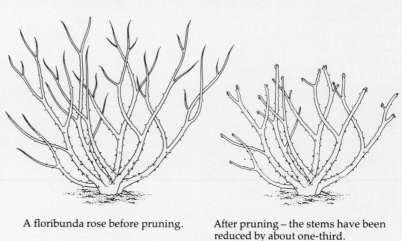

A floribunda rose before pruning.

After pruning – the stems have been reduced by about one-third.

(provided it is not too exposed) include 'Danse du feu', 'Madame Alfred Carrière, and 'Pink Perpetue'. Although receiving no direct sunlight, the bed should still be open to the sky.

General fertilizers may be used on roses, but fertilizers made specifically for roses are better. These contain the trace elements, such as magnesium, that are essential for healthy growth.

Firm planting is particularly important for bare-rooted roses planted in an exposed bed. Frequent shaking by the wind checks root development.

Chafer grubs, which feed on the roots of rose bushes, can cause serious damage before wilting and other signs of distress are apparent. As a precaution, sprinkle a soil pesticide – one containing gamma-HCH or bromophos is ideal – at planting time around the roots of the plant.

Late evening, when bees have finished working, is the best time to spray roses with a pesticide. The leaves should be dry, and you should aim to wet both the upper and lower surfaces. Combined pesticides save time and money. Systemic products have a long-lasting action and will control problems fully if they are applied in late spring and again in the summer. Some fungus diseases may overwinter on dead leaves and other debris, so clear the beds after the leaves have fallen, burning the material collected if there has been any sign of disease during the growing season.

A rose hedge will make a colorful but informal screen, but should not be planted if a neat, tightly-clipped barrier is required. Prune it to shape in early spring and, if possible, remove dead flowers during the summer. However, you should not cut off the dead flowers if you are hoping for a display or hips in the fall as well as in the summer.

Established roses can be moved with a fair chance of success if care is taken to lift a large block of soil with the roots. The plant should be moved while it is dormant.

Rose pests and diseases/1

The flowers, buds, stems, leaves and roots of roses may be attacked by a variety of pests and diseases. Many of them can be avoided by preventive spraying.

Buds and flowers

Aphids clustering on the tips of shoots may damage buds, and even prevent them from opening, but they can be controlled by preventive spraying with a systemic insecticide from spring onwards. However, an even better plan is to use an all-in-one spray that will control both aphids and fungus diseases.

Dead buds and lopsided flowers are common signs of capsid bugs. Control the pests with sprays based on dimethoate, permethrin, pirimiphos-methyl or fenitrothion. However, preventive spraying with a systemic product is preferable as the damage may be done before the signs are visible. Mottled and misshapen flowers are evidence of thrips. Control them by spraying the plants with malathion, dimethoate, permethrin or other widely-available pesticides.

Tortrix moth caterpillars bore into rose buds, destroying or distorting them; nearby leaves also become wrapped in silken threads. Spray with pirimiphos-methyl, permethrin or fenitrothion.

Powdery mildew is especially common when the soil is dry or the plants are in poor general condition. Spray with a systemic fungicide containing bupirimate and triforine. Cut out the affected growth at the end of the season.

Finally, rose flowers suffer from one fairly common trouble – the so-called balling of the flowers, when they fail to open and become discolored. This is the result of excessive or prolonged rain. Some varieties of rose are more susceptible than others.

This bloom shows typical signs of damage by thrips.

Stems and shoots

"Cuckoo-spit" on rose shoots provides protection for the nymphs of froghoppers. These sap-sucking insects are easily controlled with modern foliar insecticides.

Crown gall appears as a rough, unsightly growth on rose stems. The galls are not harmful and may simply be cut off when the plant is dormant. Then seal the wound with a pruning compound.

Canker, seen as a dark, sunken patch on stems, is caused by a fungus. First remove and burn the affected parts, and then spray the rest of the bush and those around with a copper fungicide, such as bordeaux mixture, or one based on cupric carbonate.

Roots

If a rose bush sickens or dies for no obvious reason, it is possible that chafer grubs are eating away its roots. These grubs are the larvae of chafer beetles, the adults themselves doing considerable damage to blooms.

It is difficult to control these pests without lifting the bush, although it is worth working gamma-HCH, pirimiphos-methyl or bromophos into the soil, as close to the roots as possible. Look for the grubs at planting time and dust the soil with pesticide powder or granules to prevent trouble arising.

Honey fungus is another possible cause of plants dying. For further details of this *see pp166-7.*

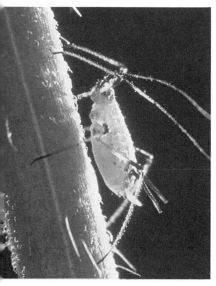 

Aphids can be one of the gardener's worst enemies.

The substance known commonly as "cuckoo spit", is in fact a secretion left to protect froghopper nymphs.

Recognizing problems

Aphids
Look for clusters of small insects, covering the flower buds and the end of shoots. These are usually green in color.

Thrips
Thrips themselves are often too small to be seen, but the edges of affected rose petals become damaged and discolored.

Froghoppers
White frothy "cuckoo spit" indicates the presence of froghoppers. Distorted growth of the plant may also be evident.

Capsid bugs
The leaves of affected plants will be distorted, and any buds will become dead and shrivelled.

Rose chafers
Examine the plants for small, square-bodied beetles. The flowers of an affected plant will be nibbled and lopsided.

Crown gall
This shows itself as a hard, wart-like growth on shoots, the main stem and roots. It is unsightly but seldom harmful.

Tortrix caterpillars
Look for holes bored in the rose bud, possibly with the maggot itself still inside. The leaves of the plant may also be hung with fine webs.

Mildew
This appears as a white coating on shoots, leaves and flowers.

Gray mold
Another fungus, which appears as gray patches and causes dieback.

Mildew can affect both the leaves and buds of roses.

Rose pests and diseases/2

The leaves of a rose provide a sensitive barometer to the plant's health. Discoloring of the leaves may occur when the plant is short of essential nutrients. Leaves may also turn yellow due to iron deficiency, which may occur on chalky or heavily-limed ground. In this event, apply sequestered iron *(see pp18-19)*.

However, leaves may also show a number of disease symptoms, as well as the damage done by pests. Taking prompt action at an early stage will give you the best chance of controlling the problem.

Leaf-cutter bees

If you see rounded segments cut out of rose leaves they have probably been removed by these small wild bees (2) to construct their nests. Although the plants may look rather unsightly, they are unlikely to suffer much harm. Dusting the leaves with malathion or gamma-HCH may prevent further damage. If you feel strongly about the matter, you will have to find the bees' nest and destroy it.

Leaf hoppers

An inspection of the underside of mottled leaves may reveal these small aphid-like insects (3), which feed on the sap of plants. Although they are seldom a major problem, it is as well to keep them under control by spraying in case the infection gets out of hand and the roses are seriously damaged. Spray the plants with malathion, pirimiphos-methyl or any of the systemic pesticides sold for aphid control.

Black spot

The name provides an accurate description of this common fungal disease (1), although the spots are sometimes brown. The condition is at its worst during warm, humid weather. The leaves may also turn yellow and fall. If this happens, they should be collected and burned, and not left on the ground over the winter or the infection may continue next year. Spray the plant with a systemic fungicide based on benomyl, propiconazole, thiophanate-methyl or bupirimate and triforine. Alternatively, use one that also contains a systemic insecticide.

Red spider

These are tiny mites (5), rather than spiders, which feed on the undersides of leaves. The signs of their presence are silvery mottling and patches on the upper surface of the leaves, together with an extremely fine web covering the mites' eggs on the reverse side. Spray the plants with a systemic pesticide as soon as you notice any of these signs.

Leaf miners

Pale blotches and serpentine blisters are caused by moth larvae (4), which feed on the leaf tissue. Pick off and burn leaves affected in this way. Pirimiphos-methyl, fenitrothion and similar sprays control the larvae if the outbreak is more extensive than usual.

Leaf-rolling sawfly

The signs of this insect's presence (6) are tightly-rolled leaves, each with a grub inside. If the outbreak is heavy the plant's development will suffer and the leaves will eventually shrivel and fall. First pick off the leaves that are already rolled, then spray the plant with a systemic insecticide.

Caterpillars

The moths of many caterpillars (7) harm roses. Damage to buds by tortrix moth caterpillars has been described on *pp132-3*, but they also damage leaves, spinning fine threads around them. These threads, together with holed and curled foliage, are indications of caterpillar damage. In addition to picking off and burning leaves with grubs on them, spray the plant with one of the common foliar pesticides such as permethrin, fenitrothion, rotenone, derris or pirimiphos-methyl.

Virus diseases

Distorted and yellow-mottled leaves (8) may be a sign of a virus infection. This is not a major problem with roses, which is fortunate as there is little treatment available. There are several forms of virus infection, which are nearly always introduced by pests that feed on the plants. For this reason alone, it is always worth keeping aphids and other pests under control even if they do not appear to be a problem. Do not propagate from infected plants.

Cockchafers

Adult rose chafers are small beetles (9) that feed on the foliage, causing a fair amount of unsightly damage. Their grubs, which live in the soil, feed on the roots of rose bushes and may destroy them. Spray or dust the plant with malathion, fenitrothion, permethrin, pirimiphos-methyl, or one of the systemic pesticides.

Rust

This fungal disease (10) does not occur very frequently. It is first visible as yellow patches on the stems and, later, on the undersides of leaves. Later still these patches turn black and young growth on the plant dies. Cut out diseased shoots, rake up and burn all fallen leaves. Spray the plant with a systemic fungicide, such as one containing bupirimate and triforine, propiconazole or pirimicarb.

Shrubs

138 Variety in shrubs
140 Shrubs to suit the site
144 Hedges
145 Rhododendrons and azaleas
146 Growing healthy shrubs
150 Propagating and pruning shrubs
152 Problems with shrubs

Variety in shrubs

A garden without shrubs would be dull indeed. They provide a backdrop for the briefer glory of annuals and other summer flowers, and their variety of shape and form brings a welcome change of contour, especially in winter when so much else is dead or cut to the ground. Many are as colorful as any border plant – in some cases, during the dreariest and coldest time of year.

Shrubs are among the most undemanding of garden plants, many needing scarcely any attention from one year to the next. With a few exceptions – which are easily avoided – they are completely hardy and also tend to be less vulnerable to disease and insect pests than many other garden plants.

It is important to choose the right shrub for your purpose. There is a vast range available, many of them deserving to be much more widely grown than they are.

For a start, do you want evergreens that retain their color and outline right through the year, or do you prefer deciduous types that bear flowers or berries, or have lovely fall tints? It is usually a good idea, if possible, to plant some of each.

What sort of soil do you have and will the site for the shrubs be in sun or shade? Like most other plants, shrubs have their preferences and you should choose species suited to the conditions you can provide.

Remember that many shrubs, such as the lovely elaeagnus and griselinia, are worth growing for their foliage alone. In some ways these provide better value than those with a brilliant but brief flowering period and leaves of no great charm.

It is a good policy to choose shrubs that provide at least two seasons of interest – continuing foliage color, perhaps, or a combination of spring flowers with either fall fruits or tints.

Shrubs for special purposes

A bed of carefully chosen shrubs, on their own or in company with hardy border plants, can provide a beautiful display.

Many shrubs make no objection if they are close-planted and then clipped to form hedges. Many of the shrubs suitable for this purpose bear flowers *(see p144)*, so why be content with a boring green privet hedge? They provide easily the

Magnolia x soulangiana, a hybrid with beautiful rose or purple blooms.

'Ville de Lyon' is a hybrid clematis that flowers throughout late summer.

Ceanothus prostratus is a creeping form of this blue-flowered shrub.

most attractive way, too, of
screening off a corner of the garden
or concealing a compost heap.

There are many climbing shrubs,
lovely plants that will cover a fence
or wall, decorate an archway or
pergola or twine their way up a
tree. Their height sets them above
the rest of the garden, and
favorite climbers, such as
honeysuckle, wisteria and the
many clematis species take full
advantage of that fact. There are
also a number of shrubs that
provide effective ground cover,
forming low, dense, spreading
growth. Few require any pruning,
or only enough to keep them
within bounds. For further details,
see p44-5.

Set on their own, in a telling
position where their particular
beauty of form, flower or foliage
may be seen to advantage, shrubs
can make superb specimen plants.
Magnolias are perfect shrubs for
this purpose.

Many shrubs will grow
contentedly in a tub, urn or
substantial trough. Planted this
way, such shrubs as camellias,
small rhododendrons, lavender,
laurel and many others can bring
year-round interest to a patio.

Heights and spreads

As well as color, shape and soil
needs, check on a shrub's eventual
height and spread when making
your decision. Some, such as the
larger magnolias, may become too
massive for a small garden.

However, you can solve many
problems by pruning and clipping.
A boxwood, for instance, will grow
unchecked but can be restricted to a
fraction of this height. Growing
shrubs in containers will also limit
their size, due to the growth of the
roots then being restricted, but
such growing conditions do not
suit most shrubs.

Shrubs to suit the site/1

Aucuba japonica 'Variegata' (spotted laurel) H 8ft, S 6ft. **Evergreen**
Speckled leaves; red berries in winter on female plants if male is planted nearby. Sun/shade. Any soil. No pruning.

Azalea – see Rhododendron.

Berberis x stenophylla (barberry) H 9ft, S 10ft. **Evergreen**
Arching sprays of golden flowers in spring; blue berries in fall. Sun/shade. Any soil. Thin out the shoots in the winter.

Buddleia alternifolia H 12ft, S 12ft. **Deciduous**
Weeping habit. Purple flowers in early summer. Sun. Any soil. Remove some shoots after flowering.

Buddleia davidii (butterfly bush) H 8ft, S 10ft. **Deciduous**
Pink, white or purple flowers in late summer. Attracts butterflies. Sun. Any soil. Cut hard back in spring.

Buxus sempervirens (box) H 10ft, S 8ft. **Evergreen**
Easily trimmed and shaped. Good for hedging and edging. Sun/shade. Any soil. Clip in summer.

Calluna vulgaris (heather) H 30in, S 30in (max). **Evergreen**
Many varieties, with different sizes and colors. Flowers in late summer and fall. Sun. Lime-free soil. Trim after flowering or in spring.

Camellia japonica H 6-10ft, S 8ft. **Evergreen**
Cup-shaped flowers in spring. Favorite varieties include 'Adolphe Audusson' (scarlet) and 'Lady Clare' (pink). Plant where shaded from early sun. Lime-free soil. No annual pruning.

S 20ft. **Deciduous**
 Campsis radicans (trumpet vine) H 30ft, Vigorous, self-clinging climber. Orange flowers, late summer. Sun. Fertile soil. Prune to size in spring.

Ceanothus x 'Delight' H 10ft, S 10ft. **Evergreen**
Mass of blue flowers in late spring. Sun/shelter. Any soil if not too alkaline. Prune lightly after flowering.

Chaenomeles speciosa H 5ft, S 4ft. **Deciduous**
White, pink or red flowers in late winter and spring. Yellow fruits in fall. Many varieties. Sun/shade. Any soil. Thin shoots after flowering.

Chimonanthus praecox H 8ft, S 10ft. **Deciduous**
Wall shrub with fragrant yellow blooms carried on bare wood in winter. Sun/shelter. Any well-drained soil. No annual pruning.

Choisya ternata H 6ft, S 6ft. **Evergreen**
Aromatic leaves; white, scented flowers in spring. May flower again later. Sun/shelter. Any soil. No annual pruning.

Cistus x purpureus H 4ft, S 4ft. **Evergreen**
Blotched, rose-colored flowers in early summer. Sun/shelter. Well-drained soil. Trim after flowering if necessary.

Clematis armandii H 30ft, S 30ft. **Evergreen**
White or pink flowers in spring. Sun/shade at base. Any soil. Thin shoots in late summer.

Clematis montana H 40ft, S 20ft (max). **Deciduous**
Vigorous climber, excellent for growing up trees. White or pink flowers in spring. Treat as *Clematis armandii*.

Clematis: large-flowered hybrids H 20ft, S 10ft (max). **Deciduous**
Great range of colors and shapes, some spring-flowering, others late summer. Study a specialist catalog which should also explain pruning differences. Other details as for *Clematis armandii*.

Clethra (sweet pepper) H 6ft, S 6ft. **Deciduous**
Creamy, scented flowers in late summer. Sun. Lime-free soil. No pruning.

Convolvulus cneorum H 30in, S 30in. **Evergreen**
Silvery leaves; white and pink flowers in summer. Sun. Any soil. No pruning.

Cotinus coggygria H 10ft, S 10ft. **Deciduous**
Feathery plumes of purple flowers in

A pink form of frangipani

Lavandula

Escallonia

Grevillea 'Robyn Gordon'

Viburnum

Hibiscus rosa-sinensis

summer. Rich fall leaf color. Sun. Any soil. Shorten over-long growths in spring.

Cotoneaster horizontalis H 2ft, S 6ft (max 6ft high on wall). **Deciduous**
Popular wall shrub; also suitable for banks. Red berries in fall and winter. Sun/shade. Any soil. Trim to shape, if necessary, in spring.

Cytisus battandieri H 12ft, S 8ft. **Deciduous**
Cone-shaped, pineapple-scented yellow flowers in summer. Sun. Any soil. Cut back a few older stems after flowering.

Daboecia cantabrica (Irish heath) H 30in, S 30in. **Evergreen**
Rosy flowers in summer. Sun/light shade. Lime-free soil. Trim in fall or spring.

Daphne mezereum H 5ft, S 3ft. **Deciduous**
Dark pink, scented flowers in early spring on bare shoots. Sun/shelter. Any soil. No annual pruning.

Deutzia H 5ft, S 5ft. **Deciduous**
Several species, all flowering in early summer. White, pink, rose or purple flowers. Sun/light shade. Any soil. Remove a few older shoots after flowering.

Elaeagnus pungens 'Maculata' H 8ft, S 8ft. **Evergreen**
A lovely foliage shrub, with yellow-centered green leaves. Sun/shelter. Any soil. No annual pruning.

Erica vagans (Cornish heath) H 2ft, S 4ft. **Evergreen**
Sprays of white or pink flowers in late summer. Sun. Unlike most heathers, tolerates a little lime. Trim in fall or spring.

Escallonia H 8ft, S 6ft. **Evergreen**
Shiny leaves; good for hedging. White, pink or red flowers in summer. Sun. Any soil. Trim after flowering.

Fatsia japonica H 10ft, S 10ft. **Evergreen**
Glossy, hand-shaped leaves. Globular white flowers in fall. Sun/shade. Any soil. No annual pruning.

Forsythia x intermedia H 8ft, S 8ft. **Deciduous**
Sprays of brilliant yellow flowers in spring. Suitable for a hedge. Sun/shade. Any soil. Remove stems that have flowered or clip hedges in late spring.

Fothergilla major H 6ft, S 6ft. **Deciduous**
Glossy leaves; "candles" of white flowers spring. fall tints. Sun/light shade. Lime-free soil. No pruning.

Fuchsia magellanica H 5ft, S 3ft. **Deciduous**
Good for seaside hedging. Pendent crimson flowers in late summer. Sun/light shade. Any soil. In all but mild areas, cut shoots back to base in spring.

Garrya elliptica H 12ft, S 10ft. **Evergreen**
Long, silvery-green catkins in late winter and early spring (those on male bushes are longest). Sun/light shade/shelter. Any soil. No annual pruning.

Gaultheria shallon H 5ft, S 5ft. **Evergreen**
Pale pink flowers in late spring, followed by dark purple berries. Spreads rapidly. Light shade. Lime-free soil. No pruning.

Genista lydia (broom) H 2ft, S 6ft. **Deciduous**
Pea-like flowers on arching sprays in early summer. Good on top of a low wall. Sun. Any soil. No pruning.

Griselinia H 15ft, S 12ft. **Evergreen**
Excellent foliage shrub or hedge for seaside gardens. Sun/shade. Any soil. No annual pruning.

Halesia carolina (snowdrop tree) H 15ft, S 20ft. **Deciduous**
Spreading branches, with clusters of white, bell-shaped flowers in late spring. Sun/shelter. Lime-free soil. No annual pruning, except to maintain shape.

Hamamelis mollis (Chinese witch hazel) H 8ft, S 8ft. **Deciduous**
Clusters of scented, golden flowers, with long thin petals in mid-winter. Sun/light shade/shelter. Lime-free soil. No pruning, except to prevent overcrowding.

Shrubs to suit the site/2

Hedera helix (ivy) H 20ft, S 20ft.
Evergreen
Many varieties with variously-shaped
and colored leaves. 'Gold Heart' is
green and yellow; 'Glacier', green and
white. Good for ground cover as well as
walls. Sun/shade. Any soil. Clip in
spring if necessary.

Hydrangea macrophylla H 5ft, S 5ft.
Deciduous
The many varieties are divided into
Hortensia (mop-headed) types, and
Lacecaps, which have flat heads of tiny
flowers surrounded by others with
larger petals. Pink, blue, crimson and
white flowers in late summer. Sun.
Moist soil. Remove old flowers and
weak shoots in spring.

Hypericum 'Hidcote' H 5ft, S 4ft.
Deciduous
Saucer-shaped golden flowers from
summer to early fall. Sun/light shade.
Any soil. No annual pruning.

Ilex aquifolium (holly) H 20ft, S 12ft.
Evergreen
Many varieties have beautifully-
variegated leaves. There are also
weeping forms. Red berries in fall and
winter on female plants if their is a
nearby male plant. Sun/shade. Any soil.
Clip to shape only.

Jasminum nudiflorum (winter-flowering
jasmine) H 10ft, S 10ft. **Deciduous**
Sprays of brilliant yellow flowers on
bare shoots throughout winter. Sun/
light shade. Any soil. Cut back shoots
that have flowered.

Kalmia latifolia (calico bush) H 8ft, S 10ft.
Evergreen
Glossy leaves; clusters of pink, bell-like
flowers in early summer. Shade. Moist
and lime-free soil. No pruning.

Lapageria (Chilean bell-flower) H 12ft,
S 3ft. **Evergreen**
A half-hardy climber, suitable only for
sheltered, nearly frost-free gardens.
Red, bell-like flowers in late summer.
Sun/shelter. Lime-free soil. No pruning.

Laurus nobilis (sweet bay) H 12ft, S 12ft.
Evergreen
Slow-growing, easily clipped to shape.
Aromatic leaves; yellowish flowers in
spring. Sun/light shade/shelter. Any
soil. Prune only for restricting or
shaping growth.

Lavandula spica (lavender) H 3ft, S 3ft.
Evergreen
Gray foliage; spikes of blue, scented
flowers in summer. Good for low
hedges. Sun. Any soil. Trim after
flowering.

Ligustrum ovalifolium (privet) H 10ft,
S 10ft. **Evergreen**
'Aureum' has green and gold leaves,
more attractive than others of the
species. Popular for hedging but also on
own. Sun/shade. Any soil. Clip hedges
in summer, otherwise no pruning.

Lonicera periclymenum (honeysuckle)
H 15ft, S 15ft. **Deciduous**
Vigorous climber. Yellow and purple
flowers in summer. Red berries. Sun/
shade. Any soil. Thin old stems
annually.

Magnolia x soulangiana H 12ft, S 12ft.
Deciduous
Superb white and rosy flowers in
spring. Sun/shelter. Lime-free soil. No
annual pruning.

Mahonia aquifolium (Oregon grape)
H 4ft, S 5ft. **Evergreen**
Clusters of fragrant yellow flowers in
spring. Black berries. Light shade. Any
soil. No annual pruning.

Parthenocissus quinquefolia (Virginia
creeper) H 60ft, S 30ft. **Deciduous**
Self-clinging wall climber with crimson
leaves in fall. Sun/shade. Any soil. No
annual pruning.

Passiflora caerulea (passion flower)
H 25ft, S 10ft. **Deciduous**
Dramatically-shaped and marked white
and purple flowers in summer. Sun and
shelter in mild area. Any soil. In spring,
cut back overgrown shoots to within
4-6in of main stem.

Pernettya H 3ft, S 3ft. **Evergreen**
Tiny, globular white flowers, early
summer. Pink and red berries in
fall. Sun. Lime-free soil. No annual
pruning.

Philadelphus 'Beauclerk' (mock orange)

Cotinus coggygria

Hamamelis mollis

Campsis radicans

Cotoneaster

Brunfelsia

Hypericum

H 4ft, S 5ft. **Deciduous**
White, fragrant flowers in summer.
These are single but there are double
forms. Sun/light shade. Any soil. Thin
out old stems after flowering.

Pieris formosa H 10ft, S 12ft. **Evergreen**
Cascades of white flowers in spring,
and brilliant red young leaves which
turn to pink and then green. Shade.
Lime-free soil. No pruning.

Pittosporum tenuifolium H 12ft, S 6ft.
Evergreen
Pale green crinkly leaves; black stems;
purple-brown flowers in spring. Good
seaside hedge. Sun/shelter from cold.
Any soil. Clip hedges in spring.

Polygonum baldschuanicum (Russian vine)
H over 20ft, S 20ft. **Deciduous**
Fast-growing climber – grows perhaps
12ft in a year. Massed sprays of pink
flowers in summer. Sun/light shade.
Any soil. No pruning.

Potentilla fruticosa H 3ft, S 3ft.
Deciduous
Small, serrated leaves; covered with
flowers throughout summer – red,
pink, yellow or orange, depending on
variety. Sun. Any soil. Remove some
old shoots each spring.

Pyracantha (firethorn) H 12ft, S 12ft.
Evergreen
Splendid as a hedge or against a wall,
having glossy leaves, white flowers in
late spring, brilliant berries in fall and
winter. Sun/shade. Any soil. Prune to
shape after flowering.

Rhododendron (inc azaleas) H & S from
a few inches to tree size. **Deciduous or
evergreen**
A vast range of flowering shrubs,
including numerous named hybrids.
(Azaleas, which are mostly deciduous,
are included.) Most rhododendrons are
evergreen. Hardiness varies and the
range of flower colors and shapes is
remarkable. Choose from a specialist
catalog (*see also p145*).

Ribes (flowering currant) H 6ft, S 5ft.
Deciduous
Pendent clusters of pink or red flowers
in spring. Dark berries in fall. Sun/light
shade. Any soil. Prune only to preserve

the plant's shape.

Rosmarinus officinalis H 6ft, S 5ft.
Evergreen
Aromatic leaves; spikes of blue or
mauve flowers in spring. Sun. Any soil.
Cut out any dead stems after winter.

Senecio laxifolius H 3ft, S 6ft. **Evergreen**
Silver-gray leaves; bright yellow flowers
in summer. Sun/light shade. Any soil.
No annual pruning.

Skimmia japonica H 4ft, S 6ft. **Evergreen**
Fragrant white flowers in spring. Scarlet
berries in fall and winter on female
plants if a male is planted nearby.
Sun/light shade. Any soil. No pruning.

Spiraea x bumalda 'Anthony Waterer'
H 3ft, S 4ft. **Deciduous**
Leaves are sometimes variegated cream
and pink; clusters of crimson flowers in
summer. Sun/light shade. Any soil. Cut
back to within 4in of ground in early
spring.

Syringa vulgaris hybrids (lilac) H 12ft,
S 10ft. **Deciduous**
Fragrant white, pink, purple, lavender
or red flower clusters in late spring.
Many varieties. Sun. Any soil. Remove
dead flowers and cut out weak shoots in
fall.

Tamarix pentranda (tamarisk) H 12ft,
S 12ft. **Deciduous**
Fine coastal plant, with glaucous
foliage. Long sprays of rosy flowers in
late summer. Sun. Any soil. In fall
remove all but a few inches of last year's
growth.

Weigela florida H 6ft, S 6ft. **Deciduous**
'Foliis Purpureus' has purple-flushed
leaves; those of 'Variegata' have creamy
margins. Flowers of both are pink and
appear in summer. Sun/light shade.
Any soil. No annual pruning.

Wisteria sinensis H 50ft or more;
indefinite spread. **Deciduous**
Supremely beautiful climber, festooned
with fragrant mauve or white flowers in
late spring. Sun/shelter. Any good soil.
Reduce side-growths to four buds in
late winter. Trim surplus shoots in
summer.

Hedges

Hedges are simply shrubs planted to create a barrier or screen and they need not be neatly clipped or symmetrical. Of the many suitable shrubs for hedging, some need only light trimming rather than close clipping. A flowering shrub may be an added bonus.

Most hedges grow to about 3ft in as many years and will continue to make steady growth. Other details will be found under shrubs *(see pp140-3)* and trees *(see pp160-1)*.

Aucuba japonica (spotted laurel) PD 2ft. Glossy leaves; berries on female plants. *Aucuba japonica* 'Nana Rotundifolia' is low-growing. Evergreen.
Berberis stenophylla PD 18in. Dense, with arching branches; golden flowers (spring); blue berries (fall). Evergreen.
Buxus sempervirens (box) PD 18in. A good dwarf hedge. Evergreen.
Chamaecyparis lawsonia PD 24in. Makes a dense, fast-growing hedge. Attractive foliage. Evergreen.
Chaenomeles speciosa PD 3ft. An informal hedge with white, pink or red flowers (late winter and spring). Deciduous.
x Cupressocyparis leylandii PD 30in. Very fast growing; easily trimmed to shape. Evergreen.
Escallonia macrantha PD 18in. Excellent seaside hedge; red flowers (summer). Evergreen.
Euonymus japonica (spindleberry) PD 18in. Good seaside hedge; glossy leaves. Evergreen.
Fagus sylvatica (beech) PD 18in. Good windbreak. Russet fall leaves (all winter). Deciduous.
Fuchsia magellanica PD 15in. Good seaside hedge. Crimson flowers (late summer). Deciduous.
Ilex (holly) PD 18in. Variegated types are recommended. A good protective hedge. Evergreen.
Hippophae rhamnoides (sea buckthorn) PD 18in. Good seaside hedge. Silvery leaves; orange berries if both male and females are planted. Deciduous.
Lavandula (lavender) PD 12in. Attractive dwarf hedge. Blue, scented flowers (summer). Evergreen.
Ligustrum (privet) PD 15in. The golden-leaved form is recommended. Evergreen.

A "tapestry" hedge of alternate plain and purple beech.

Berberis stenophylla in full flower.

Aucuba japonica 'Nana Rotundifolia'.

Philadelphus (mock orange) PD 2ft. Low-growing, informal hedge. White flowers (summer). Deciduous.
Prunus laurocerasus (cherry laurel) PD 30in. Shiny leaves; white flowers (spring). Vigorous and tall-growing. Evergreen.
Rosa (rose) PD 2ft. See *p124* for some suggested varieties.
Senecio greyi PD 18in. Good seaside hedge. Yellow flowers (summer).

Evergreen.
Spiraea thunbergii PD 18in. Informal hedge. White flowers (spring). Deciduous.
Taxus baccata (yew) PD 2ft. Slow-growing and dense. Evergreen.
Tamarix pentandra (tamarisk) PD 24in. A loose hedge or windbreak, particularly good for seaside. Deciduous.

Note: PD *indicates planting distance.*

HEDGES

Shrubs for hedges ● Growing hedges ●
Rhododendrons and azaleas and their
special needs

A mixed planting of pink rhododendrons and yellow azaleas.

Rhododendrons and azaleas

Azaleas are a branch of the rhododendron family. The majority (mainly the taller ones) are deciduous, but some of the smaller species and hybrids are evergreen. In contrast, nearly all other rhododendrons are evergreen and, as a rule, are larger shrubs and have larger flowers than azaleas.

Taken together, rhododendrons and azaleas constitute an impressive and diverse family of plants.

Both azaleas and rhododendrons share a dislike of alkaline soil and will not grow where lime is present. They also require plenty of humus in the form of compost, leaf mold or peat. The rhododendrons (as opposed to azaleas) found in most gardens are hardy hybrids, of which there are scores of named types. They flower between late winter and late summer, although the majority bloom in late spring. Colors range through every shade

of purple, pink, red, yellow, apricot and cream to white. Sizes vary substantially, but there are plenty that grow to around 6-10ft in height, making them suitable for medium-size gardens. Hardiness varies, and early-flowering varieties should not be grown in places which are exposed to late frosts in spring.

Deciduous azaleas, of which there are also many named types, mostly grow between 3ft and 8ft in height, and in fall their foliage takes on brilliant colors. The evergreen types (including the very popular Kurume hybrids) are mostly only 3-4ft high, and a good choice if space is restricted.

Types of rhododendrons and azaleas are too numerous to mention individually by name. The only satisfactory way to make your choice is by visiting a specialist nursery or consulting a catalog.

Acid, humus-rich soil is the first essential need of practically all rhododendrons and azaleas – the pH reading should be 6.0 or lower.

A mulch of peat or compost each spring will keep established plants growing and help to ensure that the soil does not dry out during the summer. A position in light, dappled shade is ideal, although this is less important than making sure that the roots always have ample moisture. If they are grown in containers, rhododendrons must be planted in an ericaceous or lime-free compost.

Container-grown rhododendrons may be planted at any time provided that the soil is suitable. Bare-rooted plants, including those which have been lifted from another part of the garden, should be planted between early fall and spring.

Little pruning is necessary for rhododendrons. However, dead stems should be removed in spring and any weak shoots cut back. Remove flower heads when they have died.

Yellowing of the leaves is a sign of chlorosis (see pp18-19). Drooping leaves indicate lack of water.

Growing healthy shrubs/1

Buying shrubs

Most large garden centers stock a range of popular shrubs. These are grown in plastic containers and may be bought and planted at any time of the year when the soil is not frozen or waterlogged. Buying shrubs from garden centres ensures that you get exactly what you want, and unhealthy or undersized specimens can be rejected. The only disadvantage is that container-grown plants usually cost more than bare-rooted shrubs.

Bare-rooted plants bought direct from a nursery are generally excellent value for money if you are able to collect them yourself. Otherwise, delivery charges may be high and you will have to trust the nursery to supply good stock. The chief adavantage is that nurseries are able to supply a great many species and varieties that seldom find their way to garden centers. Bare-rooted plants should be planted while dormant, between fall and early spring.

Mail order firms also supply shrubs and other plants at competitive prices. Selection is limited and the plants are usually small, but nevertheless it is an economical way to stock a garden. The shrubs, which are bare-rooted, are dispatched during their dormant period.

When buying container-grown plants (not plants that have simply been placed in a container), check that no large roots are protruding and that there is not a gap between the compost and the plastic. If the shrubs are bought during the spring or summer, check that the leaves and shoots are healthy and pest-free. Bare-rooted plants should have plenty of fibrous roots and be fully dormant when you buy them. Always select plants with sturdy, well-placed stems.

Soil preparation

The chief aim when planting is to provide conditions that will encourage the shrub's fibrous root system to develop. Root development will be hampered if the surrounding soil is either excessively wet or dry.

Wet, badly-drained soil can be improved by double digging or, in extreme cases, by laying drainage pipes (see pp14-15). Digging organic material into the topsoil will improve its structure and will also enable light soil to retain moisture.

If you are planting the shrubs in normal soil, the ground should be dug some weeks before planting is due, if possible with some rotted manure, compost or peat incorporated at the same time. Work a dressing of general fertilizer into the surface shortly before you begin planting.

Unless the soil is a really good loam – that is, free-draining but moisture-retentive – it is worth using a specially-prepared planting mixture around the shrubs' roots. This can be a commercial, peat-based type or alternatively you can mix your own from equal parts of soil and peat, with an added sprinkling of bonemeal. If the soil is on the heavy side, part of it can be replaced in the planting mixture by sharp sand.

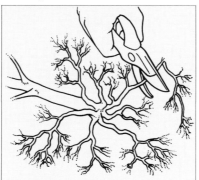

Before planting, cut off any broken or dead-looking roots.

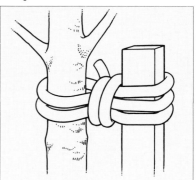

A plastic-covered clothes line makes an inexpensive tie.

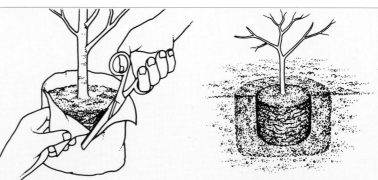

Leave the soil ball intact when removing plastic containers.

Place plenty of planting mixture around container-grown plants.

Planting

If bare-rooted shrubs arrive before you are ready to plant them, remove the packing material and heel them in to the ground temporarily. This means digging a hole or trench deep enough to take the roots, which should then be covered with soil.

To plant a bare-rooted shrub, first dig a hole several inches wider than the spread roots and sufficiently deep for the soil mark on the stem to be level with the surface of the ground. This is easily checked by placing a stick across the hole.

Loosen the soil in the bottom of the hole and then hold the shrub in position, placing some of the planting mixture over and between the roots. Shake the stem up and down so that the planting mixture settles without gaps, then put in another layer and firm it with your foot. Continue adding layers of soil in this way until the hole is filled and the shrub firmly planted.

Plant a container-grown shrub by digging an oversized hole, placing the soil ball on a layer of planting mixture, and then filling in the hole with soil and then watering it in.

Honeysuckle will climb wires, a trellis, or any similar support.

Reminders

Evergreen shrubs supplied with a wrapped ball of soil are best planted in spring or late summer, not during the winter. Try to keep the soil ball intact when planting.

Protect newly-planted evergreen shrubs from strong winds. Use plastic windbreak material, a wattle hurdle or a sacking screen.

Plant climbers and trained shrubs at least 12in from a supporting wall.

Make sure that spring-planted shrubs do not dry out. The same applies to container-grown shrubs planted during the summer.

Providing support

Most free-standing shrubs can manage without support, but those with tall stems need staking. Hammer in the stake after digging the planting hole but before planting the shrub.

Patent ties, which include buffers to place between the stem of the shrub and the stake, are easy to fasten. If several shrubs or trees need staking, an inexpensive alternative is to use lengths cut from a plastic-covered clothes line, and tie them in a figure-of-eight tie.

Shrubs planted against walls can be secured to tightly-strained wires in the same way as roses *(see pp126-7)*. However, this method is best suited to wall-trained shrubs that have fairly stiff stems. For other shrubs, such as clematis, that need closely-spaced supports, large-mesh plastic netting (4-in squares are ideal) is more suitable. First nail or screw battens to the wall at 20-in intervals. These provide air space between the foliage and the wall. Staple the netting to the battens.

Growing healthy shrubs/2

Watering

Bare-rooted shrubs planted in fall or winter require no further attention until spring, but during their first growing season the soil should not be allowed to dry out. Container-grown plants may not be affected quite as quickly by dry soil, for their roots are more developed. However, their growth may be checked by a spell of prolonged dry weather.

Liberal watering with a hose will prevent the roots of both bare-rooted and container-grown shrubs from being harmed during dry weather. You should also irrigate the soil around the planting area, as well as that immediately over the roots.

Shrubs may begin to settle a little more deeply in the soil within a few months of planting and, if secured to stakes, they could eventually become suspended by their ties. Check once or twice during the year to see that this has not happened and also that the ties remain tight enough to prevent the shrub from moving, without restricting its growth.

Mulching

Like so many other plants, ornamental shrubs benefit from a dressing of organic material spread around the root area. This is especially helpful during the first year or two, while the fibrous root system is developing and before deeper roots have grown to tap the supply of moisture at a lower level.

Mulching should be carried out in late spring, when the soil has had time to grow warm. First, remove any perennial weeds, complete with roots, and remove annual weeds with a hoe before spreading the mulch. Apply the mulch while the soil is still moist.

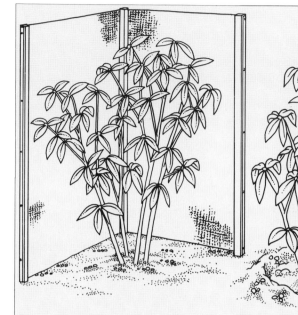

A sacking screen can be used to protect newly-planted rhododendrons.

Keep the roots of young evergreen shrubs well watered.

If you have no compost to spare for a mulch, a good layer of lawn mowings is better than nothing. Shredded bark, which is sold at garden centers, also makes an effective mulch.

Feeding

Newly-planted shrubs will not need feeding during their first year if the soil has been dressed with general fertilizer and some bonemeal was added to the planting mixture. If the bonemeal and fertilizer were omitted, scatter some general fertilizer over and around the planting area in spring and work it into the soil with the tips of a fork.

Shrubs should not normally require feeding in subsequent years, but an annual spring dressing of fertilizer will help them

Reminders

Foliar feeding – spraying a shrub with a liquid fertilizer – will give it a boost during prolonged dry weather when the roots are unable to take up sufficient nourishment.

Suckers growing from beneath the ground alongside grafted shrubs, such as lilacs or camellias, should be pulled away from the rootstock.

Sparse flowering may be due to overfeeding, especially if the plant is otherwise vigorous. On average soil, shrubs should be able to find all the nourishment they need without regular fertilizer dressings. Shrubs grown in containers are an exception.

Removing dead blooms is usually impractical, but the flowerheads of lilacs should be cut off as they fade.

GROWING HEALTHY SHRUBS/2

Watering and spraying ● Mulching ●
Feeding ● Protection ● Avoiding
problems ● Weed control

to grow if the soil is not particularly fertile. Mulching is also valuable. Any material remaining on the surface should be forked into the topsoil each fall. If possible, use manure rather than peat on poor soil.

Winter protection

A number of quite widely-grown shrubs are not fully hardy. They require a position that is sheltered from icy winds and, in some cases, they also should be protected during the winter with straw, plastic or burlap (*see pp140-3*).

Whether or not more protection is required depends, to some extent, on the garden's position. For instance, plants that thrive in mild, coastal gardens may not survive in frosty inland districts. An obvious example of such a plant is *Fuschia magellanica*, which retains its stems and foliage throughout the winter when grown near the coast but becomes, in effect, a herbaceous perennial in less favorable climates inland.

Shrubs at risk

Ceanothus is best avoided in very cold areas, although it can be partly protected by a drape of burlap in winter. Choisya should not be grown in gardens exposed to icy winds.

Cistus, too, is susceptible to frost and should be protected with burlap or plastic. Clethra grows best in a mild area. It is tender but is too large to be covered easily.

Fuschia should be cut down to ground level in late fall in areas at risk from frost, and the crown covered with peat, straw or bracken. Garrya needs to be protected with straw or burlap during its first winter. passiflora should have its crown covered with a good layer of peat or ashes during

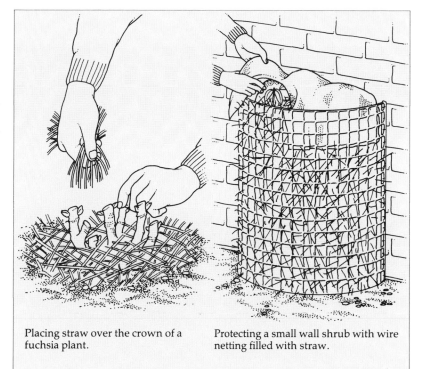

Placing straw over the crown of a fuchsia plant.

Protecting a small wall shrub with wire netting filled with straw.

the winter. Protect young growth from frost with burlap.

Caring for evergreens

Some evergreens are susceptible to frost and wind damage during their first winter, but a simple burlap wrapping will provide valuable protection. Dryness after planting is another danger, especially for spring-planted evergreens. Unlike bare-rooted deciduous shrubs, which do not produce leaves for some time after planting, evergreen species transpire moisture through their foliage right from the moment they are planted.

In addition to watering evergreen shrubs carefully, and keeping the soil moist if dry weather follows, frequent spraying of the foliage with clear water will help the shrubs through the most

dangerous conditions of dry windy weather. A simple windbreak will help if the shrubs are in an exposed position. This can be removed after a few months, when new roots have developed.

Weed control

Keep the soil beneath newly-planted shrubs free from weeds for the first year or two, (*see pp42-3*). For long-term clearance use a residual weedkiller based on simazine or propachlor. Dig out any perennial weeds first. Alternatively, apply a translocated weedkiller based on glyphosate, taking care that none of the chemical touches the shrubs. Where shrubs are grown in a lawn, keep the soil beneath them bare (except for a mulch) for the first year or two.

Propagating and pruning

Raising shrubs from seed is not the usual method of propagation. Some seeds do not germinate for as long as 18 months, and it takes much longer to produce a sizable plant by sowing than it does from a cutting. However, in spite of this, raising shrubs from seed provides a cheap and interesting means of propagation.

Raising from seed

Prepare an outdoor seedbed, with bonemeal raked into the surface, where the seeds or seedlings can remain undisturbed for a couple of years. Sow the seeds in early spring in shallow drills and cover them with netting or black thread. If you save your own seeds, place hard-coated types, such as holly berries and rose hips, in a pot of sand and stand them outside for the winter before sowing. They germinate more readily after freezing.

Cuttings

Several types of shrubs can be most easily propagated by taking hardwood cuttings in the fall. These will root outdoors. This method is suitable for berberis, buddleia, buxus, deutzia, forsythia, ligustrum, polygonum, as well as a number of other shrubs.

Remove a stem of the current year's growth, just below a bud, and then cut off the top above a bud. The final length of a cutting should be about 12in. Dip the bottom end in hormone rooting powder. If the cutting is from an evergreen, remove the leaves from its lower half.

Open up a narrow trench about 9in deep, place an inch of sharp sand in the bottom and stand the cuttings 6in apart on the sand. Replace the soil and firm it. The cuttings should have reached a suitable size for planting by the

Cuttings

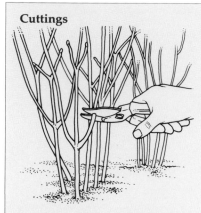

Remove pencil-thick shoots in early autumn.

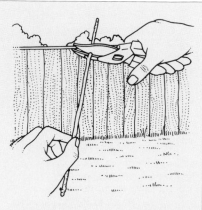

Cut just beyond the buds at each end of the shoots when trimming.

Bury two-thirds of each cutting in the trench.

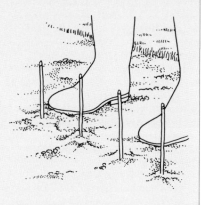

Fill the trench, then firm around it with your feet.

following fall.

An even greater number of shrubs propagate more readily if the cuttings are taken during the summer, while the tips of the shoots are still soft. Shrubs which propagate more readily from these semi-ripe cuttings include aucuba, camellia, ceanothus, chaenomeles, choisya, cistus, clematis, cotoneaster and daphne.

Remove any sideshoots that are about 6in long. Cut off the tip and the lower leaves, then trim the stem just beneath the bottom leaf joint. Dip this end in hormone rooting powder and insert the lower, leafless part of the stem into a pot containing seed compost, placing several cuttings in each pot. Water them in and secure a plastic bag over the top with a rubber band, first inserting some sticks or wires to hold the plastic clear of the leaves. Stand the pots in a warm but shaded place. Pot the cuttings individually, once they have made good roots.

PROPAGATING AND PRUNING

Raising from seed ● Raising from
cuttings ● Avoiding problems ●
Pruning

Pruning shrubs

Many shrubs need little or no
pruning from one year to the
next. Others will flower more
freely, and maintain a better
shape, if pruned annually. When
and how this is done varies from
plant to plant, the crucial point in
many cases being whether
flowers are carried on the
previous year's growth or on
shoots that have formed during
the current season.

Make all pruning cuts
immediately above an outward-
facing bud (see p130). (Individual
pruning suggestions are given on
pp140-3.) Remove dead or
diseased shoots, and any that are
weak or misplaced, even if overall
pruning is unnecessary.

When pruning shrubs that
flower on the previous season's
growth (Buddleia alternifolia, for
example), do this immediately
after flowering, cutting the
shoots that have flowered back
to the new wood. This will
encourage fresh shoots, which
will carry the following year's
blooms, to form.

Early spring is the time to
prune shrubs that flower on the
current season's shoots, such as
Buddleia davidii. Cut back last
year's shoots to within about
three buds of their base.

Neglected, overcrowded
shrubs can be rejuvenated by
cutting out old branches at the
base, leaving more space for
younger growth. This is much
better than simply shortening the
branches, which will cause even
denser growth. After hard
pruning of this sort, spread a
dressing of general fertilizer over
the root area and fork it into the
top inch or two of soil. Applying
a mulch of rotted manure will
also help. After pruning, paint
the cut ends of large branches
with a pruning sealant.

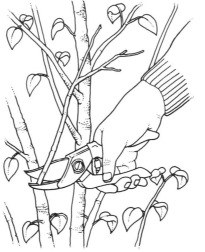

With all types of shrubs, the first step is
to cut out any weak, diseased or dead
shoots.

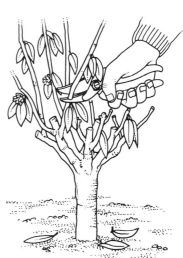

Cut back shrubs that flower on last
year's shoots. New growth will form to
carry next year's flowers.

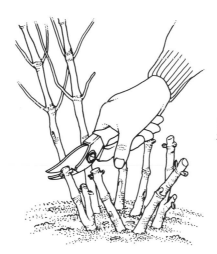

Fairly heavy spring pruning will induce
better flowers on shrubs that bloom on
the current year's growth.

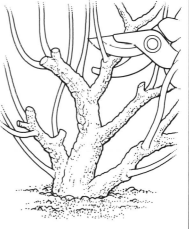

Remove some of the older branches
from neglected shrubs. If necessary,
cut them back to ground level.

Problems with shrubs/1

Soil and weather

If a shrub looks off-color, perhaps with wilting or discolored leaves. it is not necessarily diseased. As often as not the weather or soil conditions are to blame, rather than an infection. An obvious example of this is the chlorosis that affects rhododendrons, camellias and other acid-soil plants when they are planted in ground that contains lime. In these conditions the plants are unable to take up iron from the soil, and their leaves turn yellow due to lack of chlorophyll. Suitable treatment is suggested on *pp18-19*.

Another cause of yellow foliage is persistent waterlogging of the soil, which causes the leaves of the shrub to drop and is likely to retard overall growth. The shrub will eventually die if nothing is done to improve drainage. If the shrub is young, it is worth lifting it, with as large a soil ball as possible, double-digging the site, and then replanting it.

Frost damage shows as brown blotches and blisters, often with a degree of peeling, especially near the tips of leaves. The tender young spring foliage is most at risk, particularly when hard frosts occur after a spell of mild weather. However, fresh, undamaged growth will usually follow.

Young foliage is also at risk from scorch, which is caused by cold, drying winds during the spring. Scorch shows as discolored or dead patches on the leaves. In exposed gardens it is worth erecting a temporary screen on the windward side of any susceptible shrubs before the first spring foliage appears.

Wilting leaves and stems, possibly accompanied by the discoloration and fall of the leaves, indicate dryness at the shrub's roots. In addition to

A chlorotic rhododendron, the result of lime in the soil.

White curl grubs eat decayed vegetable matter and roots.

The telltale marks of coral spot.

copious watering, foliar feeding at two-weekly intervals will help the shrub to recover.

Shoots, flowers and roots

Aphids
Aphids are common pests. They usually cluster on the tips of shoots, spreading to nearby leaves. There are a number of insecticides sold specifically for aphid control. Use a systemic type for the best long-term control.

Capsid bugs
These are also sap-sucking insects but they are more active than aphids and may have moved on by the time any damage becomes apparent. Telltale signs are holed and distorted leaves, and misshapen flowers. Spraying with permethrin or dimethoate will discourage further attacks.

Chafers
Adult chafer beetles may do a certain amount of damage to

leaves, but their white grubs, which live in the soil, pose the greatest threat, feeding on the roots of plants and frequently killing them. Apply gamma-HCH, pirimiphos-methyl, bromophos or diazinon at planting time as a precaution against chafers.

Clematis wilt
This fungus disease is specific to clematis. The first signs are wilting of the shoot tips. Cut out affected growth and spray new shoots with a fungicide based on benomyl.

Coral spot
Although it lives on dead wood, this fungus may attack living trees and shrubs, where it shows as pinkish spots on the bark. Cut out and burn all affected shoots and branches and seal the wounds with pruning compound.

Die-back
There are a number of possible reasons – for example, disease, frost, damage, waterlogging – for shoots dying from the tips. Cut out affected growth and try to find and deal with the cause. Seal the wounds with pruning compound.

Honey fungus
A serious and highly infectious disease, responsible for killing many trees and shrubs. The first positive sign may be toadstools growing near the base of the tree in fall. For further details *see pp166-7*.

Woolly aphids
These pests reveal their presence by the white, waxy secretions they produce on shoots and branches. These are often followed by galls and distorted growth. The most effective treatment is to brush the affected area with malathion or one of the many commercial aphid spray liquids. Repeat as necessary.

Problems with shrubs/2

Damage to leaves and buds

Leaves are useful indicators of plant health, and often show the first signs of an infection or an attack by pests. Serious problems are the exception rather than the rule where shrubs are concerned, but it is on their leaves and buds that the pests and diseases listed here may first become evident.

Adelgids

These are extremely small aphids that frequently attack conifers, weakening the plants by feeding on their sap. Like others of the same family, they secrete honeydew on which molds may become established. They also produce a protective waxy coating – which looks like tufts of wool – that makes control more difficult. Drenching with malathion or spraying with a systemic pesticide is the most effective treatment.

Bud blast

This is a fungus disease of rhododendrons (1), which causes the buds to turn brown and then, in spring, to develop dark, bristle-like growths that carry the spores. The disease is transmitted by leafhoppers, which may be controlled by preventative spraying in late summer. Remove and burn affected buds.

Caterpillars

Several types of caterpillar can prove to be serious pests, virtually stripping a shrub of its leaves when they are present in large numbers. At the first signs of damage, spray with malathion, permethrin or fenitrothion. Alternatively, dust with derris or gamma-HCH.

Galls

This term covers a variety of lumps, raised marks and swellings (2), which are often caused by the plant's reaction to an attack by insects. Aphids or adelgids may be responsible, but some are due to the presence of gall mites and gall wasps. However, the damage is rarely severe and, as a rule, no action need be taken.

Leaf-cutter bees

These pests are mainly rose pests, but they sometimes attack other garden shrubs. They rarely do much damage (see pp134-5).

Leaf miners

Like leaf-cutter bees, these pests (3) only attack shrubs occasionally and are not a serious problem (see pp134-5).

Leaf spot

This term is used to describe a multitude of different fungal infections that show as dark spots or blotches on the leaves of plants. Black spot on roses is a familiar example of leaf spot.

Poor growing conditions, especially waterlogged soil, seem to encourage these fungal infections, and vigorous plants are less likely to be affected than weak ones. As well as trying to improve the general growing conditions, if necessary, you should also remove any dead leaves and spray the plant with fungicide.

1

6

foliage of shrubs *(see pp134-5)*. In addition to spraying with a systemic pesticide, a DNOC/gasoline wash in late winter will destroy eggs laid in the crevices of the bark.

Rhododendron bugs
When the upper surfaces of a shrub's leaves become mottled, and brownish spots develop on the reverse sides, these bugs are usually responsible (5).

The danger period is from late spring and the bushes should be sprayed immediately with malathion or derris, or dusted with gamma-HCH.

Rhododendron leafhoppers
These pests transmit bud blast from plant to plant. Spraying in late summer with a combined contact and systemic pesticide, such as one based on permethrin and heptenophos, provides the best method of control.

Scale insects
These pests (6), which look more like blisters than living creatures, gather on the stems and leaves of shrubs. Like many other sap-sucking insects, they secrete honeydew, which encourages black mold to form. Scale insects can be controlled by spraying with a systemic pesticide, and winter spraying with tar oil wash is also an effective treatment.

Vine weevils
These nighttime feeders may damage a number of garden shrubs, especially rhododendrons. They eat the leaves, creating irregular patches. During the day they conceal themselves under leaves, twigs and other plant debris on the ground, so keeping the ground clear acts as a deterrent. Dust affected shrubs, and those nearby, with gamma-HCH.

Mealybugs
These are mainly greenhouse pests (4), but they are also troublesome on some outdoor shrubs, including currants and ceanothus. Mealybugs are sapsuckers, with a protective coating of waxy "wool".
They encourage fungal infection with the honeydew they secrete. Control minor outbreaks with a brush application of malathion, or spray with a systemic pesticide.

Powdery mildew
This is a common shrub infection, which affects clematis in particular. Spraying with a systemic fungicide provides the surest means of control *(see also pp132-3)*.

Red spider mites
These tiny sapsucking insects may do considerable damage to the

Trees

158 A tree for every garden
160 The right tree for the site
162 Buying and planting trees
164 Caring for trees
166 Problems with trees

A tree for every garden

This weeping birch, *Betula pendula* 'Youngii', is a favorite tree for small gardens.

Trees can be a delight or a disaster. Choosing the right tree is only part of the story; where you put it is almost as critical. Unless you have a very small garden, you may find that it is more effective to plant several trees, rather than rely on one specimen as the focal point.

Firstly, you should decide what you want from a tree. Is it shade; shelter from wind; or simply something lovely to look at? For shade, a tree with a relatively tall trunk supporting a spread of branches is needed. For shelter, you will need upright conifers or other trees with foliage that extends to ground level. However, for those who simply want something beautiful to enhance their gardens the choice is vast, including trees with stunning fall foliage, enchanting spring blossom, attractive bark, or delicate summer foliage. You must also decide whether you want deciduous trees or evergreens – the joy of seasonal change against the assurance of color and form all the year round.

Eventual height and spread must

A TREE FOR EVERY GARDEN

Choosing suitable trees • Practical
benefits • Avoiding problems • Trees
for small gardens

always be borne in mind, together
with whether the tree is an
exceptionally fast or slow grower.
Always allow for the extent of the
shade it will cast, especially if you
have a rock garden or pool *(see
pp106-7 and 170-1)*. Also consider
whether the shade will affect your
neighbors. Tree roots may
damage drains and foundations, so
plant any trees well away from the
house. You should be especially
careful when planting willows.

Although a tree may impoverish
the soil beneath it, bulbs and a
variety of other amenable plants
can be grown around it. This will
increase its value as a focal point in
the garden.

Certain trees, notably some
species of acer, are difficult to
distinguish from shrubs. This
emphasizes the point that types of
tree vary considerably and that
some are suitable even for very
small gardens. If in doubt, visit a
good tree nursery to explain your
needs. Strolling around gardens
open to the public may give you an
idea of the choice available.

Trees for small gardens

The heights (H) and spreads (S) given
here are averages.

Acer palmatum 'Dissectum' H 8-10ft, S
10ft. Shrubby, marvellous autumn
color. Sun/shade.
Crataegus oxyacanthoides (hawthorn) H
15ft, S 15ft. Several forms, with white,
pink or red flowers and scarlet haws.
Sun/light shade.
Cryptomeria japonica 'Elegans Nana' H
3ft, S 3ft. Small form of the Japanese
cedar. Sun.
Gleditsia triacanthos (honey locust) H
15ft, S 12ft. Pretty leaves that turn
yellow in fall. Sun.
Juniperus virginiana 'Sky Rocket' H 12ft,
S to 24in. Slender, gray-leaved conifer.
Sun/light shade.
Laburnum anagyroides H 15ft, S to 12ft.
Festoons of yellow flowers in June.
Upright and weeping forms. Sun.
Malus (crab apple) H up to 15ft, S up to
12ft. Types within these size limits
include *Malus floribunda*, which has
white flowers and yellow fruits and
Malus 'Red Sentinel', which has scarlet
fruits. Sun/light shade. (Worth visiting a
tree nursery.)
Pinus mugo (mountain pine) H 6-9ft, S
6-9ft. Dark needles, glossy cones. Sun.
Prunus (ornamental almonds, cherries,
peaches and plums) Some forms of even
the larger species are suitable for small
gardens. (Visit a specialist nursery.)

Reminders

Small trees are easier to establish than
trees that are already well developed.

Trees, like other garden plants, have
their soil preferences.

When considering the question of
shade, remember that shadows are
much longer in winter.

If possible, choose a tree that will
look good for more than just a few
weeks each year.

If you have an unsuitable tree, have it
felled by an expert – do not risk injury
or damage by doing it yourself.

Purple fruits follow the lovely crimson flowers of *Malus x lemoinei.*

The right tree for the site

The heights and spreads are averages, for soil and situation can make a considerable difference to growth. Also, most trees will take a good many years to attain these sizes.

Acer griseum H 40ft, S 20ft. **Deciduous**
Peeling bark reveals orange-brown trunk beneath. Superb fall leaf color. Slow-growing, so good for lawn planting. Open position. Any soil.

Acer negundo 'Variegatum' H 20ft, S 15ft. **Deciduous**
Spreading habit; white-edged leaves. Leaves of 'Elegans' have bright yellow margins. Open position. Any soil.

Arbutus unedo (strawberry tree) H 20ft, S 15ft. **Evergreen**
Slow-growing tree with a gnarled trunk. White flowers and strawberry-like fruits (fall). Sheltered position in warm areas. Any soil.

Betula papyrifera (paper birch) H 50ft, S 20ft. **Deciduous**
For large gardens. Thinly-peeling white bark; yellow leaves in fall. Graceful habit. Any position and soil.

Caragana arborescens (pea tree) H 10ft, S 10ft. **Deciduous**
Spiny leaves; yellow, pea-like flowers in late spring. Shrubby habit. Any position and soil.

Catalpa bignonioides (Indian bean tree) H 30ft, S 15ft. **Deciduous**
Large, heart-shaped leaves; foxglove-like white flowers with yellow and purple markings (summer) followed by long seedpods. Sun/shelter. Any soil.

Cercis siliquastrum (Judas tree) H 15ft, S 12ft. **Deciduous**
Attractive, rounded leaves; pea-like rosy flowers (late spring), followed by red seedpods. Sun/shelter. Any soil.

Chamaecyparis lawsoniana (Lawson cypress) H & S wide variation. **Evergreen**
There are many varieties, from miniatures only 3ft high *(see panel)* to giants of 50ft or more. Some are columnar, some rounded, but most have flattened sprays of foliage and small cones. Best to choose from a selection at a nursery or from an illustrated catalogue. Any soil and site, provided it is not too exposed.

Corylus avellana (hazel) H 15ft, S 10ft. **Deciduous**
Shrub-like growth; yellow catkins (late winter). *Corylus avellana* 'Contorta' (corkscrew hazel) has strangely-twisted branches. Sun/light shade. Any soil.

Davidia involucrata (pocket handkerchief tree) H 20ft, S 15ft. **Deciduous**
Creamy, petal-like bracts, resembling folded handkerchiefs (late spring). But trees must be at least 10 years old. Any soil and position.

Eucalyptus niphophylla H 30ft, S 15ft. **Evergreen**
The flaking bark is gray, cream and green; the leaves are long and gray-green. White flowers (summer). Well-drained, moisture-retentive soil. Sun/shelter from cold winds.

Eucryphia glutinosa H 10ft, S 8ft. **Deciduous**
Leaves turn orange and red (fall); large white flowers (summer). Slow growing. Sun/light shade/shelter. Lime-free soil.

Ginkgo biloba (maidenhair tree) H 40ft, S 15ft. **Deciduous**
Striking, fan-shaped leaves that turn yellow in fall. Sun/shelter. Any soil. soil.

Ilex x altaclarensis (holly) H & S wide variation. **Evergreen**
Many forms (some shrubby) available in different sizes and various leaf and berry colors. 'Camellifolia', with spineless black-green leaves and large berries, is pyramidal; 'Gold King' has gold-margined leaves, scarlet berries. Any situation and soil.

Koelreuteria paniculata (golden rain tree) H 30ft, S 20ft. **Deciduous**
Yellow flowers (summer) followed by bladder-like fruits. Sun. Any well-drained soil.

Larix decidua 'Pendula' H 20ft, S 20ft. **Evergreen**
Beautifully-shaped form of the common larch, with long, weeping branches.

Illawarra flame tree

Pyrus salicifolia 'Pendula'

New Zealand Christmas tree

Catalpa bignonioides

Robinia pseudoacacia 'Frisia'

Koelreuteria paniculata

Good fall colors. Open position. Any soil

Morus nigra (black mulberry) H 20ft, S 12ft. **Deciduous**
Gnarled trunk, heart-shaped leaves. Slow-growing. Dark red berries (late summer). Sun/light shade. Any soil.

Nyssa sylvatica (tupelo) H 25ft, S 15ft. **Deciduous**
Slow-growing. Glossy leaves turn red, yellow and orange (fall). Open position. Lime-free soil.

Parrotia persica H 20ft, S 20ft. **Deciduous**
Slow-growing. Tiny red flowers (winter): fine fall colors, similar to beech. Sun/light shade. Any soil.

Paulownia tomentosa H 20ft, S 15ft. **Deciduous**
Foxglove-like, purple, fragrant flowers

Morus nigra (black mulberry) H 20ft, S 12ft. **Deciduous**
Gnarled trunk, heart-shaped leaves. *Picea pungens* 'Kosteri' H 20ft, S 10ft. **Evergreen**
Conical habit; intense glaucous-blue foliage. Cones on older trees. Shelter when young; moist, lime-free soil.

Prunus (flowering cherries) H to 25ft, S to 20ft. **Deciduous**
This very extensive group includes ornamental plums, peaches and almonds, as well as cherries. Most are spring-flowering, with either white or pink blooms, which may be single or double. Habit, bark and foliage vary, as well as the flowers, and there are weeping types.

Pyrus salicifolia 'Pendula' (weeping pear) H 15ft, S 10ft. **Deciduous**
Willow-like leaves; graceful weeping habit. Creamy flowers (spring); inedible fruits. Open position. Any soil.

Robinia pseudoacacia (false acacia) H 30ft, S 15ft. **Deciduous**
Attractive foliage; fragrant, white, pea-like flowers (early summer). 'Frisia' has golden-yellow flowers. Any situation and soil.

Salix matsudana 'Tortuosa' (dragon's claw willow) H 30ft, S 15ft. **Deciduous**

Twisted and contorted branches; narrow leaves; catkins (spring). Open position, not near buildings. Moist soil.

Sorbus 'Joseph Rock' H 15ft, S 10ft. **Deciduous**
Superbly colored fall foliage; creamy flowers (spring); yellow fruits (fall). Any position and soil.

Stuartia pseudocamellia H 25ft, S 15ft. **Deciduous**
Flaking red bark; red and yellow leaves (fall). White camellia-like flowers with yellow centers (summer). Light shade/shelter. Lime-free soil.

Thuja plicata 'Zebrina' H 30ft, S 8ft. **Evergreen**
Conical habit; slow-growing. Typical cedar foliage but banded creamy-yellow. Sun. Any well-drained soil.

Some dwarf conifers

All are slow-growing and may take years to attain the sizes stated here.

Abies balsamea 'Hudsonia' H 24in, S 30in. Compact, with aromatic foliage. Any position and soil.

Chamaecyparis lawsoniana 'Minima Aurea' H 36in, S 30in.
Conical shape, bright yellow foliage. Any position and soil.

Cryptomeria japonica 'Vilmoriniana' H 3ft, S 2ft.
Very slow-growing. Dense foliage which turns bronze-red in winter. Sun. Lime-free soil.

Juniperus communis 'Compressa' H 3ft, S 1ft.
Columnar habit; gray-green foliage. Any position and soil.

Pseudotsuga menziesii 'Fletcheri' H 2ft, S 2ft.
Flat or rounded top; blue-green foliage. Open position. Any soil.

Thuja occidentalis 'Rheingold' H 3ft, S 2ft. Conical habit; golden-amber foliage, turning darker in winter. Sun. Any soil.

Buying and planting trees

Most garden centers stock a reasonable range of the more popular species, but you will find an even greater selection, including less common varieties, at specialist nurseries. It is worth paying one a visit, bearing in mind the difference a tree will make to your garden's appearance.

Deciduous trees lifted from the ground at the nursery should be planted while they are dormant, between fall and early spring. On heavy soil, evergreens are best bought and planted in mid-to late spring, but fall planting is satisfactory in light soil. If they are sold in the containers in which they have been grown, both deciduous trees and evergreens may be planted at any time of year, as long as the soil is neither frozen nor saturated.

Container-grown trees are most likely to be found at garden centres. They should not be confused with trees lifted from the ground complete with a ball of soil wrapped in sacking or plastic to keep it in place. (Most evergreens not grown in containers are treated in this way.)

Small, young trees are the best buys. They become established more quickly than larger ones and may even catch them up within two or three years. If you are buying bare-rooted trees, with or without some surrounding soil, satisfy yourself that they have a well-developed root system with plenty of fibrous growth. If the trees are not bare-rooted, look for sturdy, close-jointed shoots and a strong main stem.

Soil preparation

Bearing in mind a tree's long life span it is worth going to a little extra trouble to ensure that the soil is in good condition before planting. All too often trees are

A young *Acer platanoides* 'Drummondii' in the bloom of health.

Planting

The tree should be planted at the same depth as the one at which it had been previously growing, whether it is in open ground or in a container. Hold the tree upright in the planting hole, and place a stick across the hole at ground level. Check that the line of the stick corresponds with the soil mark on the stem (if the tree is bare-rooted) or the level of the container. Add or remove soil from the base of the hole to adjust the tree's height as necessary. Hammer in a stake just a little from the center of the hole.

Hold the tree in place again, with its stem close to the stake, and shovel the enriched soil (*see below*) between and over the roots. When they are partly covered, shake the tree gently to eliminate any air pockets. Continue in this fashion, firming the soil by treading it until the hole is filled. Finally, secure the tree to the stake. Give the ground a thorough soaking if it is dry.

Check that the soil mark on the stem is level with the ground surface.

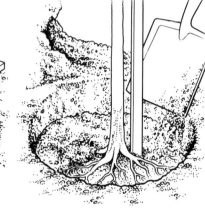

Hold the tree in place while you shovel the soil between and over the roots.

planted in ground that has not been cultivated for many years and that is consequently compacted and lacking in humus and the necessary plant foods.

Sometimes trees are planted to replace others that have died. In this case, take care to remove every trace of the previous roots and stumps to reduce the risk of honey fungus infection (*see p166*). If the previous trees were known to be infected, plant elsewhere and take steps to kill the fungus.

Poor drainage discourages root development, so the first step is to loosen the subsoil beneath the planting site. Dig an area of soil up to twice the width of the tree's root span and 10-12in deep. Place the soil on one side. With a fork, loosen and break up the subsoil in the bottom of the hole.

Now mix some thoroughly-rotted manure or compost with the soil removed from the hole, and several handfuls of bonemeal. (If compost is in short supply, buy a bag of commercial planting mixture and use this instead). You will find that the young tree's roots grow rapidly in this rich filling.

Supporting

There are two reasons for supporting a young tree. One is to prevent it being pushed over at an angle by the wind; the other is to avoid "wind rock", which prevents the roots from securing a firm hold by constantly disturbing them. Except on very exposed sites, staking is needed for only the first two or three years.

A 5-ft stake is usually sufficient to support a tree (remember that the lower 18in of the stake will actually be buried in the ground to make it stable). The stake should, in any case, fall short of the lowest branches of the tree.

A single tie, fastened near the top of the stake, is generally adequate to give a tree support. Either use a patent tie, with an adjustable strap, or a strip of burlap, which can be secured with twine.

Whichever type of tie is used, it is important not to let the stem of the tree rub against the stake. Check the tie at regular intervals to make sure it has not worked loose or is not pressing too tightly on the stem.

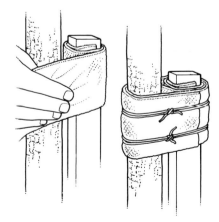

Wrap the strip of burlap around the stake first to from a cushioning pad, and then pass it around the tree itself.

Caring for trees

The first months after planting are a critical time for young trees, especially bare-rooted specimens that have been planted while they are still dormant. Young trees are easily overlooked, for they are seldom in a border with other plants and nothing much is expected of them for a year or two after planting.

Make sure you keep a careful eye on any young trees, and always check whether they are at risk from excessive exposure. Provided that they are properly staked, they should not suffer any damage from normal wind. However, recurrent gales on a cold, exposed site may wither the young foliage on the trees when the buds break. Consider a temporary windbreak of hurdles or perforated plastic sheeting if necessary (see pp26-7).

If trees are planted in the fall, watch for loosening of the soil by frost, due to repeated freezing and thawing over the winter. If this happens, wait until the soil is no longer sticky and then firm it with your feet.

A mulch of compost, rotted manure or shredded bark will help to keep the soil moist during the summer. Alternatively a circle of plastic sheeting may be placed over the planting area and hidden with a layer of lawn clippings. Apply either type of mulch while the soil is damp and after it has warmed up in late spring.

If prolonged dry weather makes watering necessary, give the young trees a really good soaking – enough to go right through the topsoil. Spraying the young leaves with clear water two or three times a day will also check dehydration during warm, windy weather.

Spraying the trees with tar oil wash in winter will kill moss and lichen on trunks of mature trees. However, you should take care not to spray nearby grass and plants.

Container-grown trees need frequent watering during dry weather.

A circle of plastic sheeting can be used as a mulch for young conifers.

Conifers and evergreens

Newly-planted evergreens are at greater risk than deciduous trees. Not having a true dormant period, there is continuing moisture loss through their foliage – even while the disturbed roots are trying to become settled and established in the new site. For the same reason, it is vital not to let the root ball become dry before planting.

Light overhead spraying several times a day is especially helpful for conifers and other evergreens at times when moisture loss is likely to be greatest. Its effect will be longer lasting if the trees are protected from strong winds, although nothing elaborate is

Reminders

Watch out for aphids, as they damage the shoots of young trees.

Cut away any dead wood at source. Remove living, but badly-placed, branches in winter.

Examine tree ties at intervals to check that they are not too tight.

Do not allow grass to grow above a tree's rooting area for a year or two after planting.

necessary. The temporary windbreak can be removed when new growth shows that the roots have become established.

When a tree is suffering from

dehydration, the first sign of trouble is browning of the foliage, often accompanied by drooping. If this happens, spray the tree with clear water to give it immediate relief. Then water the ground well and provide some shelter for the tree from the wind.

Trees planted in containers are particularly at risk, as the compost is likely to dry out very rapidly. Check the compost every day or two in dry weather, and remember that evergreens continue to lose moisture through their foliage during even the coldest months.

Considerable care is necessary if you move a young conifer or evergreen that has already become established in the garden. This should be done in spring. It is important to lift as large a clump of soil as possible with the roots. Enlist a helper to slide a sheet of sacking or thick plastic under the tree while you lever it up with a spade, as this is difficult for one person. Replant the tree at once in a previously-prepared hole, with plenty of peat or planting mixture around the roots.

Pruning

Compared with many shrubs, trees rarely need pruning. However, a little may be necessary for very young trees, and also for trees that become damaged.

It is quite normal for low-level shoots to grow from the main stem of a young tree. It is best to leave these for a year or two, as they help the tree to develop, but they should be cut off flush with the trunk once the tree is established.

Suckers – shoots that emerge from below ground level – sometimes occur with trees that have been grafted on to a different root-stock. This is often the case with crab apples and ornamental cherries. Suckers are harmful as

well as unsightly, and should be pulled or cut off cleanly at their source. If necessary, first scrape some soil away from the roots to see where they start.

The most likely occasions for pruning an older tree are when a branch has been damaged or is growing where it is not wanted. It is important to do this correctly, or you may cause further harm. A

purpose-made pruning saw is the best tool to use.

First cut off all but 12in or so of the branch and then cut the stump cleanly from the trunk. Always cut part of the way through the branch first from the underside, then from above. This prevents the bark tearing as the branch falls. Afterwards, paint the cut with pruning compound to seal it.

A simple windbreak helps to prevent the excessive moisture loss that is so damaging to young trees.

Securing branches with burlap strips will protect young conifers from being damaged by snow.

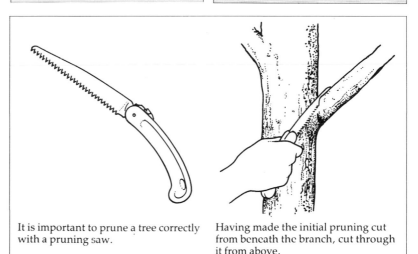

It is important to prune a tree correctly with a pruning saw.

Having made the initial pruning cut from beneath the branch, cut through it from above.

Problems with trees

Trees are among the least troublesome of plants, usually outliving everything else in the garden yet demanding the minimum of attention. They are capable of shrugging off the effects of a variety of insect pests, although there are a few diseases that may do more permanent damage or even prove fatal.

Not all tree problems are caused by pests or diseases. There are also the so-called physiological disorders brought about by unsatisfactory growing conditions. These may include unsuitable soil, inadequate drainage, drought and excessive exposure. For instance, few young trees take kindly to direct planting in heavy clay. As well as attending to drainage, plenty of peaty planting mixture is needed to assist development of their fibrous roots.

The first few years, while the root system is becoming established, are certainly the most critical. Waterlogged soil and exposure to persistent cold winds are other possible causes of a tree's failure to grow early in life. In addition, it is necessary to choose species that are suitable for the particular site. Many of the points already made about shrubs, which suffer from similar disorders (*see p152*), are also applicable to trees.

Bracket fungi are parasitic and can harm living trees.

Tree pests and diseases

Many of the pests and diseases that affect shrubs (*see pp152-5*) are also liable to affect trees. These may hardly be noticed on a mature tree, and often do little harm, but a heavy infestation of sapsucking insects, such as aphids, can severely check a young tree's progress.

Capsid bugs and adult chafers are generally less harmful. However, as a basic precaution against the root-eating chafer grubs, treat the soil with a granular pesticide when you plant a tree.

Honey fungus is fairly common and kills trees and shrubs alike. Black strands, like laces, will be found on and around the roots of affected plants. Veins of white fungal growth spread beneath the bark near ground level. Control, aimed at preventing the spread of infection, consists of removing and burning the affected growth, including the roots, and then treating the soil with formalin or with a commercial emulsion.

Gall wasps are particularly active on trees, but the swellings that result are unsightly rather than harmful. Caterpillars are likely to be more of a problem, and spraying or dusting (*see pp154-5*) should not be delayed if they are present in large numbers.

Further tree problems

Apple canker
Although this mainly affects apple trees, it also occurs on beech, mountain ash and poplars. The bark shrinks and cracks, sometimes causing whole branches to die. Cut out any small branches affected and paint the wound with pruning compound. On stems or larger branches, pare back to healthy

An advanced case of canker.

wood and then paint the wound
with pruning compound.

Bark splits

These may be due to extreme cold
or severe fluctuations in soil
moisture. The danger is that
disease spores may enter the wood
and cause more serious problems.
If you find the split just after it has
formed, paint it immediately with
pruning compound, working the
compound well into the crack. If
the crack has been present for some
time, cut out any dead wood before
treating it with pruning compound.
Improve the soil, if necessary, by
feeding and mulching.

Conifer spinning mites

These tiny insects cause conifer
needles to become discolored and
then fall. The mites spin fine webs
similar to those of red spider mites.
They may be controlled by spraying
with a systemic insecticide.

Dutch elm disease

This fungus infection is carried by
the elm bark beetle, and there is no
practical remedy. The leaves of an
affected tree become limp and
discolored, and then die. Only
elms are affected. If only a few
branches develop the symptoms of
the disease, it may be worth cutting
them off and sealing the wounds
with pruning compound. Usually,
however, it is necessary to fell and
burn the tree.

Fireblight

This very serious disease will
gradually cause leaves to wither
and shoots to die back. Eventually,
the whole tree will die. Fireblight
may affect hawthorne, mountain
ash, apple and pear, trees as well as
a number of shrubs. If you suspect
the disese you should report it.

Peach leaf curl

This first shows as prominent red
blisters on the leaves of prunus

species followed by white spores.
The overall vigor and growth of the
tree may be affected. To kill
overwintering spores, which will
damage the young growth in
spring, spray in late winter with a
copper fungicide or one based on
mancozeb. Repeat the treatment
two weeks later and also again
before the leaves drop in fall.

Shothole

This is caused by a fungus
infection, and seldom occurs on
strong-growing trees. It is confined
to prunus species. The
characteristic holes are preceded by
brown spots and patches, and a
brown margin remains when the
dead area disintegrates. Regular
spraying with a fungicide will
control the infection. Spraying with
a foliar feed will serve as a quick-
acting tonic, but the tree should
also be fed annually with a general
fertilizer and mulched with manure
in late spring.

Silver leaf

This is another fungus disease that
attacks prunus trees, but it may
also affect a number of other
species. The name is an apt
description of the effect the disease
creates, but further symptoms
include die-back of shoots and
whole branches, with a scaly
fungus on the bark. A dark stain
may be seen on diseased wood
when a branch is cut. Treat by
pruning back to at least 6in beyond
the point where the stain is visible,
and then paint the wound with
pruning compound.

Tar spot

This affects only acers, and shows
as black spots or blotches on the
leaves. The spores overwinter on
fallen leaves, so these should be
collected and burned in fall. The
young leaves should be sprayed
with a fungicide as the buds break
in the spring.

Water gardens

170 Creating a water garden
172 Making the pool
174 Fountains and waterfalls
175 Bog gardens
176 Stocking the pool
178 Waterside plants
180 Caring for pool plants
181 Fish for garden pools
182 Seasonal care of pools
184 Water garden problems

Creating a water garden

A pool brings a different dimension to the garden, providing a fresh source of interest and an opportunity to grow new plants. It also attracts a variety of wildlife. The special fascination of a water garden makes it a focal point and it is often the first thing to catch a visitor's eye. Water also has a tranquil quality, which will reflect your mood when you wish to relax.

Water plants have a quiet sort of beauty, less emphatic than the summer border, but entirely in keeping with their surroundings. The planting area can extend beyond the water itself to the ground immediately around it. You can make a bog garden, if you wish, and create fountains and waterfalls. For extra interest, fish can also be introduced to the pool, and such visitors as newts, frogs, dragonflies and water beetles ensure that there is always something new and entertaining to watch.

It should be stressed that you do not need a stream or any other natural supply of water for a garden pool, and no more than an occasional top-up with fresh water is necessary. If you like the idea of a fountain or miniature cascade, this can be supplied by a small pump that simply circulates the existing pool water. Introducing fresh water in any quantity upsets the pool's biological balance.

A garden pool can be formal or informal in appearance and, within limits, as large or as small as you wish. However, it is important to make it deep enough to avoid drastic temperature fluctuations.

Pool construction is within the capabilities of any gardener. The soil removed when you dig the pool can be used to build a rock garden alongside. Only topsoil should be used; any subsoil should be dumped elsewhere. As explained on *pp172-3*, a flexible

A pool where the emphasis is on waterside plants.

liner provides the most satisfactory way of constructing a pool of almost any shape.

Management of a garden pool is not hard work but it is time-consuming, so there is no point in creating a water garden unless you are prepared to give it the amount of attention it requires. Work can be kept to a minimum by taking initial care over the siting, design and stocking of the pool.

The position of the pool is of vital importance. It must be open to the sun for most of the day and in a place where fall leaves will not drop in great numbers. Avoid natural hollows, where water pressure from the soil beneath the pool may disturb the liner.

CREATING A WATER GARDEN
Size and shape ● Site ● Position ●
Fountains and waterfalls

The water hawthorn is in flower throughout summer.

A poolside hosta sets off a yellow water lily.

Types of water plants

Water lilies are the best-known water plants, but there are many others from which to choose. You will also need plants to supply the water with oxygen and help to prevent it from becoming green. Water plants are divided into various categories, depending on the depth of water they need or their particular function.

Deep-water plants
There are plenty of fully hardy water lilies that flower throughout the summer. The types suitable for garden pools should be planted in 12-18in of water, although as little as 3in is enough for some miniatures. There are many named hybrids. Make your choice from a specialist supplier's catalog. There are also a few other plants which grow in the deepest part of the pool, including aponogeton and marsilea (nardoo).

Marginal plants
These are plants that grow in the shallower water – anything from surface level to about 9in deep. They should be grown on shelves set around the edges of the pool. A few will even grow in damp soil at the pool's edge.

Submerged oxygenating plants
These are invaluable if you intend to have fish. They release oxygen into the water, provide a certain amount of food for the fish, and provide protective cover for their offspring. They also help to limit the growth of green algae.

Floating plants
There are few plants that spend part or all of their lives floating on the pool surface. However, there are only one or two that are both hardy and decorative.

Making the pool

As well as being in an open position (unshaded for a good part of the day) and away from trees, a pool must be on level ground. Check this with a level when deciding the site. If the ground is not level, part of the liner will remain visible.

The minimum satisfactory depth for a pool is 15in, but ideally it should be a few inches deeper than this. The surface area is not critical, but the smaller the pool, the more difficult management becomes. Although a 5ft x 4ft pool is feasible, the water in one twice this size will maintain a more even temperature and cause fewer problems.

The shape of a pool is not very important, as long as it is kept simple. Underwater, the sides should drop at quite a steep angle, with shelves around part of the edge about 9in below water level for marginal plants. These will be grown in containers, so the shelves need be only 8-9in wide.

There are a number of ways of constructing a garden pool. Concrete, the traditional material, may at first seem to be the most robust but it does have disadvantages. Settlement or frost may result in hair cracks in the concrete, which in turn lead to leaks. Also, making a concrete pool is fairly hard work.

Ready-made fiberglass pools are very easy to install. First, dig a hole slightly larger than the pool, then place the pool in position, and fill the space around the outside with soil. Unfortunately, most of these pools are too small to give consistently good results in gardening terms.

Pool liners made of butyl rubber are the most satisfactory. Polyvinyl chloride, especially the reinforced grades, is reasonably satisfactory, although it does not last so long. Polyethylene will only last for a year or two.

A watertight and natural-looking pool can easily be made with a liner.

MAKING THE POOL
Choosing a design ● Choosing
materials ● Making a water garden

Constructing a pool with a liner

Before ordering the liner, mark out the proposed
shape of the pool to ensure that it will be in
proportion to its surroundings. Use pegs and
string to mark out a rectangular shape but a
hose is better for showing a curved outline.
Experiment, if necessary, with a variety of shapes
and sizes until you are satisfied. A kidney-shaped
pool looks attractive and it is certainly best to avoid
fussy outlines.

Now take the measurements to use as a basis for
ordering the liner. The length of the liner should
be that of the pool, plus twice the pool's maximum
depth. The width of the liner should be that of the
pool, again plus twice the pool's maximum depth.
The same rule applies even if you have chosen an
irregular outline, but be sure to base it on the
maximum length and the maximum width.

For instance, the liner for the pool shown here
should be 13ft long (10ft + 36in) and 9ft wide (6ft
+ 36in).

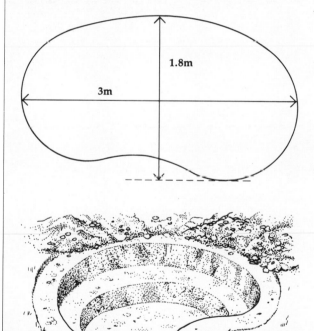

1 Dig the hole, leaving shelves around part or all of the
sides. Strip off a 2in layer of lawn (or soil) from the edges if
you intend to lay paving stones to cover the edges of the
liner. Remove any protruding stones and cover the bottom
surface of the pool with damp sand to provide a smooth bed
for the liner.

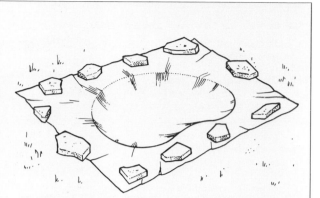

2 Lay the liner evenly over the hole, with its center just
touching the base of the pool. Do not press it into shape.
Place bricks or fairly heavy stones around the edge of the
liner to hold it in place while it is filled with water. Make
sure that these weights do not hang over the pool's edge.

3 Position the end of the hose over the pool and turn on the
water. The weight of the water will stretch the liner, press it
into shape and smooth out any wrinkles. Some of the bricks
or stones can be lifted as the pool fills, but leave sufficient to
keep the liner taut while you are still filling the pool.

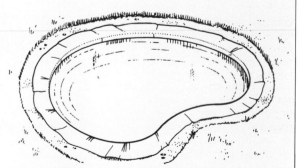

4 When the pool is full, remove the remaining bricks and
trim the edge of the liner to shape, leaving a flap around the
edge. This should be covered with paving stones, bedded
on mortar and laid to project an inch or two over the edge.
Alternatively, if you wish, the lawn can extend right up to
the water's edge.

Fountains and waterfalls

Besides making a pool more attractive, running water is good for fish as it increases the water's oxygen content. Oxygen may fall into short supply during hot weather, causing the fish to become distressed. The splashing of a fountain or waterfall will help to prevent this from happening. However, most plants prefer still water, and so should be planted away from any turbulence.

The pump supplying the fountain or waterfall may be a submersible type, which is placed on a plinth on the bottom of the pool, or a surface type, which is housed in a small chamber near the pool edge. Submersible types are theeasieest to install. A fountain jet can be mounted directly on to the pump, while a waterfall or cascade is supplied by means of a concealed tube that runs from the pump to the head of the fall. Some pumps will supply a fountain and waterfall simultaneously.

Surface pumps have a greater output than most submersible pumps and are therefore better suited to larger pools. It is essential to follow the maker's instructions regarding installation and use of both types of pumps so that they will function correctly.

Various types of fountain jets are available. Cascades and waterfalls can be made from stones cemented together, but it is important to make sure that the joints between the stones are completely watertight. Settlement makes this difficult, so it is best to use a rubber or polyvinyl chloride liner when making a watercourse. Alternatively, you can buy ready-made concrete, fiberglass or plastic units.

To minimize the movement of water, put a submersible pump (or the suction hose supplying a surface pump) near where the water enters the pool.

A cleverly-constructed cascade tumbling over rocks.

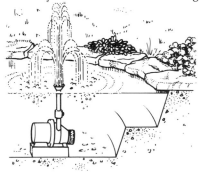

A fountain jet may be attached directly to a submersible pump. Stand the pump on one or more bricks so that the jet is just above the surface of the pool.

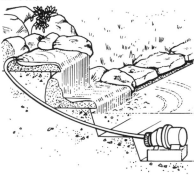

To supply a cascade or waterfall, a concealed pipe is taken from the pump to the highest point. Check that the pump's maximum lift (measured from water level) is sufficient.

Making a bog garden

A variety of moisture-loving plants enjoy the damp ground beside natural pools. Similar conditions can also be created by a garden pool, although maintaining this rather specialized environment requires some care. As a result, bog gardens, as they are called, are for real plant enthusiasts.

The plants that grow happily in a bog garden do not require permanently soggy and stagnant soil; they do best in moisture-retentive soil that floods occasionally but that has some drainage to allow partial drying in the interim.

The easiest way to create these conditions is to remove up to about 12in of the topsoil from an area alongside the pool. Ideally, this should be done, or at least planned, when the pool itself is being constructed. Place some lining material in the hole you have made (polyethylene will do, as it won't be exposed to sunlight). Turn up the edge of the lining by about 6in. Make some slits or pierce holes in the bottom of the liner for drainage. Now replace the topsoil, mixing a generous amount of peat with it. These conditions will suit plants that need relatively dry surface soil but prefer damp soil father down. For plants that need damper soil near the surface, a section of the liner edge can be turned up to ground level.

Rainfall should keep the soil sufficiently moist for much of the year, but frequent watering may be needed during the spring and summer. Spraying with a long length of perforated plastic tubing, which can be snaked around the bed, is better than overhead watering. If unobtrusive black tubing is used it may be left in place throughout the summer.

Trollius 'Goldquelle' requires moist soil at root level.

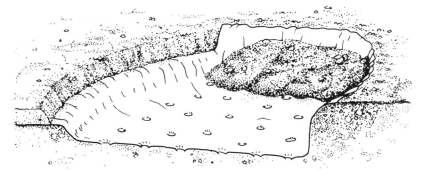

Position the bog garden so that it will be behind or at the side of the pool when seen from the usual viewpoint. The base and liner can be arranged to slope very slightly towards the area where you plan to grow plants with the greatest need for moisture; the edge of the liner should be turned up more on this side. However, some drainage holes are needed even here.

Stocking the pool

Water lilies

These beautiful plants begin to flower in late spring or early summer and continue flowering until late summer. Their blooms open during the morning but close again towards the end of the afternoon. Each flower lasts for a few days and many are scented.

Lilies serve a practical function as well as being decorative. Their spreading leaves, which float on the surface, shade the water and help to prevent the excessive growth of green algae, which so frequently causes problems in water gardens.

The lilies sold for outdoor pools are completely hardy and remarkably easy to grow. They are mostly hybrids and are available in a wide range of colors. The required planting depths provided in the lists below actually refer to the depth of the water above the compost in the containers.

Large pools (Depth 1-3ft; spread up to 4ft)
Gladstoniana (white); Charles de Meurville (red); Colonel A J Welch (yellow); Colossea (pink); Conqueror (red).

Medium pools (Depth 9-24in; spread up to 3ft)
Albatross (white); Amabilis (pink); Attraction (red); *Brackleyi rosea* (pink); Escarboucle (red); *Marliacea albida* (white); *Marliacea chromatella* (yellow); *Marliacea rosea* (pink); Masaniello (pink); Mme Wilfron Gonnere (pink); Moorei (yellow); Mrs Richmond (pink); Rene Gerard (red); Sunrise (yellow); *Tuberosa rosea* (pink).

Small to medium pools (Depth 6-18in; spread 24in)
Andreana (orange-red); Atropurpurea (red); *Caroliniana perfecta* (pink); Firecrest (pink); Froebeli (red); Gloriosa (red); Gonnere (white); Indiana (copper-red); James Brydon (red); *Laydekeri fulgens* (red); Lucida (pink); *Odorata alba* (white); *Odorata sulphurea* (yellow); *Odorata turicensis* (pink); Pink Opal (pink); Rose Arey (pink); Rosennymphe (pink); Sioux (peach); William Falconer (red).

The blooms of Charles de Meurville

Patio pools and tubs (Depth 3-12in; spread 12in)
Aurora (orange); Candida (white); Ellisiana (red); *Laydekeri purpurata* (red); *Laydekeri rosea* (pink); *Odorata minor* (white); *Pygmaea alba* (white); *Pygmaea helvola* (yellow).

Other deep-water plants

The flowering plants listed here should also be planted in the deep part of the pool. The depths (D) given here refer to the depth of water above the compost in containers.

Aponogeton distachyum (water hawthorn) (D 6-24in). Black-centered, fragrant white flowers in spring and summer, with sometimes even a few in winter. *Nymphoides peltata* (D 4-18in) Dainty, bright yellow flowers, rather like miniature water lilies; mottled leaves.

Orontium aquaticum (golden club) (D 3-15in) Bright yellow flamelike flowers on white stems; blue-green leaves.

Marginal plants

There are many plants that flourish best in fairly shallow water and, for this reason, are grown in containers placed on shelves around the edge of the pool.

Acorus calamus variegatus H 2½-3ft, PD 2-6in. Iris-like plant with sword-like foliage; variegated forms.
Alisma plantago (water plantain) H 2ft, PD 0-6in. Small pink and white flowers (summer).
Butomus umbellatus (flowering rush) H 2-3ft, PD 2-5in. Long leaves; pink flowers (mid- to late summer).
Caltha palustris (marsh marigold) H 12in, PD 0-2in. Bright yellow flowers (late spring).

Caltha palustris flowers earlier than most other water plants.

Cotula coronopifolia (golden button) H 6-9in, PD 0-4in. Small yellow flowers throughout summer.
Eriophorum angustifolium (cotton grass) H 12-18in, PD 0-2in. Evergreen foliage, with silky white heads.
Glyceria spectabilis variegata H 2ft, PD 0-5in. A grass with attractively-striped leaves.
Iris laevigata H 2ft, PD 2-4in. Blue flowers (summer). Several named varieties with different colors.
Iris pseudacorus (yellow flag) H 3ft, PD 0-4in. Sturdy grower; yellow flowers (late spring).
Mentha aquatica (water mint) H 9-12in, PD 0-3in. Scented leaves; lilac flowers (late summer).
Mimulus luteus H 12-18in, PD 0-3in. Yellow flowers throughout summer.
Myosotis palustris (water forget-me-not) H 6-9in, PD 0-3in. Deep blue flowers (summer).

Pontederia cordata (pickerel weed) H 18in, PD 2-5in. Spearhead leaves; blue flowers (late summer).
Saggitaria japonica (arrowhead) H 12-24in, PD 3-6in. White, yellow-centered flowers (summer).
Scirpus zebrinus (zebra rush) H 2ft, PD 3-6in. Green and white striped foliage.

Note: H *indicates height*, PD *indicates depth of water over compost.*

Oxygenating plants

These submerged plants are strictly functional, their chief value being to help keep the water clear. They are usually supplied as mixed collections, to ensure that at least some will find the conditions of any particular pool to their liking. Some of the most effective oxygenating plants are ceratophyllum,

elodea, lagarosiphon and potamogeton. Placed in small containers, plants should be planted at a rate of one bunch of unrooted cuttings per 2 square feet of surface area.

Floating plants

Recommended types include *Azolla caroliniana* (fairy moss), a small floating fern which turns red in fall; *Hydrocharis morsus ranae* (frogbit), which has lily-like leaves and small white flowers; and *Stratiotes aloides* (water soldier), which surfaces only in summer, when it displays its spiny leaves and white flowers. Avoid eichhornia and trapa, both of which have to be wintered indoors. Species of lemna (duckweed) have a tendency to be rampant growers and consequently are also best avoided.

Waterside plants

'Fanal' is one of the many lovely forms of the hybrid *Astilbe x ardensii*.

The flowers of *Lysichiton americanum*.

Aruncus sylvester in full flower.

The setting of a pool is as important as the design if you are to achieve a natural effect. Choose carefully from the many waterside plants available to enhance your own pool. Some may be true bog plants, needing soil that is constantly wet (but never stagnant), while other types simply require a moist soil for their roots.

Fortunately, many moisture-loving plants can adapt to different conditions, having evolved to cope with seasonal changes. However, it is worth choosing and positioning waterside plants with some care to make the most of the conditions you can provide.

Remember that ferns are ideal for planting by the pool. They bring a cool beauty to the poolside, and are easy to grow. Ferns are especially suitable if part of the area by the pool is shaded, although some will grow in sunshine.

Think about the contours of your pool when deciding what to plant and where. Two or three large rocks, partially embedded in the soil, will give the pool a three-dimensional quality and provide natural territory for trailing or scrambling plants – or ferns, if other conditions are right.

Pool-side ferns

All the ferns described here are deciduous. Heights (H) and spreads (S) given are average.

Adiantum pedatum (maidenhair fern) H 18in, S 15in. Light shade; peaty soil.
Athyrium filix-femina (lady fern) H 2ft, S 2ft. Light shade; humus-rich soil that always remains moist.
Dryopteris filix-mas (male fern) H 4ft, S 3ft. Shade; moist, humus-rich soil.
Matteuccia struthiopteris (shuttlecock fern) H 3-4ft, S 3ft. Light shade; moist soil.
Osmunda regalis (royal fern) H 6ft, S 5ft. Sun/light shade; damp soil.

Iris kaempferi needs soil that is not too wet in winter.

Waterside plants

This list includes plants whose needs vary. Some of the marginal plants described on *pp176-7* are also suitable for waterside planting in wet soil, depending on their recommended planting depths. The heights (H) and spreads (S) given here are averages.

Aconitum napellus H 3-4ft, S 15in. Spikes of blue flowers (summer). Sun/light shade; moisture-retentive soil.
Anagallis tenella (bog pimpernel) H 1in, S 12in. Creeping habit; pink flowers (early summer). Sun; permanently moist soil.
Aruncus sylvester (goat's beard) H 4ft, S 2ft. Creamy-white flowers (summer). Sun/shade; permanently moist soil.
Asclepias incarnata (swamp milkweed) H 3½ft, S 2ft. Leafy stems; pink flowers (summer). Sun; moist, peaty soil.
Astilbe x ardensii H 2-4ft, S 12-18in. Attractive foliage; feathery plumes of white, pink or red flowers (summer). Sun/shade; moist soil.
Filipendula rubra H 4-5ft, S 2ft. Hand-shaped leaves; spires of pink flowers (summer). Sun/light shade; moisture-retentive soil.
Gunnera manicata H up to 10ft, S 12ft. Rhubarb-like plant; bottlebrush flower spikes (late spring, early summer). Sun/light shade; deep, moist soil. Protect crowns in winter.
Hosta (plantain lily) H 1-3ft, S 2-3ft. Many species and varieties, with glaucous and variegated foliage; white or lilac flowers (summer). Light shade/sun; humus-rich, moisture-retentive soil.
Iris cristata (crested iris) H 6in, S 6in. Lilac-blue flowers with orange blotch (spring). Light shade; moisture-retentive soil.
Iris kaempferi H 2ft, S 12in. Large white or blue flowers (summer). Sun; moist, lime-free soil that does not flood in winter.
Iris sibirica H 2-3ft, S 2ft. Many varieties with white, blue or purple flowers (early summer). Sun; moist soil.
Lysichiton americanum (skunk cabbage) H 30in, S 2ft. Long glaucous leaves; yellow blooms (spring). Sun; constantly moist soil.
Lysimachia punctata H 30in, S 2ft. Yellow flower spikes (summer). Sun/light shade; moist soil. Invasive.
Lythrum salicaria (purple loosestrife) H 3-4ft, S 2ft. Spires of red-purple flowers (summer). Sun/light shade; damp or wet soil.
Mimulus cardinalis (monkey flower) H 18in, S 9in. Scarlet and yellow flowers (summer). Sun; constantly damp soil.
Monarda didyma (bee balm) H 30in, S 12in. Red, pink or white flowers, attractive to butterflies (summer). Sun/light shade; moisture-retentive soil.
Primula beesiana H 2ft, S 1ft. Carmine flowers (early summer). Sun/light shade; moisture-retentive soil.
Primula florindae (giant cowslip) H 3ft, PD 15in. Yellow, bell-like flowers (summer). Sun/light shade; moisture-retentive soil.
Primula japonica H 24in, S 12in. White, pink or red flowers (early summer). Sun/light shade; moisture-retentive soil.
Rheum palmatum (ornamental rhubarb) H 5ft, S 3ft. Spreading leaves; creamy-white flowers (early summer). Sun; moisture-retentive soil.
Rodgersia pinnata H 2-3ft, S 2ft. Handsome foliage; white or pink astilbe-like flowers (summer). Light shade; moist soil.
Trollius (globe flower) *see p95.* This border plant grows best where the soil remains moist throughout summer, and is excellent for pool edges.

Caring for pool plants

Planting and aftercare

The easiest and most reliable way to stock a new pool is to use a collection of plants selected by a specialist water garden center. This is cheaper than buying plants separately and you will be assured of a balanced collection – water lilies, marginals, submerged oxygenating plants and floating plants – which can also be selected to suit the size of your pool. Some nurseries even include water snails in their collections. Planting should be carried out between spring and late summer, while the plants are in active growth.

The newly-filled pool should be allowed to stand empty for a week before plants are introduced. It is best to grow the plants in special containers made from perforated plastic, and of a size to suit the particular species. The container can then be lowered into the water and placed in the appropriate position. For a water lily, the container should be lowered, in stages, to the bottom of the pool; a

marginal plant should be placed on a shelf or on a plinth of bricks.

Ordinary garden soil is suitable for planting, although heavy soil is more suitable than light. Line the containers with coarse burlap if the soil is light.

Do not add manure, garden compost or ordinary fertilizer to the soil – any of these aggravate the problem of green water. The only satisfactory plant foods are those that contain no nitrogen. A type of commercial fertilizer, which is rich in phosphate, is sold by most plant suppliers.

When planting, set the plants firmly in the compost, afterwards spreading a layer of gravel over the surface. Lower the containers gently into the water so that you do not disturb the soil in them. Water lilies should be placed on bricks at first, and then lowered gradually over a period of weeks so that their new leaves are closer to the surface.

Plant submerged oxygenators as they are supplied – in rootless bunches – placing them in a small container such as a seed tray. Press the plants firmly into the soil, if

Marginal plants may be placed on a plinth of bricks if the pool does not have a shelf.

necessary securing them with stones. Floating plants should simply be placed in the water.

The pool water almost invariably turns green after planting and will stay that way until the plants have grown sufficiently to make conditions less suitable for algae to thrive. This may take a few weeks but the condition will correct itself in due course.

Planting a water lily

1 Before planting, cut off the old leaves and trim back the thick roots, but not the fine ones. This may have been done by the supplier.

2 Plant the lily firmly with a trowel, with the crown just above the surface. Plant tuberous-rooted varieties with the tuber almost horizontal.

3 After planting, spread a layer of gravel over the surface to prevent fish disturbing the soil. Lower the plants only gradually over several weeks.

Fish for garden pools

Fish add extra colour and interest to any garden pool.

Golden rudd are surface feeders. There is also a silver variety.

There are some very beautiful varieties of fish that are suitable for garden pools. Fish are not essential for a pool but, by feeding on mosquito larvae, they prevent it from becoming a mass breeding ground for these pests.

The most suitable and attractive types of pool fish are goldfish and golden orfe, the former being brightly colored and the latter spending much of their time close to the surface of the pool. Goldfish are mostly orangy-red, although some are silver or yellow, or have black markings. They breed readily. Orfe are a very distinctive orange-salmon color and do not breed so freely under pool conditions.

Shubunkins are similar to goldfish, but have a mottled coloring. Comets, or comet longtails, are a variety of goldfish which have flowing tails and large fins. Both of these are good choices for garden pools. However, carp should be avoided, as they grow very rapidly and may do considerable damage to plants in a small or medium-sized pool.

Water snails

Opinions differ on the value of water snails in the garden pool. They are quite effective scavengers, eating uneaten fish food and other decaying matter, but some may damage plants. Some varieties are less beneficial than others, the least satisfactory variety being the freshwater whelk (*Limnaea stagnalis*).

Looking after fish

Wait for a few weeks after planting the pool before introducing the fish. This gives the plants – particularly submerged oxygenators – a chance to become established. The pool should be stocked at a rate of not more than 2-3in of fish to each square foot of pool surface area.

Fishes' feeding requirements vary with the time of year. They should not be fed at all during mid-winter, but supplementary feeding is essential in fall and spring. During the summer, the amount of feeding necessary will depend on the size of the pool and the number of fish. The fish usually enjoy a daily feed, but a medium-sized pool, well stocked with plants, provides a good deal of natural nourishment. During the summer, it will not matter if the daily feed is occasionally missed – and can even be left for a couple of weeks at vacation time. Commercial pellets, which float on the surface water are the most satisfactory form of food.

Seasonal care of pools

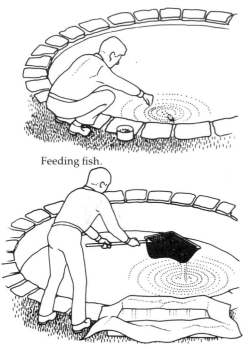

Feeding fish.

Transferring fish to a temporary pool.

Removing blanket weed.

Spring

Spring comes slowly to the pool, although waterside and bog garden plants may be divided, or new ones bought and planted, from early spring onwards. However, water lilies and marginal plants should not be planted until late spring or early summer.

As a rule, the first real sign that spring has arrived is that the water turns green. The rising temperature of the water, coupled with the fact that oxygenating plants and water lilies have yet to begin their spring growth, provide just the right conditions for the growth of algae - the near-microscopic form of plant life that makes the water green.

Changing the water is no solution, for the new water will soon turn green again as the algae reproduce. It is also better to avoid chemical treatment unless the problem proves unusually persistent. Green water may be unsightly but it harms neither plants nor fish and, if left, it should eventually clear by itself.

The warmer spring weather will also waken fish from their winter torpor. They should be fed as soon as they become active and take food readily: they will be at a low ebb after the winter and can easily succumb to fungus infections. Feeding will give the fish increased resistance to infection but, if necessary, there are also preventative treatments that can be added to the water. In late spring you should begin in-pool planting and every three or four years give the pool a good "spring clean" and divide the plants.

When you clean the pool, first make a temporary pool for the fish, using a sheet of plastic either supported by a timber frame or placed in a hollow. Take care to protect the fish from cats. Then pump out the water from the pool and scoop out mud and debris.

To divide water lilies, cut pieces of new growth, each with a growing shoot, from the old crown. Replant these in fresh soil.

Summer

Early to midsummer is the main planting season for water lilies and marginal plants. With the water becoming warmer and the hours of daylight longer, they will soon become established and grow rapidly. Remember that they prefer still water and that water lilies will grow better if the plants are not submerged too quickly.

Blanketweed is a form of algae whose long strands grow to an extent where they threaten to choke both plants and fish. The easiest way to clear the weed is by poking a long stick into the strands, twirling it around, and lifting out as much weed as possible. Remove dead flowers and foliage, which may otherwise pollute the water.

During hot weather the pool may need fairly frequent topping-up with water – this is particularly important to prevent damage to plastic pool liners. You should also keep an eye on the fish, which may suffer from lack of oxygen during hot, sultry weather. Spraying the surface of the pool forcefully with a hose, or fixing the hose so that it trickles from a foot or so above the water will help. A more permanent solution is to install a fountain or a waterfall, the essential point being that the falling water should create a splash.

Fall

Dead leaves, flowers and other rotting vegetation can be a hazard to fish. During the winter, when the pool may be covered with ice for days at a time, toxic gases from this material are trapped. Also, the very process of decomposition takes oxygen from the water. To check this problem, cut off the withered stems and leaves of marginal plants before they fall into the water, and pull off the dead leaves and stems of water lilies.

To prevent other dead vegetation and leaves falling into the pool, secure small-mesh netting over it, keeping the edges of the netting close to the ground so that leaves cannot be blown beneath it. Failing this, remove any fallen leaves from the surface of the water as often as possible. A rectangle of netting secured on the prongs of a garden fork, which is a convenient scoop.

Fish need to be in prime health to be able to withstand the long, cold months of winter when they do not feed, and therefore need a good diet. Commercial pellets of fish food provide this, although some people like to supplement the food with a diet of chopped earthworms or shreds of boiled fish. Do not give the fish more than they will eat readily in three or four minutes.

Cut down the waterside plants, dividing them where necessary as you would any other herbaceous perennials. Remove any submersible pumps, clean them thoroughly and store them in a dry place for the winter. Surface pumps, too, should be disconnected and serviced.

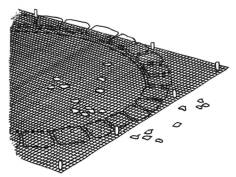

Netting to catch leaves.

Winter

There is little work required in the water garden during the winter. The plants around the pool, and those in the water, require no attention. Nor do fish, although they should be fed through the fall as long as they take food.

The formation of ice is the main cause for concern during the winter. Ice can damage the pool itself and harm the fish. The pools structurally at risk are those with concrete shells. As frozen water expands, the ice creates sufficient lateral pressure to crack concrete walls or open joints in the pool. This, in turn, frequently causes leaks, although the cracks themselves may be difficult to detect. Pools with polyvinyl chloride or butyl rubber liners are not at risk. To reduce the pressure of ice and prevent cracks, float logs on the surface, before the freezing temperatures of midwinter set in The logs should be resilient enough to take up the pressure as the ice forms, but their elasticity varies, so you will need to use several.

Low temperatures do not harm hardy fish such as orfe or goldfish, which go into a state of torpor throughout the winter and remain that way until the water becomes warm again. However, ice formation on the surface of the pool can endanger the fish by trapping the dangerous gases given off by decaying vegetation in the water.

The best solution to this problem is to install an electric pool heater that maintains an ice-free patch. The cable used for a fountain or cascade can be used to operate it.

If the pool does become frozen, do not break the ice by hitting it. The shock waves you create may harm the fish.

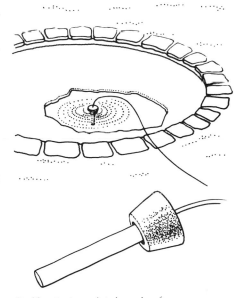

Pool heater to maintain an ice-free patch.

Water garden problems

Green water has been referred to already, being by far the most frequent problem in water gardens. The water in every pool turns green occasionally – especially in spring – and it is virtually impossible to create a new pool without this happening. Persistent greening is most likely to happen in pools of below average size.

Beginners often think that they must have done something wrong, and that an instant remedy should be available. However, the condition is not a result of any wrong treatment and the best cure is to leave the pool to right itself.

Sudden greening of the water is due to an increase of algae, which feed on the dissolved mineral salts in the water. Algae prosper in full light but are inhibited by the shading effect of water lily leaves or other waterside plants. Submerged oxygenating plants compete with algae for the mineral salts in the water. Once they become established, or have made fresh spring growth, they deprive the algae of their essential food. The combined effect of a reduction of light and food will usually destroy the algae quite rapidly.

However, if the pool has not been sited and planted in a suitable way, the problem may be more difficult to solve. For instance, a shaded position will discourage the growth of oxygenating plants and the water may stay green for much longer than usual. Too few water lilies, or oxygenators, will inevitably lead to green water. Compost or manure added to the planting soil also provides a rich diet for algae.

Provided that the pool has been planted correctly, the green water should clear after just a few weeks. However, if the water remains green, and there are no obvious faults in your pool management, you may find that the only solution is to use a proprietary algicide to solve the problem.

Leaking pools

If a concrete pool leaks, it is better to seal the whole surface than attempt to patch a single crack. You may find that there are other invisible cracks, while the concrete itself may be porous.

After emptying and cleaning the pool, apply a special primer, followed by a coat of plastic paint. Both are sold by water garden specialists. There are also rubber-based paints that do not require primer. If you decide to construct a new concrete pool, be sure to add a waterproofing material to the mix.

If a polyvinyl chloride liner is accidentally pierced, repair it with a patch of the same material, using plastic adhesive. A special repair tape is sold for butyl liners.

Fish pests and diseases

Diseased or unhealthy fish are usually a result of bad management. Polluted water is the most likely cause of this problem, due to an accumulation of rotting material on the bottom of the pool or to contamination with garden chemicals. This, and inadequate or incorrect feeding, will lay the fish open to attack by fungus spores, which can be seen as a gray film or growth on parts of the fishes' bodies. A commercial fungus treatment, used as a bath for affected fish or added to the pool itself, will be necessary.

Anchor worms are parasites about ¼-in long, which attach themselves to fish. These, and the smaller fish lice, should be removed with tweezers, while you hold the fish gently in a wet cloth. Then treat the water with a commercial medication. The great diving beetle, and its equally ferocious larvae, are both capable of killing quite large fish. The adults are accomplished flyers. If seen, in or out of the water, they should be caught and killed.

A heron can clear a pond of fish in a very short time and may visit country, or even suburban, gardens. Netting is the surest means of protecting the fish against this predator.

Plant pests and diseases

Blackfly frequently cluster on water lilies and marginal plants during the summer. One of the many commercial aphid controls may be used if there are no fish in the pool. However, if there are fish, or if you prefer not to harm the pool's other residents, wash blackfly off the plants by squirting them forcefully with a hose.

Water lily beetles, which are dark brown and about ¼-in long, cause great damage to the leaves and flowers of water lilies. Fortunately, they are not particularly common in garden pools. Spray the lilies with malathion if there are no fish; otherwise you will have to remove the damaged foliage, complete with beetles and grubs.

Water lily leaf spot, a fungal disease, appears as brown spots and patches on the foliage. It occurs most frequently during damp summers. Little can be done except to remove and burn the affected leaves as soon as you see them.

Visitors to garden pools

Sooner or later a garden pool may well attract frogs and toads, both voracious eaters of insect pests and an asset to any gardener. Both breed in spring, but a proportion of the tadpoles they produce will be eaten by fish.

Newts may also take up residence in the pool. There are

WATER GARDEN PROBLEMS

Pollution ● Weeds ● Plant pests and
diseases ● Fish pests and diseases ●
Pool visitors

Palmate newts are attractive creatures, found mainly in acid-soil areas.

The lovely dragonfly

three types of newt – smooth,
palmate and great crested – and all
spend most of their lives on land.
They breed in spring and, on the
whole, can be considered an asset,
although they do eat young fish.

Waterboatmen – brownish
creatures about ⅔-in long, which
swim with a rapid paddling action –
prey on small fish and are best
netted and destroyed. Despite their
appearance, dragonflies are quite
harmless and will eat substantial
numbers of flying insects during
their brief lives.

Frogs spend most of their time in the damp growth near a pool or ditch.

Index

Page numbers in *italic* refer to illustrations.

Abies balsamea 'Hudsonia', 161
Acaena, 44
  microphylla, 45, 111
Acanthus, 17, 31, 92
Acer, 27, 33, 167
  griseum, 160
  negundo 'Variegatum', 160
  palmatum 'Dissectum', 159
Achillea, 17, 29, 33, 92
  filipendulina, 29
acid soils, 20-1
  weeds of, 13
Aconitum, 31, 92
  napellus, 179
Acorus calamus variegatus, 176
adelgids, 154
Adiantum, 31
  pedatum, 178
Aethionema 'Warley Rose', 111
African lily, 29
Agapanthus, 29, 92
Ageratum, 15, 82
Ajuga, 31
  reptans, 43, 45
algae, 72
Alisma plantago, 176
alkaline soil, 18-19
  flowers of sulphur for, 18, 19
  improving, 19
  iron deficiency, 18, 19
  plants for, 19
  weeds of, 13
Allium moly, 102, *103*
alloxydim sodium, *46*, 47
alpine plants, 77, 106-13
  alkaline soil, 19
  light soils, 17
Althaea, 15, 92
Alyssum saxatile, 29, 111
Amaryllis belladonna, 102
aminotriazole, 47
ammonium sulphamate, 47
Anagallis tenella, 179
Anchusa, 92
Androsace, 111
Anemone, 19, 30, 92
  blanda, 31
  Coronaria, 102
annuals, 37, 76, 78-83
  alkaline soils, 19
  light soils, 17
  for moist soil, 15
Antirrhinum, 82, *82*
ants, 72, 116
aphids, 115, 116, 133, 153
Aponogeton distachyum, 176
apple canker, 166, *167*
Aquilegia, 92, *95*
Arabis albida, 111

Arbutus, 17, 33
  unedo, 160
Armeria, 29, 33, 111
  caespitosa, *113*
Artemisia, 92
Aruncus sylvester, *178*, 179
Asclepias incarnata, 179
ash, 23
aspect, 10
asphalt, patios, 35
Asplenium, 31
Aster, 19, 92
  x *frikartii*, *94*
Astilbe, 14, 15, 30, 92
  x *ardensii*, *178*, 179
Athyrium, 31
  filix-femina, 15, 178
Aubretia, 111
Aucuba, 31, 33, 104
  japonica, 144
  japonica 'Nana Rotundifolia', 140
azaleas, *20*, 21, 30, 104, 145, *145*
Azolla caroliniana, 177

baby's breath, 92
barberry, 29, 31, 140
bark split, 167
bay laurel, 31, 142
bear's breeches, 17, 31, 92
beech, 30, 144
bees, 51, 134, 154
Begonia semperflorens, 82
bellflowers, 19
Bellis perennis, 85
Berberis, 27, 29, 31, 33, *140*
  x *stenophylla*, 140, 144, *144*
Bergenia, 19, 29, 31
  cordifolia, 45
Betula, 17, 27
  papyrifera, 160
  pendula 'Youngii', *158*
biennials, 76, 84-5
  light soils, 17
bilberry, *21*
birch, 17, 27
birds, 34, 48, 50, 51
bird's-foot trefoil, 38, *39*
black mulberry, 161
black root rot, 118
black spot, 134
black-eyed Susan, 82, *83*

blackfly, 116
bladder campion, 13
blanket flower, 29, 92
bluebells, 102
blueberry, 21
bog gardens, 175
bonemeal, 23
box, 31, 35, 144
bricks, patios, 35
Brompton stocks, 84, 85
broom, 17, 33, 141
Brunnera, 31, 92
buckler fern, 31
bud blast, 154
Buddleia, 19
  alternifolia, 140
  davidii, 51, 140
bulb flies, 116
bulb scale mites, 118
bulbs, 76, 96-103
  acid soils, 21
  alkaline soils, 19
  light soils, 17
  for moist soil, 15
  shady areas, 31
  shady positions, 30
Butomus umbellatus, 176
buttercup, creeping, 13
butterflies, 51
butterfly bush, 140
Buxus, 31, 35
  sempervirens, 140, 144

cages, 48-9
Calceolaria, 82
calcifuges, 18
  in tubs, 21
Calendula, 79
calico bush, 140
Callistephus chinensis, 82
Calluna, 21, 29
  vulgaris, 140
Caltha palustris, 15, 176, *177*
Camellia, 18, 21, 31, 34, 104
  'Donation', *21*
  japonica, 140
Campanula, 19
  carpatica, 111
  medium, 85
  persicifolia, 92
Campsis radicans, 140
canary climber, 89

candytuft, 17, 79
canker, 132
Canterbury bell, 85, *85*
capsid bugs, 116, 132, 133, 153
Caragana arborescens, 160
carnation, 17, 33
Carpinus, 19
Catalpa, 35
  bignonioides, 160, *161*
caterpillars, 116, 135, 154
catnip, 92
cats, 34, 49
Ceanothus, 29, 33
  x 'Delight', 140
  prostratus, *139*
Celosia, argentea cristata, 82
Centaurea, 29, 30, 79, 92
Cerastium, 111
Cercis siliqquastrum, 160
Chaenomeles, 31
  speciosa, 140, 144
chafers, 72, 116, 132, 133, 153
chalky soil, 18-19
  flowers of sulfur, 18, 19
  improving, 19
  plants for, 19
Chamaecyparis, 27, 33
  lawsoniana, 144, 160
  lawsoniana 'Mimima Aurea', 161
Cheiranthus, 17, 85
  'Orange Bedder', *84*
chemical weedkillers, 40, 43
cherry laurel, 144
chickweed, 13, 38, *38*
Chilean bell-flower, 142
Chimonanthus praecox, 140
china aster, 82
Chionodoxa, 104
chlorosis, 18, 152, *152*
Choisya, 19
  ternata, 104, 140
Chrysanthemum, 33, 91
  carniatum, 79
  maximum, 92
  'Nobleman', *91*
cinquefoil, 19, 33
Cistus, 17
  x *purpureus*, 140
Clarkia, 19, 79
clay soils, 14-15
  acid, 20-1
cleavers, 38
Clematis, 31
  armandii, 140
  montana, 140
  'Ville de Lyon', *139*
clematis wilt, 153
Clethra, 21, 140
climbers, 77, 89
  town gardens, 35
cloches, for shade, 28
club root, 118
coastal gardens, 32-3
cockchafers, 135
Colchicum, 30
  autumnale, 102

cold gardens, 26-7
coltsfoot, 13, *40*
columbine, 92
comfrey, 45
compost
  alkaline soils, 19
  bins, 23, *23*
  for containers, 104-5
  light soils, 17
  making, 23
coneflower, 30
conifer spinning mites, 167
conifers, 161, 164
contact weedkillers, 46
container plants, 104-5
Convallaria, 15, 31, 92
Convolvulus, 17, 29
  cneorum, 140
coral spot, 153, *153*
Coreopsis, 92
  tinctoria, 79
corms, 76, 96-103
cornflower, 79, 92
Cornish heath, 141
Cornus, 15, 33
Cortaderia, 29, 92
Corylus avellana, 160
Cosmos, 19, 82
Cotinus, 19
  coggygria, 140
Cotoneaster, 19, 31, *143*
  cordifolia, 45
  dammeri, 45
  horizontalis, 141
cotton lavender, 17
Cotula coronopifolia, 177
crab apple, 19, 35, 159
cranberry, 21
crane's bill, 33, 92, 111
Crataegus, 17, 27
  oxyacanthoides, 159
crazy paving, patios, 35
creeping buttercup, 13
Crinum x *powellii*, 102
Crocus, 17, 102, 104
crown gall, 132, 133
crown imperials, *97*
Cryptomeria japonica, 159
  japonica 'Vilmoriniana', 161
cuckoo spit, 132, 133
cultivators, using, 22
x *Cupressocyparis leylandii*, 33, 144
cuttings, 88, 150
cutworms, 116
Cyclamen, 19, 31
  coum, 102
cypress, 33
Cytisus, 17, 33
  battandieri, 141

D

Daboecia, 21, 31
  cantabrica, 141
daffodil, 102
Dahlia, 19, 82, 90
  'Elegant Star', *77*
  'Glow', *90*
dalapon, 47
Daphne, *141*
  mezereum, 141
Davidia involucrata, 160
day lily, 29, 30, 92
dead nettle, 31
deer, 49
Delphinium, 19, 92
  ajacis, 79
design, 10
Deutzia, 31, 141
Dianthus, 17, 33, 92
  alpinus, 111
  barbatus, 85
  caryophyllus, 82
  deltoides, 111
Dicentra, 31, 92
dichlorbenil, 47
dichlorophen, 47
die-back, 153
digging, 22, *22*, 42
Digitalis, 31, 85
diquat, 47
diseases
  flowers, 118-9
  lawns, 73
  roses, 132-5
  shrubs, 152-5
  trees, 166-7
division, 88
docks, 40
dogwood, 15, 33
Doronicum, 29, 31, 92
double digging, 14
downy mildew, 118, *119*
dragon's claw willow, 161
drainage, 12
  alkaline soils, 18
  heavy soils, 14
  paths, 11
dried blood, 23
dry gardens, 28-9
Dryas octopetala, 111
Dryopteris, 30, *31*, 31
  filix-mas, 178
Dutch elm disease, *166*, 167
dwarf conifers, 161
dwarf thistle, 13

E

earthworms, 72
earwigs, 116
Eccremocarpus, 89, *89*
Echinops, 29, 92
eelworm, 118
Elaeagnus, 27, 29, 33, 35
  pungens 'Maculata', *27*, 141
elm, 167
Epimedium perralderianum, 45
Eranthis, 31
  hyemalis, 102
Erica, 21, 29, 33
  vagans, 141
Erigeron, 92
  macranthus, 111
Erinus, 111
  alpinus, *113*
Eriophorum angustifolium, 177
Eryngium, 29, 33, 92
Escallonia, 19, 29, 33, 35, *140*, 141
  macrantha, 144
Eschscholzia, 79, *79*
Eucalyptus niphophylla, 160
Eucryphia, 21
  glutinosa, 160, *160*
Euonymus, 31, 33
  fortunei, 45
  japonica, 144
Euphorbia, 33, *95*
  robbiae, 45
  wulfenii, 33, 92
evening primrose, 84, 85
exposed gardens, 10, 26-7

F

Fagus sylvatica, 144
fairy rings, 55, 72
fall crocus, 30
false acacia, 161
fat hen, 38
Fatsia, 31, 33
  japonica, 141
Felicia, 17
  bergeriana, 82
fences, 11

ferns, 31, 178
fertilizers, 22, 114
  alkaline soils, 18
  lawns, 56
  light soils, 17
  liquid, 22
  shrubs, 148
  types, 23
Filipendula rubra, 179
fireblight, 167
firethorn, 31, 143
fish, 184
flax, 17, 79, 92
flea beetles, 116
fleabane, 92
flowering cherry, 19, 35, 159, 161, 167
flowering currant, 15, 31, 143
flowers, 75-135
flowers of sulfur, alkaline soils, 18, 19
foliar feeds, 22
foot rot, 119
forget-me-not, 31, 84, 85
forking, 22, 42
Forsythia, 19, 27, 31
  x *intermedia*, 141
Fothergilla, 15, 21, 31
  major, 141
fountains, 174
foxglove, 31, 34, *76*, 85
Fritillaria, 30
  meleagris, 15, 102, *103*
froghoppers, 117, 132, 133
frost, 10, 26-7, 152
frost pockets, 27
Fuchsia, 31
  magellanica, 33, 141, 144, 149
fusarium patch, *72*, 73

G

Gaillardia, 29, 92
  pulchella, 82
galls, 154
Garrya, 31, 35
  elliptica, 141
Gaultheria, 21, 27, 31
  procumbens, 45, *45*
  shallon, 27, 141
Gazania, 17, 82
Genista, 33
  lydia, 141
Gentiana, 15

Index

septemfida, 111
Geranium, 29, 30, 31, 33, 92, 111
  endressii, 45
geraniums *(Pelargonium)*, 81
Geum, 30, 92
  'Lady Stratheden', *93*
Ginkgo biloba, 160
Gladiolus, 17, *76*, 99, 102
Gleditsia tricanthus, 159
globe thistle, 29
Glyceria spectabilis variegata, 177
glyphosate, 47
Godetia, 19, 79
golden rain tree, 160
golden rod, 30, 94
goosegrass, 38
grape hyacinth, *97*, 102
gravel, patios, 35
greenhouses, 11
Griselinia, 31, 33, 141
grit, soil drainage, 14
ground cover, 31, 37, 43, 44-5
ground elder, 13, 40
groundsel, 38
Gunnera manicata, 15, 179
Gypsophila, 17, 29
  elegans, 79
  paniculata, 92

hairy bittercress, 38
Halesia, 21
  carolina, 141
Hamamelis, 31, 35
  mollis, 141
hares, 160
hawthorn, 17, 27, 159
hazel, 160
heath, 29
heather, 29, 33, 104
heavy soil, 14-15
  double digging, 14
  drainage, 14
  dryness, 28
  heat, 28
  liming, 14
  plants for, 15
  weeds of, 13
Hebe, 33, *33*
  pinguifolia, 45
Hedera, 31, 35, *141*
  helix, 45, 142
hedges, 144-5
  seaside gardens, 32, 33

Helenium, 92
  'Coppelia', *93*
Helianthemum, 29
  nummularium, 112
Helianthus, 92
Helleborus, 31, 34, 92
Hemerocallis, 29, 30, 92
herbaceous plants, 76
hillside gardens, 10
Hippophae rhamnoides, 33, 144
hoeing, 42
hoes, *42*
honesty, 31, 85
honey fungus, 132, *152* 153
honeysuckle, 19, 29, 31, 35, 142
hoof and horn, 23
hop, 35
hop manure, 16
hornbeam, 19
horsetail, 13, *41*
Hosta, 15, 31, 34, 92, 104, *171*, 179
hot gardens, 28-9
houseleeks, 112
Humulus, 35
humus, 12
  light soils, 16, 17
hurdles, 11, 28, 32
Hyacinthus, 17
Hydrangea, 15, 33
  macrophylla, 142
Hydrocharis morsus ranae, 177
Hypericum, 29, 31, *143*
  calycinum, 45
  'Hidcote', 142
  patulum forrestii, *29*

Iberis, 17, 79
  sempervirens, 112
Iceland poppy, 85
Ilex, 29, *143*, 144, 161
  x *altaclarensis*, 160
  aquifolium, 142
Indian bean tree, 160
Ipomoea, 89, *89*
Iris, 19, 29, 33, 100
  cristata, 179
  danfordiae, 100
  kaempferi, 179, *179*
  laevigata, 177
  pseudoacorus, 177
  pumila, 100
  reticulata, 100, 104
  sibirica, 15, *100*, 179

iron deficiency, 18, 19
ivy, 31, 35, 45, *141*, 142

japonica (Chaenomeles), 31
Jasminum, 31, 35
  nudiflorum, 142
Jew's mallow, 31, 35
Judas tree, 160
Juniperus, 17, 33
  communis, 109
  communis 'Compressa', 161
  virginiana 'Sky Rocket', 159

Kalmia, 15, 21, 31
  latifolia, 142
Kerria, 31, 35
kingfisher daisy, 82
Kniphofia, 17, 33, 92, *95*
knotgrass, 13, 38, *39*
knotweed, 31, 33, 45
Koelreuteria paniculata, 160, 161

labor-saving gardens, 37
Laburnum, 27, 35
  anagyroides, 159
lacewings, 51
lady fern, 178
lamb's tongue, 13, 45
Lamium, 31
  maculatum, 45
Lapageria, 21, 142
Larix decidua 'Pendula', 160
larkspur, 79
Lathyrus, 19, 79, 89, *89*
laurel, 33
Laurus, 31, 33
  nobilis, 142

Lavandula, 19, 33, *140*
  spica, 142
Lavatera trimestris, 79
lawns, 34, 36, 37, 53-73
  acid soils, 20
  aerating, 57
  diseases, 73
  fairy rings, 55, 73
  feeding, 56
  grass for, 66-7
  maintenance, 56-7, 62-3
  moss, 55, 70-1
  mower damage, 55
  mowers, 58-9, *58*, *59*, 60-1
  mowing, 58-9
  new, 66-9
  pests, 72
  problems with, 55
  raking, 57
  repairing, 64-5
  scarifying, 57
  seeding, 69
  top dressing, 56
  trimming edges, 59
  turfing, 68
  watering, 56
  weak growth, 55
  weeds, 55, 70-1
Lawson cypress, 144, 160, 161
leaf miners, 117, 134, 154
leaf mold, light soils, 16
leaf spot, 119, 154
leaf-cutter bees, 134, 154
leafhoppers, 134
leaf-rolling sawfly, 135
leatherjackets, 72, 117
leopard's bane, 29, 31, 92
Leucojum, 15, 30
  aestivum, 102
Leucothoe, 21, 31
Lewisia, 111
  cotyledon, 112
Leyland cypress, 33
light soils, 16-17
  manuring, 16, 17
  mulching, 16, 17
  plants for, 17
  weeds of, 13
Ligustrum, 31
  ovalifolium, 142
lilac, 27, 142
Lilium, 18, 101
  auratum, 21, 101
  canadense, 21
  candidum, 101
  regale, 101
  rebellum, 21
  tigrinium, 21
lily-of-the-valley, 15, 31, 92
lime-haters, 18
  in tubs, 21
liming, 14, 20, 21
  light soils, 17
Linaria, 92
ling, 29
Linum, 17

grandiflorum, 79
  grandiflorum 'Rubrum', *78*
  narbonnense, 92
liquid fertilizers, 22
Lithospermum, 77
  diffusum, 112
Livingstone daisy, 17, 82
loam, 12
Lobelia, 15
  erinus, 82
Lonicera, 19, 29, 31, 35
  periclymenum, 142
Lunaria, 31, 85
Lupinus, 19, *76*, 92
Lychnis, 112
Lysichiton americanum, *178*, 179
Lysimachia, 15, 31
  nummularia, 45
  punctata, 179
Lythrum salicaria, 179

M

Macleaya, 15
Magnolia, 21, 139
  x *soulangiana*, *138*, 142
Mahonia, 31, 104, *141*
  aquifolium, 142
maidenhair fern, 31, 178
maidenhair tree, 160
mallow, 92
Malus, 19, 35, 159
  x *lemoinei*, *159*
Malva, 92
manuring
  alkaline soil, 19
  heavy soil, 14
  light soils, 16, 17
  sandy soil, 16, 17
maple, 27, 33, 159, 160, 167
marsh marigold, 15, 176, *177*
Metteuccia, 31
  struthiopteris, 178
Matthiola bicornis, 79
  incana, 82, 85
mealybugs, 118, *118*, 155
Meconopsis, 30, 92
Mesembryanthemum, 17
  criniflorum, 82
Mexican orange, 19, 104, 140
Michaelmas daisy, 92
mildew, 119, *119*, 132, 133, 155
millipedes, 117

Mimulus, 15
  cardinalis, 179
  luteus, 177
mock orange, 19, 27, 31
moist soil
  plants for, 15
  see also heavy soil
moles, 49, 72
Monarda didyma, 179
monkshood, 31, 92
morning glory, 89, *89*
Morus nigra, 161
moss, in lawns, 55, 70-1
moss campion, 112
mountain avens, 111
mowing lawns, 58-9
  mowers, 37, 58-9, *58*, *59*, 60-1
mulching, 28
  light soils, 16, 17
  sandy soil, 16, 17
  weed suppression, 42-3
mullein, 29, 94
Muscari armeniacum, 102, *103*
mushroom compost, 14, 19
Myosotis, 31, 85
  palustris, 177

N

Narcissus, 19, 30, 102, 104
nasturtiums, 77, 79, 89, *89*
neglected gardens, 36-7
Namesia, 19
Nemophila, 79, *79*
Nepeta, 92
Nerine, 17
netting, 48-9
nettles, 40
New Zealand burr, *44*, 45
Nicotiana, 82
Nigella, 79
night-scented stock, 79
nitrate of soda, 23
nitro-chalk, 20, 23
nitrogen, fertilizers, 23
Nomocharis, 21, 31
nutrients
  alkaline soils, 18
  light soils, 17
  soil, 12
Nymphaea, 176
Nymphoides peltata, 176
Nyssa, 21
  sylvatica, 161

O

Oenothera biennis, 85
Olearia, 33
Onoclea, 31
Oregon grape, 142
organic material, 12
  alkaline soils, 18
  heavy soils, 14
Origanum amanum, 112
Orontium aquaticum, 176
Osmunda, 15, 31
  regalis, 178
Oxalis adenophylla, 112

P

Pachysandra terminalis, 45
Paeonia, 94
  lactiflora 'White Wings', *95*
pampas grass, 29, 92
Papaver, 19
  naudicaule, 85
  orientale, 94
  rhoeas, 79
paper birch, 160
paraquat, 47
Parrotia persica, 161
Parthenocissus, 31
  quinquefolia, 142
pasque flower, 112, *112*
Passiflora caerulea, 142
passion flower, 142
paths, 11
patio gardens, 35, *35*
patios, 10
  seaside, 32-3
Paulownia, 161
paving slabs, patios, 35
peach leaf curl, 167
pearlwort, 13
peat
  acid soils, 20
  alkaline soils, 18
  light soils, 16
Pelargonium, 81, *81*
Penstemon, 29, 33, 82, 94
peony blight, 119

perennials
  alkaline soils, 19
  dividing, 88-9
  dry soil, 29
  light soils, 17
  for moist soil, 15
  seaside gardens, 33
periwinkle, 30, *31*
Pernettya, 21, 143
persicaria, 38, *39*
pesticides, 116-18
pests
  animals, 48-9
  flowers, 115, 116-19
  lawns, 72
  pools, 184
  roses, 132-5
  shrubs, 152-5
  trees, 166-7
pets, 49
Petunia, 76, 82, *83*
pH levels, 114
  acid soils, 20, 21
  alkaline soils, 19
  testing, 13
Philadelphus, 19, 27, 31
  'Beauclerk', 143
Phlox, 30, 94
  drummondii, *80*, *82*
  sublata, 112
phosphate, fertilizers, 23
Picea, 21, 27
  pungens 'Kosteri', 161
Pieris, 15, 21, 31
  formosa, 143
pinks, 17, 33, 111
Pinus, 27, 33
Pittosporum, 33
  tenuifolium, 143
plantain, 13, *40*
plants
  for acid soils, 21
  for alkaline soils, 19
  for dry soil, 29
  for ground cover, 31, 45
  for heavy soils, 15
  for light soils, 17
  for pools, 176-9
  for rock gardens, 111-12
  for shady positions, 30-1
  for town gardens, 35
plastic mulch, 16, 17
plume poppy, 15
pocket handkerchief tree, 160
polyanthus, 46
Polygonum, 31, 33, 94, *142*
  affine, 45, 112
  baldschuanicum, 143
Polystichum, 31
Pontederia cordata, 177
pools, 170-85
  maintenance, 182-3
  making, 172-3
  plants for, 176-9
  problems, 184
  wild life, 51, 184-5

Index

poppy, 19, 79, 85, 94
position, 10
pot marigold, 79
potash, fertilizers, 23
Potentilla, 19, 33, *143*
  fruticosa, 143
powdery mildew, 132, 133, 155
primrose, *85*, 94
Primula, 15, 31, *85*
  beesiana, 179
  denticulata, 94
  florindae, *15*, 179
  japonica, 179
  vulgaris, 94
privet, 31
propachlor, 47
propagation, shrubs, 150
pruning
  roses, 130-1
  shrubs, 150-1
  trees, 165
Prunus, 19, 35, 159, 161, 167
  laurocerasus, 144
Pseudotsuga menziesii
  'Fletcheri', 161
Pulsatilla, 19
  vulgaris, 112, *112*
Pyracantha, 31, 143
Pyrethrum, 17, 94, *94*
Pyrus salicifolia, 27
  salicifolia 'Pendula', *160*, 161

R

rabbits, 49
raised beds, 109
Ranunculus asiaticus, 102
red deadnettles, 38, 39
red hot pokers, 17, 33, 92
red spider mite, 134, 155
red thread, 73, *73*
residual weedkillers, 46
Rheum palmatum, 179
Rhododendron, 15, 18, *20*, 21, 30, 31, 143, 145, *145*
rhododendron bugs, 155
rhododendron leafhoppers, 155
Ribes, 15, *15*, 31, 143
Robinia pseudoacacia, 161
  pseudoacacia 'Frisia', *161*
rock cress, 111
rock gardens, 106-13
  alkaline soil, 19
  building, 106-7

plants for, 77, 111-13
raised beds, 109
scree beds, 108
soils, *16*
rock rose (*Cistus*), 17
rock rose (*Helianthemum*), 29, 112
Rodgersia pinnata, 179
root cuttings, 88
Rosa, 31, 35, 120-35, 144
rosemary, 27, 29, 104, 143
roses, 31, 35, 120-35, 144
  bourbons, 123
  buying, 125
  caring for, 126-9
  climbers, 123, 125, 127
  disbudding, 129
  diseases, 132-5
  floribunda, 123, 124
  hybrid tea, 122, 124
  miniature, 122, 125
  pests, 132-5
  pruning, 130-1
  ramblers, 123, 125
  shrub, 122, 124
  standard, 126
  suckers, 128
  varieties, 124-5
  watering, 129
Rosmarinus, 27, 29
  officinalis, 104, 143
rowan, 27, 33
royal fern, 15, 31, 178
Rudbeckia, 30, 94
  hirta, 82
  'Marmalade', *93*
Russian vine, 143
rust, 119, 135

S

Saggitaria japonica, 177
St John's wort, 29, 31
Salix matsudana 'Tortuosa', *160*, 161
Salvia, 19, 29, 82, *83*
  x *superba*, 94
sandy soil, 16-17
  manuring, 16, 17
  mulching, 16, 17
  plants for, 17
Santolina, 17, 33
  chamaecyparissus, *17*
Sanvitalia, 82
  procumbens, 82

Saponaria ocymoides, 112
Saxifraga, 31, 112
scale insects, 155
scarifying lawns, 57
scarlet pimpernel, 13
Scilla, 104
  nonscripta
  sibirica, 102
Scirpus zebrinus, 177
scree beds, 108
screens, 11
sea buckthorn, 144
sea holly, 33, 92
seaside gardens, 10, 32-3
seaweed, 16
Sedum, 29, 94
  spathulifolium, 112
Sempervivum, 112, *113*
Senecio, 31, 33
  greyi, 144
  laxifolius, 143
sequestered iron, 18, 19
shade, 10
  creating, 28, *28*
shady gardens, 30-1
shasta daisy, 92
sheds, 36
shelter belts, 26
shepherd's purse, 13, 38
shoddy, 16
Shortia galacifolia, 112
shothole, 167
shredded bark, 16
shrubs, 37, 136-55
  acid soils, 21
  alkaline soils, 19
  buying, 146
  for cold areas, 27
  diseases, 152-5
  dry soil, 29
  feeding, 148
  hedges, 144-5
  light soils, 17
  maintenance, 148-9
  for moist soil, 15
  mulching, 148
  pests, 152-5
  planting, 147
  propagating, 150
  pruning, 150-1
  seaside gardens, 32, 33
  shady areas, 31
  soil conditions, 152
  supporting, 147
  town gardens, 35
  weed control, 149
Sidalcea, 94
Silene acaulis, 112
silver leaf, 167
simazine, 47
sink gardens, 108-9
sites, 10
Skimmia, 31, 104
  japonica, 143
slugs, 115, 117
smoke tree, 19

snails, 117
snow, protection by, *26*
snow-in-summer, 111
snowdrop tree, 141
snowflake, 15, 30
soakaways, 14
soapwort, 112
sodium chloride, 47
soil, 10, 12-23, 114
  acid, 21-2
  alkaline, 18-19
  digging, 22
  fertile, 12-13
  fertilizers, 22, 23
  heavy, 14-15, 28
  humus, 12
  light, 16-17
  maintaining healthy, 22-3
  nutrients, 12
  organic matter, 12
  testing, 13
  town gardens, 34
Solidago, 30, 94
Sorbus, 19, 33
  aria, 27
  aucuparia, 27
  'Joseph Rock', *160*, 161
sorrel, 13
sow thistle, 38, *39*
Spanish broom, 29, 33
Spartium, 29, 33
speedwell, 13, 30, 94
spiders, 51
spindle, 31
Spiraea, 27
  thunbergii, 144
Spiraea x *bumalda* 'Anthony Waterer', 143
spleenwort, 31
sprinklers, 28, *28*
spruce, 27
spurge, 33, *33*, 45, 92, *95*
spurrey, 13
squirrels, 49
Stachys, 29, 30, 31, 94
  lanata, 45
steps, 11
stonecrop, 94, 112
Stratiotes aloides, 177
strawberry tree, 17, 33, 160
Stuartia pseudocamellia, 161
subsoil, 12
  heavy soils, 14
sulfate of ammonia, 20, 23
sulfate of potash, 23
sun, 10
sun traps, 32-3
superphosfate, 23
sweet peas, 19, 78, 79, 89, *89*
sweet pepper, 140
sweet william, 85
Symphytum grandiflorum, 45
Syringa, 27
  vulgaris, 142
sword lily, 17, *76*, 99, 102

T

Tagetes, 82
Tamarix, 17, 33, *140*
    pentandra, 142, 144
tar spot, 167
Taxus baccata, 144
testing soil, 13
thistles, 13, 40, *41*
thrift, 29, 33
thrips, 117, 133
Thuja occidentalis 'Rheingold', 161
    plicata 'Zebrinia', 161
Thunbergia alata, 82, *83*
Thymus, 29
    serpyllum, 112
Tiarella cordifolia, 45
toad flax, 92
toads, 51
tobacco plant, 82
tools, buying, 37
topsoil, 12
    alkaline soils, 18
town gardens, 34-5
translocated weedkillers, 46
trees, 158-67
    acid soils, 21
    alkaline soils, 19
    for cold areas, 27
    diseases, 166-7
    light soils, 17
    maintenance, 164-5
    pests, 166
    pruning, 165
    seaside gardens, 32, 33
    town gardens, 35
trellis, 11

Ttillium grandiflorum, *110*, 112
Trollius, 30, 94, 179
    'Goldquelle', *175*
Tropaeolum, 79, 89, *89*
    majus, 89
    peregrinum, 89
trumpet vine, 140
tubers, 77, 96-103
tubs, calcifuges in, 21
tulip fire, *118*, 119
Tulipa, 17, 99, 102
    'Red Shine', 97
tupelo, 161
2.4.3-T weedkiller, 47
2.4-D weedkiller, 47

UV

utility areas, 10

Vaccinium, 21
Verbascum, 29, 94
    'Pink Domino', *93*
Verbena, 19, *19*, 82
Veronica, 30, 33, 94
    prostrata, 45
Viburnum, 35, *141*
Vinca, 31
    major, *44*, 45
    minor, *44*, 45
vine weevil, 117, 155
Viola, 31
    labradorica, 45
virginia creeper, 31, 142
virus diseases, 125
Viscaria, 79

W

wallflowers, 17, 20
wasps, 51
water gardens, 170-85
    maintenance, 182-3
    making, 172-3
    plants for, 176-9
    problems, 184
    wild life, 51, 184 5
water hawthorn, *171*, 176
water lilies, 176, *176*
waterfalls, 174
watering, 28, *28*, 115
    lawns, 56
    roses, 129
    shrubs, 148
weedkillers, 40, 43, 46-7
    applying, 46
    for lawns, 71
    types, 47
weeds, 10, 115
    annual, 38-9
    dealing with, 42-3

ground cover, 44
    in lawns, 55, 70-1
    perennial, 40-1
    rosebeds, 129
    as soil indicator, 13
weeping pear, *160*, 161
Weigela, 29, 31
    florida, 142
wheel barrows, 37
whitebeam, 27, 33
whitefly, 117
wind, 10
windbreaks, 26, 32
windy sites, 26-7
    seaside, 32-3
wireworms, 117
Wisteria, 19, *19*
    sinensis, 142
witch hazel, 31, 35, 141
woodlice, 117
woolly aphids, 153

YZ

yarrow, 17, 29
yew, 144

Zinnia, 82
    'Dasher Scarlet', *83*

Acknowledgments

The Paul Press Limited and the authors would like to thank the following persons and organizations, to whom copyright in the photographs noted belongs:

10 (tr) Heather Angel; 11 S & O Mathews; 12 Harry Smith Horticultural Photographic Collection; 14 (tr) Heather Angel; 15 (l) Bruce Coleman; 16 (tr) Harry Smith; 17 Adrian Dames; 18 Heather Angel; 19 (bl) Harry Smith, (tr) Bruce Coleman; 20, 21 Harry Smith; 26 Heather Angel; 27 (tr) Ardea, (br) Harry Smith; 29, 30 Heather Angel; 33 (tr) Heather Angel, (br) Harry Smith; 34 Harry Smith; 35 (bl) Harry Smith, (tr) Heather Angel; 36, 37 Harry Smith; 38 Heather Angel; 39 (tl) Ardea, (tr) NHPA, (br) Heather Angel; 40 (bl) NHPA, (tr) Heather Angel; 41 NHPA; 43 Heather Angel; 44 (tr) Harry Smith, (br) Heather Angel; 45 Harry Smith; 46 Holt Studios; 48 (tr) Harry Smith, (bc, br) Holt Studios; 49 Smith Collection; 54, 55 Harry Smith; 58 (br) Holt Studios; 66, 67 Bruce Coleman; 70 Levington Research Centre; 71 Holt Studios; 72 (tr) Levington Research Centre, (br) NHPA; 73 (tl) Levington Research Centre, (tc) Photos Horticultural, (bl) Heather Angel; 76, 77, 78, 79, 80, 81, 83, 84, 85 (tc, c) Harry Smith, (br) S & O Mathews; 87 Bruce Coleman; 89, 90, 91, 92, 93 (r) Harry Smith; 93 (l) S & O Mathews; 94 (b) Harry Smith, (t) S & O Mathews; 95 (t) Harry Smith, (b) S & O Mathews; 100 NHPA; 101, 102, 103, 104 Harry Smith; 105 (tl, bl) Harry Smith, (c) S & O Mathews; 106, 108, 109, 110, 111 Harry Smith; 112 S & O Mathews; 113, 122, 123, 124, 125, 128 Harry Smith; 132 Holt Studios Ltd.; 133 (tl) Oxford Scientific Films Ltd., Ardea; 136 Harry Smith; 138 Ardea; 139, 144, 145, 147 Harry Smith; 152 (tr) Holt Studios Ltd., (br) NHPA; 153 Adrian Davies; 156, 160, 161 Harry Smith; 166, 167(c)Adrian Davies; 167 (t,b),170, 171, 172, 174, 175, 176, 177, 178, 179 Harry Smith; 181 Bruce Coleman; 185 NHPA.

Key: (t) top; (b) below; (l) left; (r) right; (c) centre.